THE ALPHABET

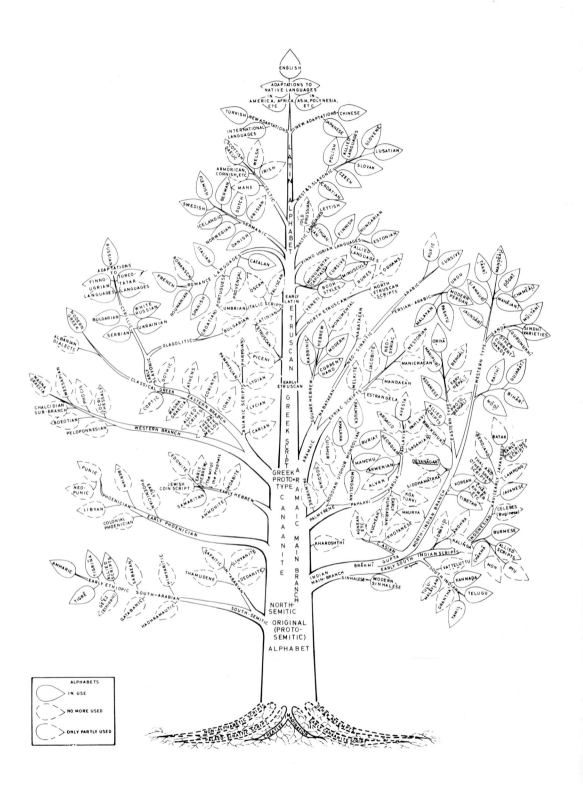

THE
ALPHABET

A Key to
the History of Mankind

DAVID DIRINGER
D.Litt. (*Flor.*), M.A. (*Cantab.*)

THIRD EDITION
completely revised with the collaboration of
REINHOLD REGENSBURGER

VOLUME 2

FUNK & WAGNALLS
NEW YORK

Copyright 1968 by David Diringer

Library of Congress Catalog Card Number: 68-22369

Published by Funk & Wagnalls, *A Division of*
Reader's Digest Books, Inc.

First published by Hutchinson & Co.
(Publishers) Ltd. in April 1948

Second edition, revised April 1949
Reprinted (with amendments) January 1953
Reprinted (with amendments) October 1953
Third edition (completely revised, in two volumes) 1968

Printed in Great Britain

CONTENTS

In this illustration volume the sections are numbered to correspond exactly with the chapter headings in the text volume, and the illustrations are numbered serially within sections. Each illustration is marked with two numbers separated by a dot. The first is the section number and the second is the specific number. The index to the whole work is in the text volume, where illustrations are referred to by page numbers shown in italic type.

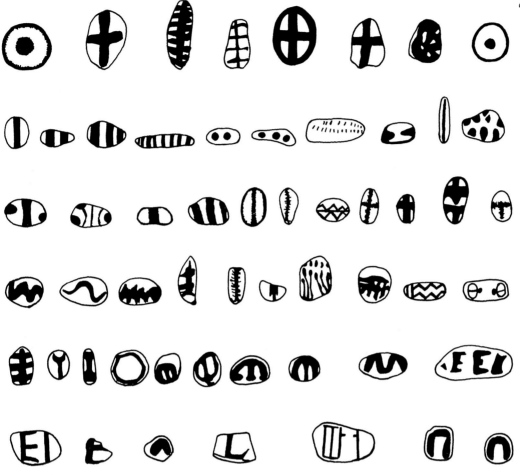

Introd. 1. *a* Azilian signary: coloured pebbles from Mas d'Azil, Ariège (Southern France). *b* Prehistoric geometric signs from Portugal.

a

b

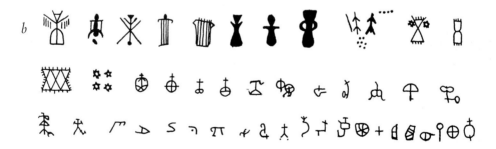

Introd. 2. Prehistoric conventionalized figures and geometric symbols from *a* Italy and *b* Spain.

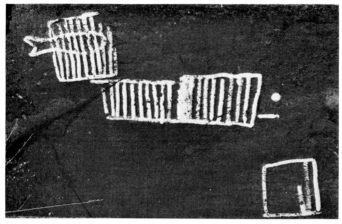

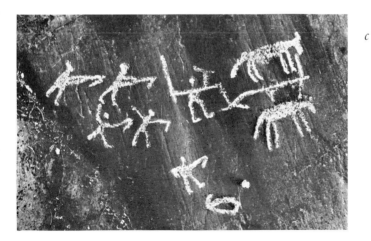

Introd. 3. Prehistoric rock-carvings from Val Cammonica (Italian Alps). *a* Fish trapped. *b* Plan of village. *c* Work in the fields.

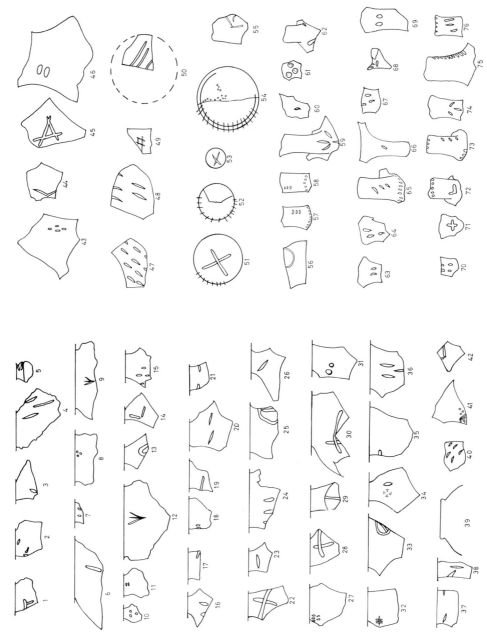

Introd. 4. Prehistoric geometric symbols from Palestine.

4

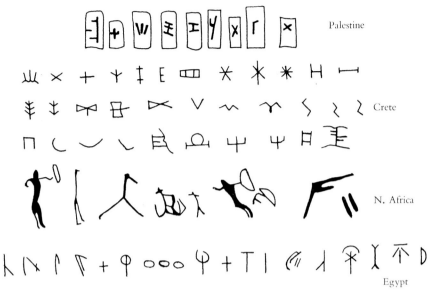

Introd. 5. *a* Prehistoric geometric symbols and conventionalized figures.

Introd. 5. *b* Prehistoric geometric symbols from Southern Rhodesia.

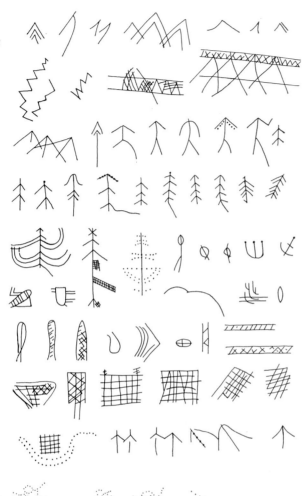

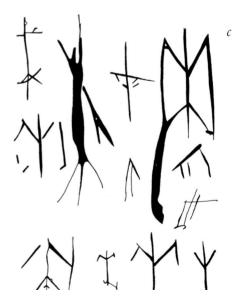

Introd. 6. Prehistoric symbols from Katanga (Congo) *a* engraved, *b* punched, and *c* painted.

Introd. 7. Petroglyphs from Afghanistan.

Introd. 8. Petroglyphs from Hoshangabad (India).

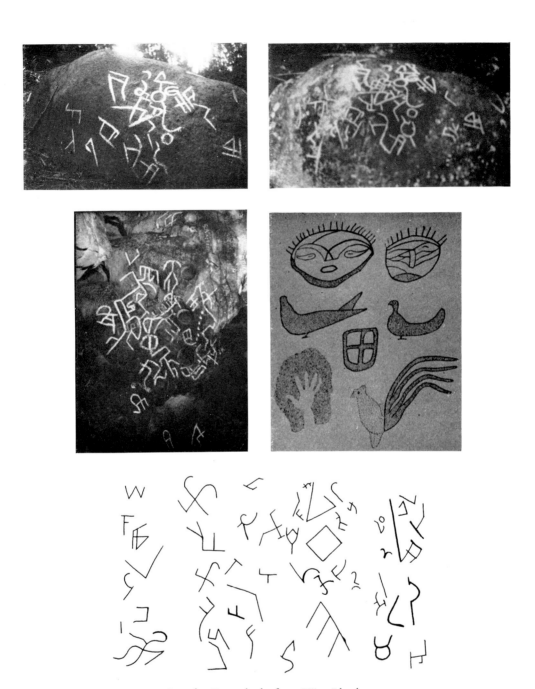

Introd. 9 Petroglyphs from Fijian Islands.

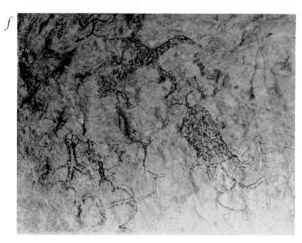

Introd. 10. Petroglyphs from New Zealand. *a* and *b* Weka Pass shelter, *c* Monkey Face Reserve, *d* Ford's shelter, *e* Awamoko Stream, *f* Dogsheads Rock Cave.

Introd. 11. Conventionalized figures of men and animals, animated objects and geometrical symbols from rock-paintings or carvings in the U.S.A. *a* to *d* California, *e* Arizona, *f* Bahamas, *g* Brazil, and *h* Australia.

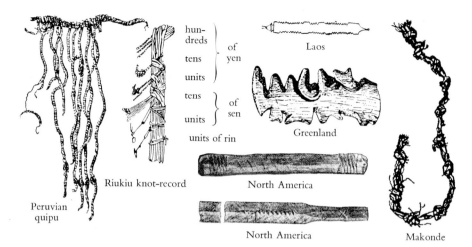

hun-
dreds
tens   } of
            } yen
units

tens   } of
units   } sen

units of rin

Laos

Greenland

North America

North America

Peruvian
quipu

Riukiu knot-record

Makonde

Introd. 12. *a* Peruvian *quipu*; Riukiu knot-record; notched stick from Laos; 'geographical map' from Greenland; Makonde knot-record; notched sticks from North America.

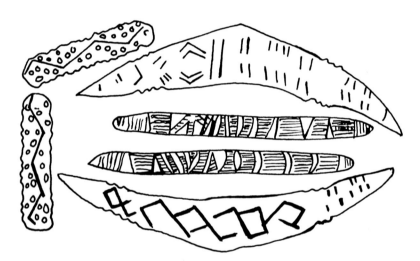

Introd. 12. *b* Australian notched sticks.

Introd. 12. *c* The Penn Wampum belt (Historical Society of Pennsylvania).

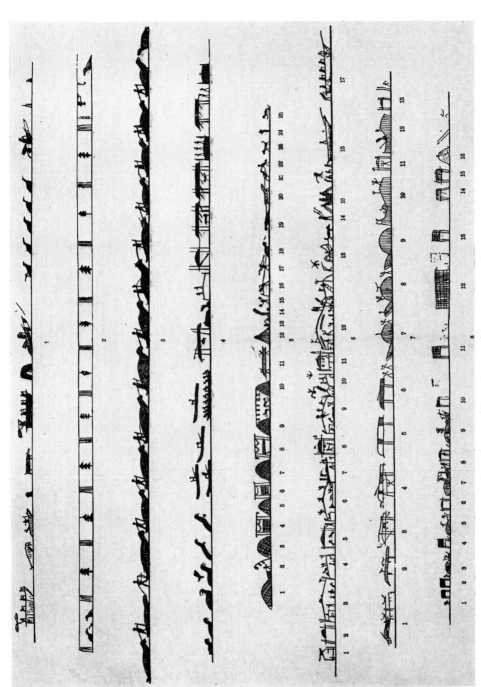

Introd. 13. Eskimo pictographic carvings on ivory.

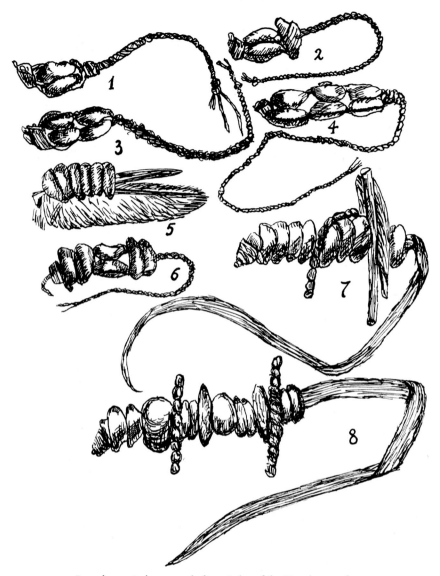

Introd. 14. *Aroko* or symbolic epistles of the Yoruba people.

1 Two cowries, strung back to back (message of reproof for non-payment of debt).
2 Two cowries, face to face, followed by one above, facing upwards (message from
a creditor to a bad debtor). 3 Four cowries, in pairs, face to face (message of good will
from a native to his brother abroad, asking for a personal interview). 4 Six cowries,
face to face (message from a general of the Jebu force to a native prince abroad).
5 Letter from a native prince of the Jebu Ode to one of his cousins abroad. 6 Another
Jebu message. 7 Message from the king Awnjale to his nephew abroad. 8 Message of
peace and good news from the king of Jebu to the king of Lagos, after his restoration to
the throne, on the 28th December, 1851.

14

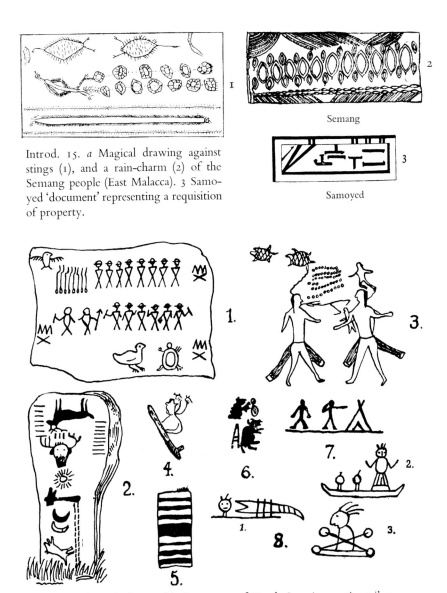

Introd. 15. *a* Magical drawing against stings (1), and a rain-charm (2) of the Semang people (East Malacca). 3 Samoyed 'document' representing a requisition of property.

Semang

Samoyed

Introd. 15. *b* Ideographic documents of North American native tribes.

1 Indian expedition. 2 Tomb-board of Indian Chief. 3 Letter of a man called Turtle-Following-His-Wife to his son named Little-Man. 4 The French General Maynadier (a man with a hat, indicating a European; the two heads of a deer at the top right-hand side, indicate the name 'Many Deer'). 5 The winter 1858–59 as indicated in a Dakota (a North American Indian tribe) 'winter count': the Dakotas bought in that winter many *Mexican blankets* from John Richard. 6 Message of a North American Indian: 'Bad-Bear (a name) died at a buffalo hunt'. 7 Message of a native from Alaska: 'No eating is in tent'. 8 (1 to 3) Ideographs from the Delaware 'Chronicle' *Walam Olum*.

Introd. 16. The modern and astute advertiser turns to a pictographic appeal for his rubber goods.

a

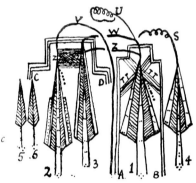

b

c

Introd. 17. Picture stories of native tribes: *a* ideographic document of North American Indians; *b* symbolic proverbs of the Ewe (West African people); *c* sad love-story of a Yukaghir girl; *d* Dakota 'winter-count' chronicle (drawing by Kedma Diringer).

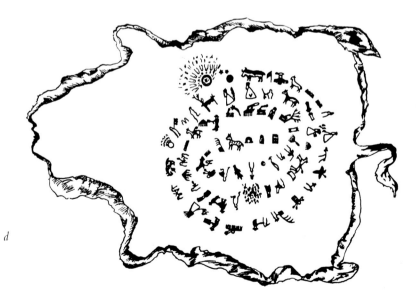

d

1

2

a

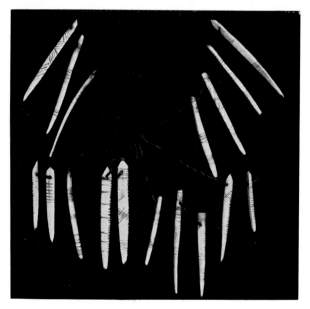

b

Introd. 18. *a* 1, Song Record-stick from Ogaga, Oklahoma, U.S.A. 2, Cheyenne Record-stick (Museum of the American Indian, New York).
b Arapahoe Record-sticks (Museum of the American Indian, New York).
c Marked bone spikes from Tahltan (Alaska).

c

Development of Cuneiform Signs

Meaning in Sumerian	English	Original Pictograph	Pictograph after turning 90°	Archaic form (c. 2500 – c. 2350) on clay	Archaic form (c. 2500 – c. 2350) on stone or metal	Ancient Babylonian	Classic Assyrian
gir	dagger, lancet, razor						
an, dingir	heaven, god						
lú	man						
sal, munus	pudendum woman						
kur	mountain						
gem	slave-girl						
sag	head						
ka, dug	mouth, to speak						
a	water						
du, gub	to go, to stand						
mushen	bird						
ḫa, ḫa	fish, may						
gud	ox						
she	barley						

1.1. Origin of cuneiform characters.

1.2. Archaic Sumerian pictorial tablets, from Kish (*a* obverse; *b* reverse), Uruk-Warka (*c* and *d*), possibly from Umma (*e*) and Jemdet Nasr (*f*).

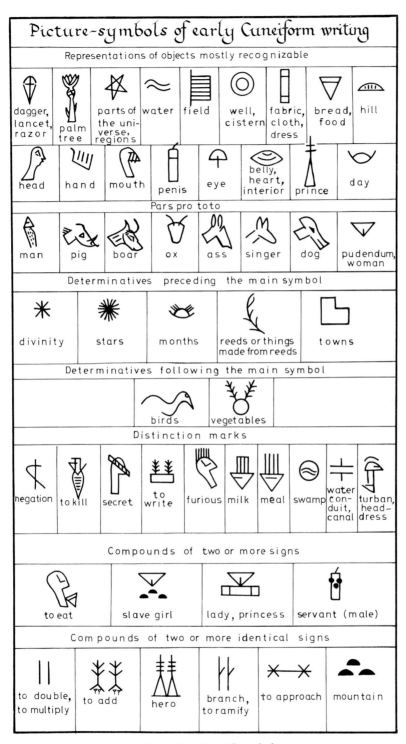

1.3. Sumerian pictorial symbols.

NO.	A	TU	GAR	NO.	A	TU	GAR
1				9			
2			(REC 417)	10			
3				11			
4				12			
5				13			
6				14			
7				15			
8				16			

1.4a. Examples of cuneiform homophones.

	1		2		3		4		5		6
	7		8		9		10		11		12
	13		14		15		16		17		18

1.4b. Examples of cuneiform determinatives (for full explanation see text, p. 18).

	1		2		3		4		5		6
	7		8		9		10		11		12
	13		14		15		16		17		18
	= a 19		= e 20		= i 21		= o 22		= u 23		

1.4c. Assyrian cuneiform symbols (1–18) for syllables and (19–23) vowels (1, ba; 2, da; 3, ga; 4, kha 5, ka; 6, qa; 7, la; 8, ma; 9, na; 10, pa; 11, ra; 12 and 13, sa; 14 and 15, sha).

1.5. Early cuneiform writing on soft material: inscribed brick of Eannadu, King of Lagash (modern Tell Lo, southern Mesopotamia).

23

1.6. Assyrian sculptures from the royal palace at Ashur, representing scribes. (*above*) Scribes in the act of writing; (*below*) two scribes writing out lists of booty.

1.7. *a–e* Cuneiform tablets of various shapes; *f* Extract from Hammurabi's *Code of Laws* showing the stylus.

a

1.8. *a* Pillar on which is inscribed
Hammurabi's Code of Laws (18th
cent. B.C.). *b* Baked clay prism
of Sennacherib, King of Assyria
(705–681 B.C.), inscribed with
the account of his invasion of
Palestine and the siege of
Jerusalem.

b

1.9. *a* Nippur archaic cylinder and grammatical text; *b* Sumerian flood tablet from Nippur (both from University Museum, Philadelphia).

a

b

a

b

1.10. *a* Fragments of the Lipit-Ishter Law Code, the oldest law-code in man's history; *b* Sumerian tablet from Nippur with the story of the Creation and the Flood (both from University Museum, Pennsylvania).

1.11b. Fragmentary tablet containing the Babylonian account of the Flood (British Museum K3375).

1.11a The Fourth Tablet of the Assyrian account of the Creation and the Flood (British Museum No. 9301b).

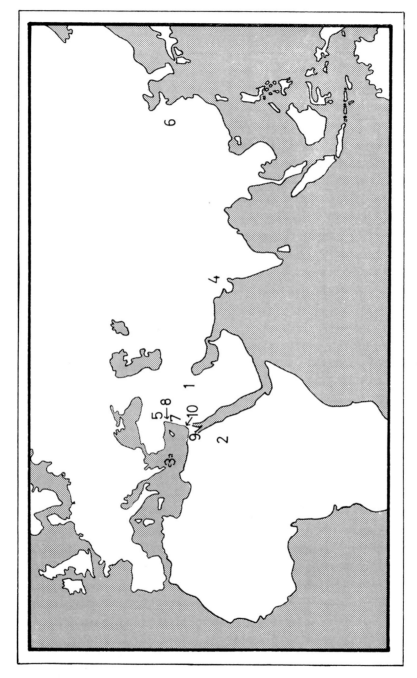

Map I. MAIN SYSTEMS OF WRITING 3000–1000 B.C.

1 Cuneiform scripts (Mesopotamia and surrounding countries). 2 Egyptian scripts (Hieroglyphic, Hieratic, Demotic). 3 Cretan and Mycenaean scripts. 4 Indus Valley scripts. 5 Hittite Hieroglyphic scripts (Asia Minor and N. Syria). 6 Chinese scripts. 7 Byblos pseudo-hieroglyphic script. 8 Ugarit cuneiform alphabet. 9 Palaeo-Sinaitic script. 10 North Semitic alphabet.

1.12*b*. Neo-Babylonian chronicle; Fall of Nineveh (British Museum 21901).

1.12*a*. Letter from Tushratta, King of Mitanni to Amenophis III, King of Egypt (British Museum 29791).

31

1.13. The 'Sun-god Tablet', showing the worship of the 'sun-god', and inscribed with a record of the restoration of the temple of Sippar by the Babylonian king Nabu-apal-iddina (ca. 870 B.C.).

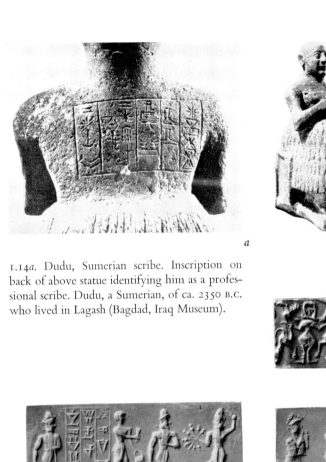

a

1.14*a*. Dudu, Sumerian scribe. Inscription on back of above statue identifying him as a professional scribe. Dudu, a Sumerian, of ca. 2350 B.C. who lived in Lagash (Bagdad, Iraq Museum).

b

c

d

e

f

1.14*b–f*. Cuneiform seals preserved in the British Museum.

1.15a. Proto Elamite tablet (British Museum 120486).

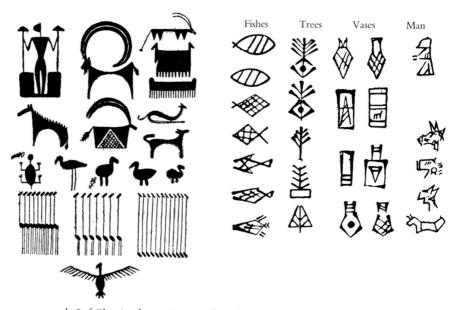

1.15b. *Left* Elamite decorative motifs, *right* early Elamite pictorial symbols.

1.15c. Inscribed Elamite brick (British Museum 90529).

1.16*a*. Darius inscription.

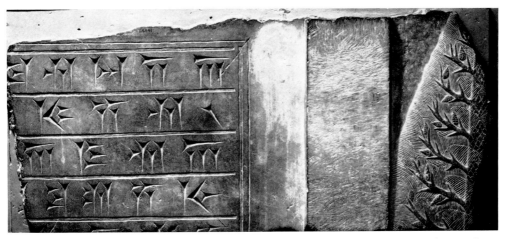

1.16*b*. Slab with inscription in Persian Cuneiform script, with text of Xerxes; *right*, part of a tree (from Persepolis, British Museum 118841), *see* also 11.1.

(1) $D(a)$-a-$r(a)$-$y(a)$-$v(a)$-u-$š(a)$ (2) $x(a)$-$š(a)$-a-
$y(a)$-$ϑ(a)$-i-$y(a)$ (3) $v(a)$-$z(a)$-$r(a)$-$k(a)$ (4) $x(a)$-
$š(a)$-a-$y(a)$-$ϑ(a)$-i-$y(a)$ (5) $x(a)$-$š(a)$-a-$y(a)$-$ϑ(a)$-i-$y(a)$-a-$n(a)$-
a-$m(a)$ (6) $x(a)$-$š(a)$-a-$y(a)$-$ϑ(a)$-i-$y(a)$ (7) $d(a)$-$h(a)$-$y(a)$-u-
$n(a)$-a-$m(a)$ (8) Vi-i-$š(a)$-$t(a)$-a-$s(a)$-$p(a)$-$h(a)$-$y(a)$-a (9) $p(a)$-
u-$ç(a)$ (10) $H(a)$-$x(a)$-a-$m(a)$-$n(a)$-i-$š(a)$-i-$y(a)$ (11) $h(a)$-$y(a)$
(12) i-$m(a)$-$m(a)$ (13) $t(a)$-$č(a)$-$r(a)$-$m(a)$ (14) a-ku-u-$n(a)$-u-$š(a)$

*Dārayavauš xšāyaϑiya vazrka xšāyaϑiya xšāyaϑiyā-
nām xšāyaϑiya dahyunām Vištāspahya puça Haxāmanišiya hya imam
tačaram akunauš*

1.17a. Darius inscription, *above* transcribed from 1.16a, *below* deciphered. Translated into English, this reads:—

Darius, the great King, the King of Kings, the King of the countries, son of Hystaspes, the Achaemenid, who built this palace.

(1) $X(a)$-$š(a)$-$y(a)$-a-$r(a)$-$š(ȧ)$-a (2) $x(a)$-$š(a)$-a-
$y(a)$-$ϑ(a)$-i-$y(a)$ (3) $v(a)$-$z(a)$-$r(a)$-$k(a)$ (4) $x(a)$-$š(a)$-a-$y(a)$-
$ϑ(a)$-i-$y(a)$ (5) $x(a)$-$š(a)$-a-$y(a)$-$ϑ(a)$-i-$y(a)$-a-$n(a)$-a-$m(a)$ (6)
$D(a)$-a-$r(a)$-$y(a)$-$v(a)$-$h(a)$-u-$š(a)$ (7) $x(a)$-$š(a)$-a-$y(a)$-$ϑ(a)$-i-
$y(a)$-$h(a)$-$y(a)$-a (8) $p(a)$-u-$ç(a)$ (9) $H(a)$-$x(a)$-a-$m(a)$-$n(a)$-i-
$š(a)$-i-$y(a)$

*Xšayāršā xšāyaϑiya vazrka xšāyaϑiya xšāyaϑiyānām
Dārayavahauš xšāyaϑiyahya puça Haxāmanišiya*

1.17b. Xerxes inscription, *above* transcribed, *below* deciphered. Translated into English, this reads:—

Xerxes, the great King, King of Kings, of Darius, the King's son, the Achaemenid.

2.1. Egyptian scribe. This statuette only 5.3 cm. high, was found by Mariette at Saqqara in a tomb of the period of the Fifth Dynasty. (Louvre Museum, Salle du scribe).

2.2a. Limestone relief: Four scribes with papyrus rolls and reed pens (18th Dynasty).

2.2b. Limestone relief: Scribes and village elders (Saqqara, 6th Dynasty).

2.3a. Both sides of the ceremonial palette of King Narmer (*c.* 2900 B.C.).

2.3b. The plaque of Akha or Akhai (*c.* 3000 B.C.).

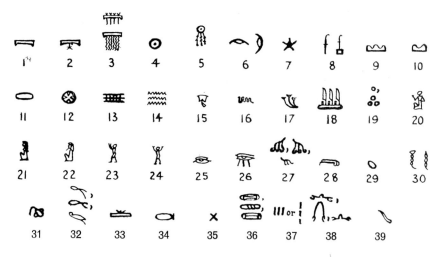

2.4. Hieroglyphic determinatives.

1. Heaven, Sky, Ceiling, what is above. 2. Night sky with a star hanging like a lamp from it, darkness, night. 3. (above) Sky slipping down over its four supports, storm, hurricane; (below) rain or dew falling from the sky. 4. Sun, the sun-god Ra, day period, time in general. 5. Shine, rise (of a luminary), being of light. 6. Moon, month. 7. Star, morning star, hour, time for prayer, pray. 8. Flourish, blooming, year, time in general, last year of a King's reign. 9. Foreign country, desert. 10. Mountain. 11. Island. 12. City, town. 13. Nome, District. 14. Water, watery mass of the sky. 15. Skin, hide. 16. Worm. 17. Plant, vegetable, herb, dried up. 18. Field, garden. 19. Grain, corn. 20. Man, first person sing. 21. Woman, first and second person sing. 22. God or divine person. 23. Pray, worship, adore, entreat, praise. 24. High, lofty, exalt, make merry. 25. To see. 26. To weep, tear, grief. 27. Hair (of men and animals), bald, lack, want, lacuna (in manuscripts), colour, complexion. 28. Phallus, front, male, masculine, procreate. 29. Women, godessess, cities. 30. Sweet, pleasant. 31. Incense. 32. Roll of papyrus, tie up, bind together, come to an end. 33. Roll of papyrus (tied round the middle), book, deed, document, register, group together, abstract ideas. 34. Oval round a royal name, known as *cartouche*. 35. Pair of tallies, count, tally, reckon, pass by, depart. 36. Bread, cake. 37. Sign of the plural 38. Negation, no, not, nothing, lack, want, need. 39. Horn.

soldier (army) eye giraffe horn swallow beetle flower sun

mountain corner foot sandal arch plough bread

to beat to fly to eat to go to fight to row to weep

to dominate to direct upper Egypt to find old age fresh
to govern south

m—n m—s sh— n—w kh—n w— kh— m— i— t—y

2.5a. Hieroglyphic word signs. 1, symbols representing things shown
2, ideographs representing actions associated with things shown; 3, symbols
representing abstract ideas; 4, hieroglyphic bi-consonantal signs.

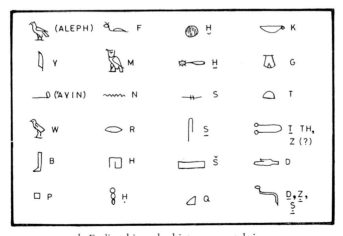

2.5b. Earliest hieroglyphic consonantal signs.

a

b

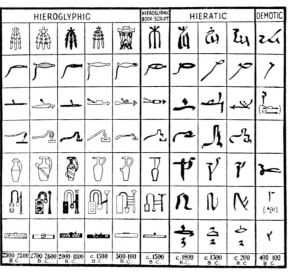

c

2.6. *a* The Palermo Stone. *b* The Stone of Israel. *c* Development of Egyptian signs (from G. Moeller).

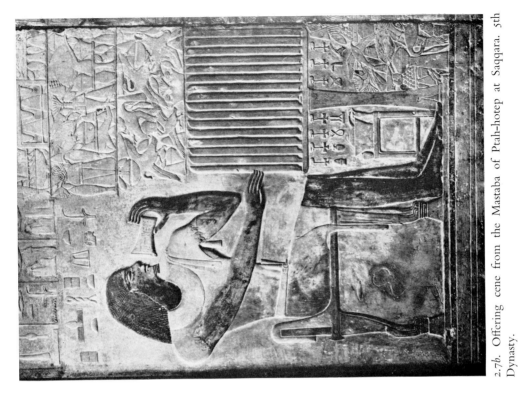

2.7b. Offering cene from the Mastaba of Ptah-hotep at Saqqara. 5th Dynasty.

2.7a. False door from the tomb of Iry, an official connected with the Great Pyramid of Cheops at Giza, fifth–sixth Dynasties.

2.8a. Egyptian hieroglyphic papyri: Ani Papyrus, sheet 3 (British Museum, Pap. 10470).

2.8b. Egyptian hieroglyphic papyri: Khă Papyrus (Turin Egyptian Museum).

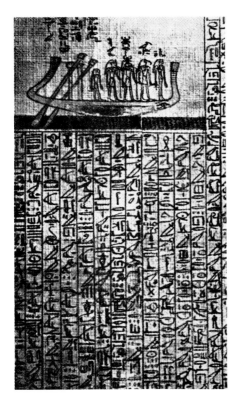

2.9. Papyri written in late hieroglyphic writing.

a Nu Papyrus (British Museum, 10447).

2.9*b*. *Book of the Dead* written in the so-called cursive hieroglyphs, belonging approximately to the Eighteenth Dynasty (Trinity College Library, Dublin).

45

2.10a. *Book of the Dead* of the Saitic period (Trinity College Library, Dublin).

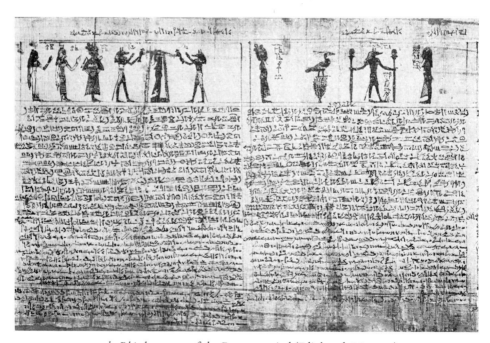

2.10b. *Rhind papyrus*, of the Roman period (Edinburgh Museum).

2.11a. Earliest known fragments of hieratic Papyri (Cairo Museum).

2.11b. Early hieratic Papyrus, Fifth Dynasty (Berlin Papyrus 9874).

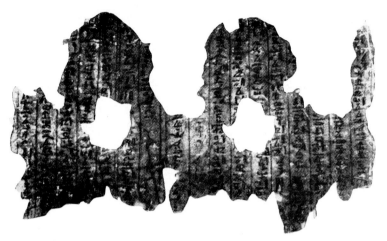

2.12*a*. Earliest extant book written on leather. Hieratic manuscript attributed to Sixth Dynasty (Cairo Museum).

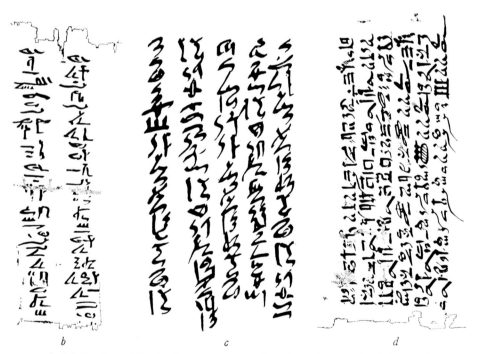

b   c   d

2.12*b*. *left* Portion of Berlin Papyrus 9010, attributed to the period of the Sixth Dynasty, *centre* Berlin Papyrus 3024, attributed to the period of the Middle Kingdom, *right* Berlin Papyrus 3033, Early New Kingdom.

2.13. *a (above) Papyrus Anastasi 7*, half of sheet 6, *recto* (British Museum 10222).
b (below) Rhind Mathematical Papyrus (British Museum 10057 and 10058).

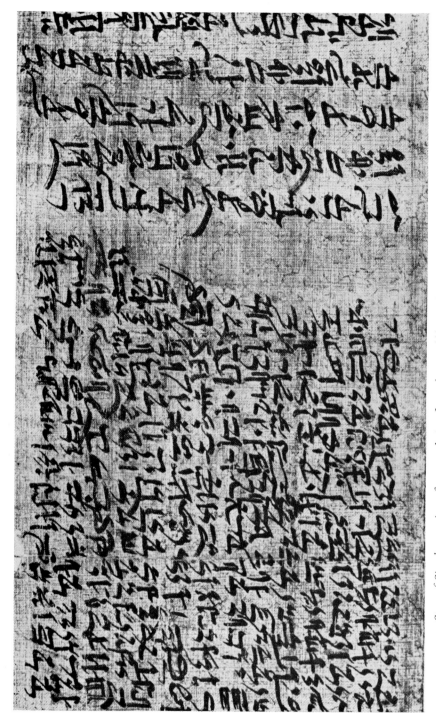

2.14. *Story of Si-nuhe*, portion of a copy dating from the Twelfth or Thirteenth Dynasty. (Berlin Papyrus 3022).

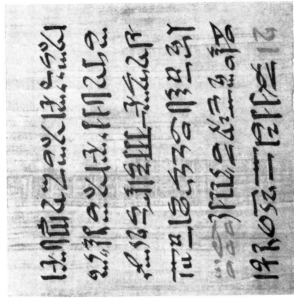

2.15. a (left) *Papyrus Ebers*, belonging to the period of the early Eighteenth Dynasty (University of Leipsig). b (above) Portion of *Papyrus Ebers*.

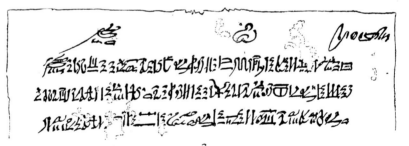

2.16a. Page of hieratic writing from the *Great Harris Papyrus* (British Museum).

2.16b. Detail from a school exercise book written in hieratic, with the teacher's corrections.

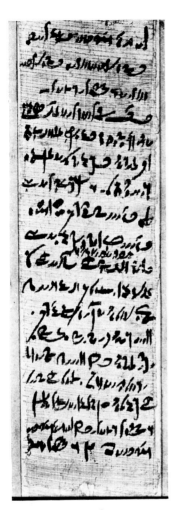

obverse

reverse   b

obverse

reverse   c

2.17. *a* Demotic document on wood. *b*, *c* Two wood labels of mummies written in demotic. Note the two lines of Greek on the reverse of *c*.

2.18. Rosetta stone (British Museum).

PTOLEMY

(P T O L M I S)
1 2 3 4 5 6 7

DEMOTIC

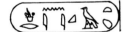

HIEROGLYPHIC

CLEOPATRA

(K L E O P A T R A)
1 2 3 4 5 6 7 8 9

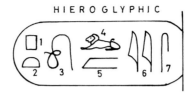

10 FEMININE ENDING
11 DETERMINATIVE FOLLOWING A FEMININE NAME

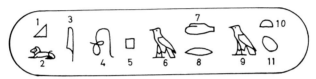

BERENICE ALEXANDER AUTOCRATOR

TIBERIUS DOMITIAN GERMANICUS TRAJAN

2.19. Decipherment of Egyptian hieroglyphic writing: decipherment of certain imperial names and titles.

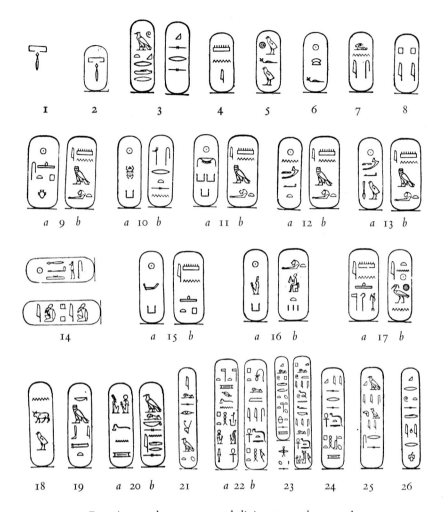

2.20. Egyptian royal names. *a* royal-divine name; *b* personal name.

1-2, Pharaoh. 3, *Autókratos* and Caesar (*Kaísaros*). 4, Mena or Menes (1st dyn.). 5, Khufu or Cheops (4th dyn.). 6, Khaf-ra or Chephren (4th dyn.). 7, Unas or Unis (5th dyn.). 8, Pepi I (6th dyn.). 9, Amen-em-hat I (12th dyn.). 10, Usertsen I or Sesonchosis (12th dyn.). 11, Amen-em-hat II (12th dyn.). 12, Amen-em-hat III (12th dyn). 13, Amen-em-hat IV (12th dyn.). 14, Apepa I or Apophis (a chief king of the Hyksos). 15, Amen-hetep or Amenophis I (18th dyn.). 16, Hat-shepset-khnem-Amen (Queen Hatshepsu). 17, Amen-hetep Neter Heq Uast or Amenophis IV (Akhnaton) (18th dyn.). 18, Necho (26th dyn.). 19, Cambyses (27th dyn.). 20, Alexander the Great. 21, Queen Arsinoë (Ptolemies). 22, Ptolemy V Epiphanes. 23, Cleopatra VII with her son Caesarion. 24, Augustus. 25, Caligula. 26, Claudius.

Class A

Class B

A   B

C   D

3.1. Cretan pictographic inscriptions.

57

3.2a. Main symbols of Linear A.

3.2b. Linear A sign list according to Caratelli.

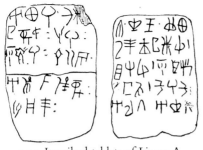

3.3a. Inscribed tablets of Linear A.

3.3b. Inscription in ink of Linear A.

Linear A

3.3c. Vase from Orchomenus (an ancient city in Boeotia) with inscription in Linear A.

Orcho-menos	Crete Pictogr.	Crete Linear A	Crete Linear B

3.3d. The Orchomenus signs compared with Cretan symbols: Cretan pictographic signs, Linear A and Linear B.

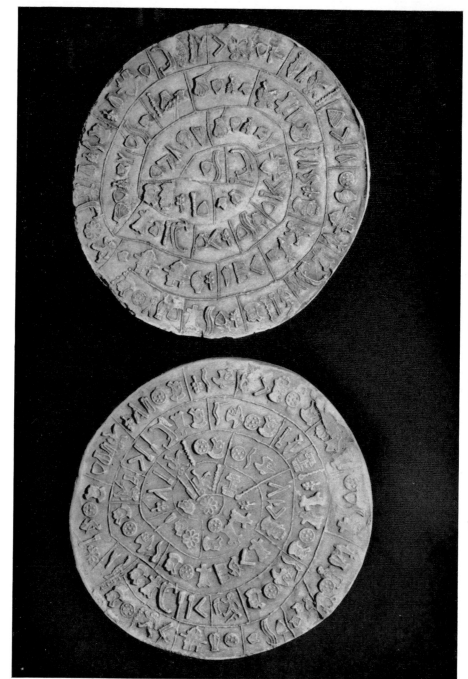

side *a*   3.4. Phaistos Disc (from a cast).   side *b*

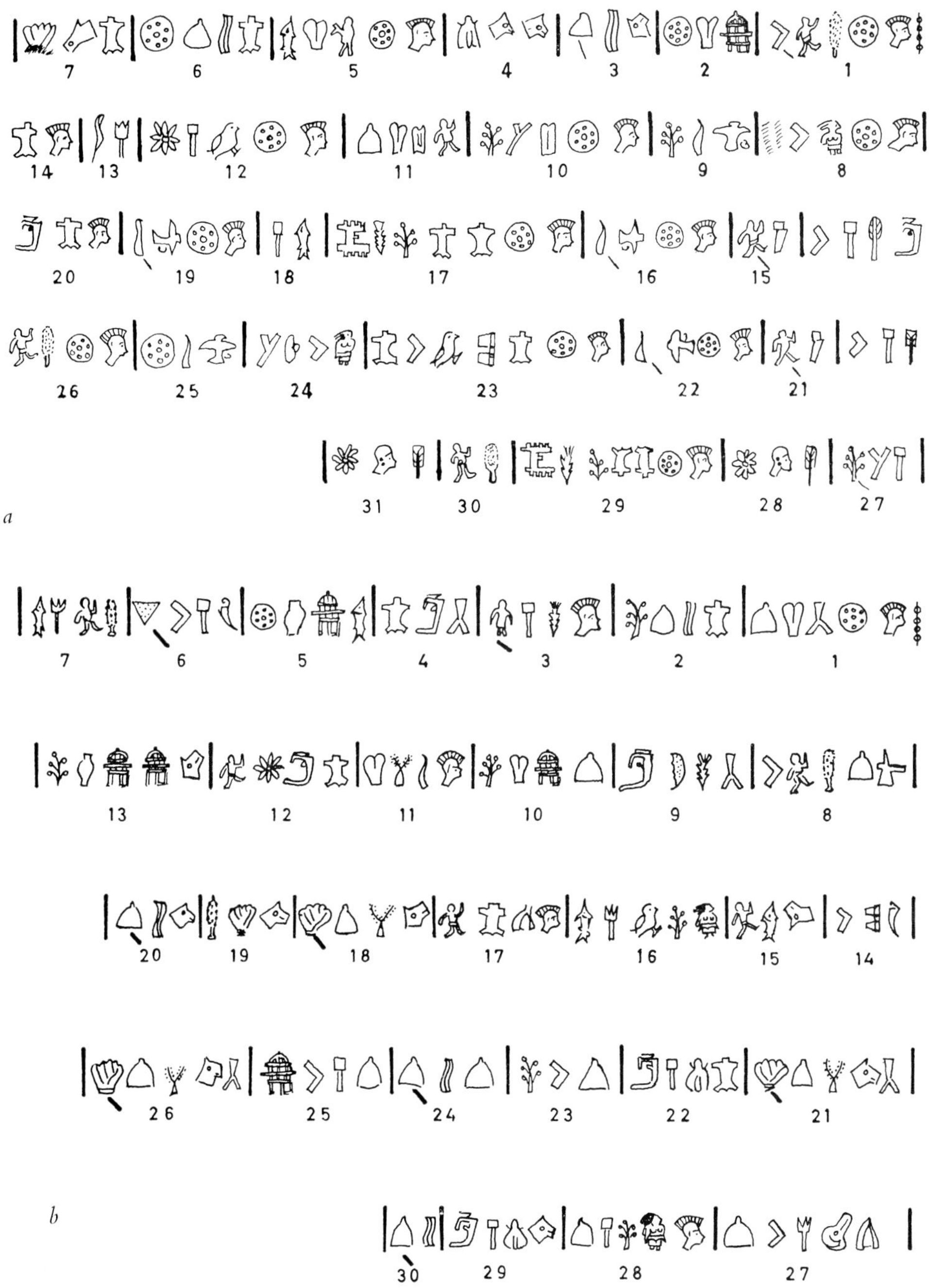

a

b

3.5. The symbols of both faces of the Phaistos disc, according to Professor Schwartz. *a* corresponds to 3.4*a* and *b* corresponds to 3.4*b*.

3.6b. Frequency table

Rows 1–15:

NO.	PICTOGRAM	I	M	F	T
1	(symbol)	19	0	0	19
2	(symbol)	0	13	4	17
3	(symbol)	2	3	1	6
4	(symbol)	1	3	7	11
5	(symbol)	0	7	5	12
6	(symbol)	1	4	1	6
7	(symbol)	0	5	1	6
8	(symbol)	8	3	0	11
9	(symbol)	1	5	0	6
10	(symbol)	4	6	8	18
11	(symbol)	0	2	1	3
12	(symbol)	0	1	0	1
13	(symbol)	2	1	3	6
14	(symbol)	5	8	2	15
15	(symbol)	0	1	0	1

Rows 16–30:

NO.	PICTOGRAM	I	M	F	T
16	(symbol)	0	1	4	5
17	(symbol)	2	2	0	4
18	(symbol)	2	3	0	5
19	(symbol)	0	3	3	6
20	(symbol)	0	4	7	11
21	(symbol)	0	2	0	2
22	(symbol)	0	2	1	6
23	(symbol)	0	3	0	3
24	(symbol)	1	9	1	11
25	(symbol)	0	1	3	4
26	(symbol)	1	3	0	3
27	(symbol)	0	0	1	1
28	(symbol)	0	4	3	7
29	(symbol)	2	2	0	4
30	(symbol)	2	0	0	2

Rows 31–45:

NO.	PICTOGRAM	I	M	F	T
31	(symbol)	0	4	0	4
32	(symbol)	0	0	2	2
33	(symbol)	0	2	0	2
34	(symbol)	0	1	0	1
35	(symbol)	0	2	0	2
36	(symbol)	4	1	0	5
37	(symbol)	0	0	1	1
38	(symbol)	0	2	0	2
39	(symbol)	2	0	0	2
40	(symbol)	0	0	1	1
41	(symbol)	0	0	1	1
42	(symbol)	0	1	0	1
43	(symbol)	0	4	0	4
44	(symbol)	1	1	0	2
45	(symbol)	0	1	0	1

3.6b. The frequency of the various symbols (I = initial, M = medial, F = final, T = total) according to Prof. Schwartz.

3.6a. Professor Schwartz' attempted decipherment of the Phaistos disc.

62

4.1. Selection of inscribed seals from Indus Valley.

4.2. Seal inscriptions from Indus Valley.

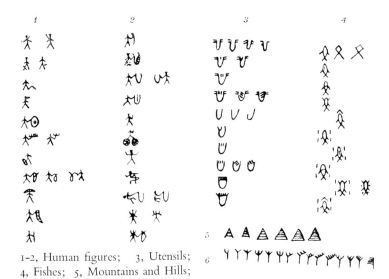

1-2, Human figures;   3, Utensils;
4, Fishes;   5, Mountains and Hills;
6, Trees.

4.3*a*. Stylized Indus Valley symbols.

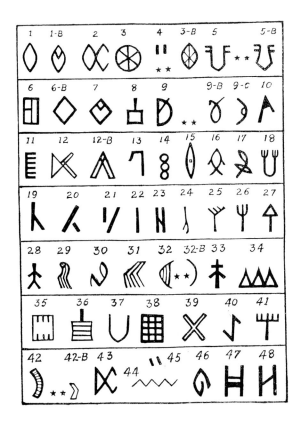

4.3*b*. Attempted deciperment by S. K. Ray, New Delhi: the uniliteral symbols of the Indus Valley.

Indus Valley	Easter Island	Indus Valley	Easter Island	Indus Valley	Easter Island	Indus Valley	Easter Island
I	II	III	IV	V	VI	VII	VIII

4.4. De Hevesy's comparison of Indus Valley symbols with Easter Island script.

5.1. Hittite hieroglyphic inscriptions carved in relief. *a*. The most beautiful inscription from Carchemish, ninth century B.C. *b*. Another Carchemish inscription, eighth century B.C.

a

b

5.2. Broken door jamb, inscribed in raised Hittite hieroglyphs: dedication of Temple of Goddess Kubaba by Kaluwas, King of Carchemish, c. 900 B.C. (British Museum).

5.3a. Hittite hieroglyphic inscription engraved on stone.

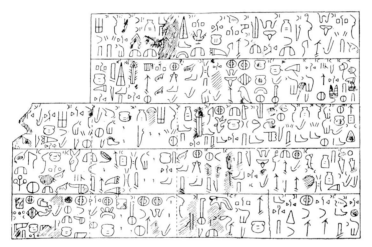

5.3b. Late Hittite hieroglyphic inscription, about 600 B.C., from Bulgar Dagh (Bulgarmaden).

Mon	Curs	Mon	Curs	Mon	Curs	Mon	Curs

5.4*a*. Comparison of Hittite hieroglyphic cursive signs with monumental symbols.

	Crete	Hitt.		Crete	Hitt.		Crete	Hitt.		Crete	Hitt.

5.4*b*. Comparison of Hittite hieroglyphic symbols wth Cretan pictographic signs.

ox ax stool sacrifice calf vase warrior goat vine land noble(?)

city con-queror(?) god import-ance(?) king palace prince river sove-reign(?) to speak great monu-ment (?)

5.5a. Hittite ideographic symbols.

5.5b. Hittite hieroglyphic sylla-bary according to I. J. Gelb.

	a	e	i	u	Vowel uncertain
Vowels					
Nasals					
ᵓ					
ḫ					
k/g					
l					
m					
n				III III III = nu / = nú	
p/b					
r					
s/z	= sa / = sá				
t/d				= tx / = tx́	
w					
Syllables of unknown value					

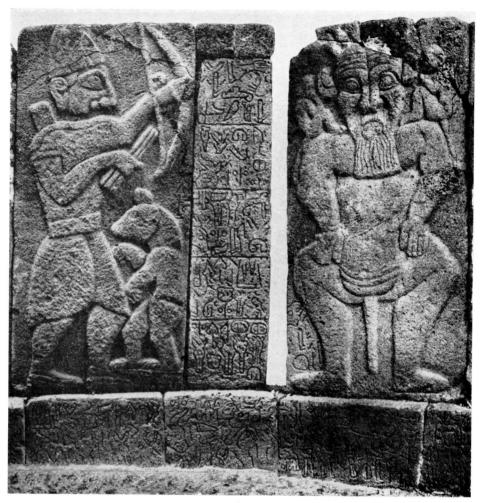

5.6. Hittite inscription from Karatepe.

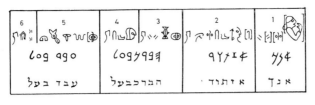

6	5	4	3	2	1
עבד בעל		הברכבעל		אזתוד	אנך

11	10	9	8	7
מלך דננים		אורך	אדר	אש

17	16	15	14	13	12
[מעל]	ל	לאב ולאם	לדננים	בעל	פעלנ

20	19	18
רמ אנך		אית דננים

29	28	27	26	25	24	23	22	21
ועד	מבא		ל ממצא שמש			ארץ עמק אדד		ירהב אנך

37	36	35	34	33	32	31	30
[וכן]	ומנעם	ושבע	כל נעם לדננים			רכן	בימתי וכן

40	39	38
עקרת פער		ומלאאנך

5.7. Transliteration of the Karatepe Hittite, Phoenician bilingual, as well as transliteration into modern hebrew.

73

(1) *kan*, sky, dry; *yang*, the first element, the creative element; Grand-father, life, favourable presage

(2) *tui*, water, sea, lakes, light

(3) *li*, fire, sun, heat, the creative element of heat and light

(4) *ch'en*, thunder, mother of lightning and heat, hard

(5) *hsü*, wind, movable, wood

(6) *k'an*, water, rivers, liquid element, cool, cold, moon

(7) *kên*, mountains, hills, element which hinders movement

(8) *kun*, earth, terrestrial element; *yin*, the second element, the element of destruction; Grand-mother, bad presage.

6.1*a*. Chinese mystic trigrams *pa kua*.

command   vow, oath   refusal   refuse   usur-
                                          to marry pation

6.1*b*. Chinese hand gestures.

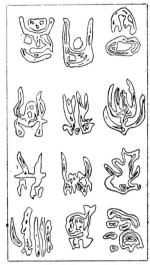

The 'Yü Tablet'

Stone drum inscription

Archaic characters on
bronze and bone

character *ti*, 'sovereign ruler'

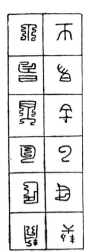

Hsiao   Ta
chuan   chuan

Bronze inscrip-
tion from Shang-
Yin period

Ancient characters engraved on
fragments of bone

6.2. Early Chinese inscriptions on stone, bronze and bone.

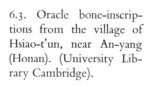

6.3. Oracle bone-inscriptions from the village of Hsiao-t'un, near An-yang (Honan). (University Library Cambridge).

76

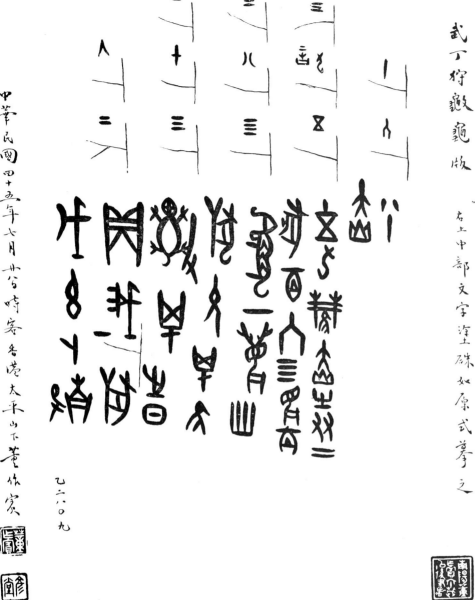

6.4. Copy of the inscriptions of divination on the ventral part of a tortoise shell on the occasion of a hunt at Kwei, by King Wu-ting of the Yin (Shang) Dynasty, 1450–c. 1000 B.C. The hunt yielded one tiger, 40 deer, 164 foxes, 159 fawns, a brace of pheasants and 18 double-red birds.

77

| Hsing shu. | K'ai shu. | Ts'ao shu. | Li shu. | Shan fang ta chuan | Chuan |

6.5. Main types of Chinese writing.

PICTOGRAMS							
MAN, ANIMALS, AND PARTS OF THE HUMAN BODY							
MAN	WOMAN	CHILD	MOUTH	NOSE	EYE	HAND	FOOT
HORSE	TIGER	DOG	ELEPHANT	DEER	SHEEP	SILKWORM	TORTOISE
NATURAL AND ARTIFICIAL OBJECTS							
SUN	MOON	RAIN	LIGHTNING	MOUNTAIN	RIVER	GRAIN	WOOD
VASE	TRIPOD	BOW	ARROW	SILK	BOOK	ORACLE	OMEN

IDEOGRAMS			
FIGHTING (MAN AGAINST MAN)	PLOUGHING (MAN+PLOUGH)	HUNTING (WEAPON+ANIMAL)	SUCKLING (WOMAN NURSING CHILD)
SUNSET (SUN+GRASSES)	BRIGHT (MOON+WINDOW)	WRITING BRUSH (HAND+BRUSH)	SCRIBE (HAND+OBJECT)
	ABOVE	BELOW	

PICTOGRAM + PHONETIC ELEMENT			
BLACK HORSE (HORSE+li)	SACRIFICE (SPIRIT+ssu)	PREGNANCY (WOMAN+jen)	HUAN RIVER (RIVER+huan)

HOMOPHONES	
(lai, "WHEAT," FOR) lai "TO COME"	(feng, "PHOENIX," FOR) feng "WIND"

6.6. Examples of Chinese pictograms, ideograms, pictograms combined with phonetic elements, and homophones.

Ancient	Modern		Ancient	Modern	
☉	日	*jih* sun	朩	木	*mu* tree
☽	月	*yüeh* moon	雨	雨	*yü* rain
山	山	*shan* mountain	矢	矢	*shih* arrow
子 子	子	*tzu* child	門 門	門	*mên* door, gate
巴 巴	巴	*pa* great serpent	冊 冊	冊	*ts'ê*, bundle of inscribed sticks, volume, book, scroll

Hsiang symbols

Ancient	Modern		Ancient	Modern	
卍	方	*fång* zone square		言	*yên* word, to talk
勿	勿	*wu* no	中 中	中	*chung* middle
Ⅰ	一	*yi* one			
Ⅱ	二	*erh* two	畺	畺	*chiang* border, limit, frontier
Ⅲ	三	*san* three			

Chih Shih symbols

Ancient	Modern	Ancient	Modern	Ancient	Modern
東東	東東	奻奻	奻女	馬馬馬	馬馬
2 × East = everywhere (*tung*)		2 × women = quarrel (*wǎn*)		3 × horse = to gallop (*ch'êng*)	

Ancient	Modern	Ancient	Modern		Ancient	Modern	Ancient	Modern	
口	口	鳥	鳥	鳴	人	言	信		明
kò mouth		*niaò* bird		= *ming* to sing	*jên* man	*yên* word	= *sin* true		

Ancient	Modern	Ancient	Modern	
☉ 日	日	☽ 月	月	明
jih sun		*yüeh* moon		= *ming* bright, clear

Hui i symbols

6.7. Classification of Chinese characters.

后 司 人 尸
hêú *szú* *jén* *shih*
prince officer, man, corpse
clerk person

Chuan chou symbols

nine basic strokes of Chinese
writing

來 足 故 古 女 汝
lâi *tsu* *ku* *kú* *nŭ* *jŭ*
grain, foot, cause used in- old woman used in- you
also also stead of stead of
to come be sufficient

Chia chieh symbols

心忄 *hsin*   水氵 *shiŭ*   言 *yên*
heart   water   to talk

工 *kūng*   忄工 *k'ūng*   江 *kiāng*   訌 *hûng*
worker   impatience   torrent, flood   quarrel

由 *yu*   忄由 *yeû*   油 *yeû*   詋 *chou*
from   sad   oil   to pray

甫 *fou*   惠 *fou*   浦 *pu*   誧 *fū*
table land,   to have fear   branch of   to talk together
huge   a river   to decide

果 *kò*   慄 *kò*   渓 *k'o*   課 *k'ó*
fruit   to go   river   to examine
                                                          to investigate

Hsing shêng symbols

6 8. Classification of Chinese characters.

Table of 300 Chinese primary elements (read in ten vertical columns, numbered 1–300):

1–30	31–60	61–90	91–120	121–150	151–180	181–210	211–240	241–270	271–300
一 1	匕 31	尢 61	子 91	斤 121	弗 151	缶 181	北 211	亞 241	垂 271
丨 2	冫 32	中 62	中 92	戶 122	冊 152	至 182	丸 212	金 242	瑟 272
丶 3	卅 33	井 63	心 93	午 123	皿 153	辛 183	谷 213	來 243	旁 273
丿 4	力 34	刀 64	午 94	牛 124	且 154	衣 184	豕 214	兔 244	寅 274
乀 5	勹 35	才 65	牛 95	今 125	目 155	交 185	豆 215	希 245	魚 275
乙 6	乃 36	广 66	今 96	不 126	自 156	亥 186	呂 216	易 246	鳥 276
乚 7	又 37	弋 67	不 97	木 127	臣 157	糸 187	克 217	夋 247	鹿 277
亅 8	乂 38	丸 68	木 98	开 128	四 158	虫 188	臣 218	函 248	咢 278
乁 9	乂 39	凡 69	开 99	水 129	只 159	束 189	囚 219	鹵 249	率 279
了 10	卩 40	凡 70	水 100	火 130	民 160	卡 190	酉 220	离 250	离 280
卜 11	卜 41	无 71	火 101	犬 131	凸 161	虍 191	卯 221	禼 251	殻 281
二 12	丩 42	毛 72	犬 102	爪 132	出 162	舟 192	臼 222	祭 252	壺 282
亠 13	丁 43	口 73	爪 103	夭 133	丙 163	自 193	角 223	象 253	象 283
人 14	丂 44	回 74	亢 104	壬 134	朮 164	自 194	囟 224	舄 254	舄 284
八 15	厂 45	尸 75	六 105	凶 135	禾 165	耳 195	豸 225	焉 255	焉 285
入 16	三 46	己 76	文 106	日 136	矛 166	臣 196	豕 226	昝 256	昝 286
八 17	彡 47	巳 77	方 107	曰 137	永 167	而 197	采 227	爲 257	爲 287
儿 18	巛 48	弓 78	万 108	月 138	永 168	而 198	尚 228	巢 258	巢 288
几 19	彳 49	马 79	勿 109	巴 139	瓜 169	丙 199	革 228	樂 259	樂 289
九 20	个 50	幺 80	欠 110	玉 140	戊 170	囱 200	肩 229	鼠 260	鼠 290
九 21	小 51	小 81	气 111	主 141	矢 171	西 201	盾 230	蜀 261	蜀 291
十 22	勹 52	宀 82	毛 112	玄 142	冬 172	冃 202	車 231	齊 262	齊 292
七 23	久 53	巾 83	手 113	白 143	疋 173	肉 203	貝 232	壽 263	壽 293
冂 24	夂 54	屮 84	半 114	臼 144	皮 174	臼 204	百 233	齒 264	齒 294
冖 25	夕 55	山 85	丰 115	瓦 145	穴 175	甘 205	身 234	署 265	署 295
口 26	巾 56	巾 86	斗 116	田 146	它 176	囟 206	良 235	龍 266	龍 296
凵 27	土 57	土 87	升 117	由 147	宁 177	由 207	辰 236	龜 267	龜 297
厶 28	互 58	工 88	廾 118	甲 148	米 178	曲 208	乖 237	燕 268	燕 298
女 29	大 59	干 89	牙 119	冉 149	羊 179	羽 209	飛 238	鬲 269	羽 299
匚 30	矢 60	也 90	予 120	曲 150	兂 180	兆 210	隹 239	羋 270	爵 300

6.9. 300 Chinese primary elements.

一丨丶丿乙亅 二亠人儿入八冂冖冫几凵刀力勹匕匚匸十卜卩厂厶又 口囗土士夂夊夕大女子宀寸小尢尸屮山巛工 己巾干幺广廴廾弋弓彐彡彳 心戈戶手支攴文斗斤方无日 日月木欠止歹殳毋比毛氏气水火爪父爻爿片牙牛犬 玄玉 瓜瓦甘生用田疋疒癶白皮皿目矛矢石示内禾穴立 竹米糸 缶网羊羽老而耒耳聿肉臣自至臼舌舛舟艮色艸虍虫血行衣 西 見角言谷豆豕豸貝赤走足身車辛辰辵邑酉釆里 金長 門阜隶隹雨青非 面革韋韭音頁風飛食首香 馬骨高髟鬥 鬯鬲鬼 魚鳥鹵鹿麥麻 黃黍黑黹黽鼎鼓鼠鼻齊齒龍龜龠

6.10. The 214 keys of Chinese writing.

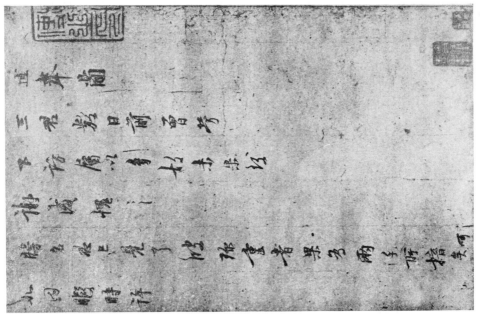

6.11b. Liu P'u (A.D. 967–1028) Sung Dynasty. Part of personal letter.
Born in Ch'ien Tung, led a hermit life at West lake. Emperor Sen Tsung conferred on him the posthumous title Ho-Chin Shing Sheng.

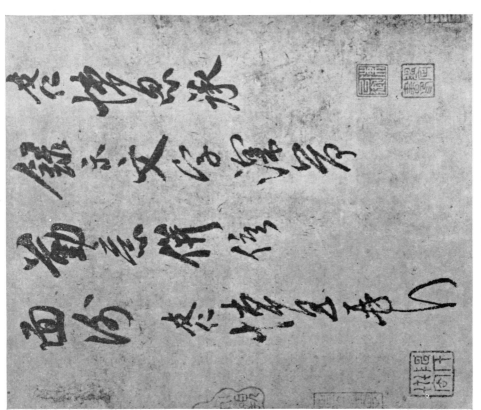

6.11a. Note of thanks to a friend, written by Mi Yu-Jen (son of Mi Fei) A.D. 1086–1165; vice minister of war under Emperor Kao Tsung—Southern Sung Dynasty.

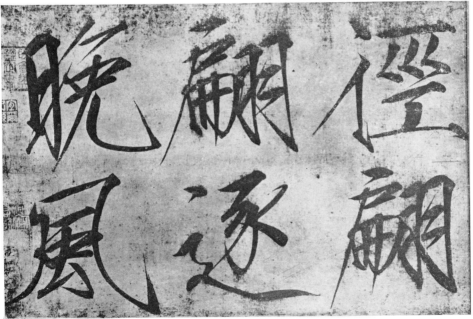

6.12. *a* (above) Part of a poem on *Autumn Flowers* by Emperor Huei Tsung (A.D. 1082–1135) the eighth ruler of the Sung Dynasty (1102–1125) named Chao Chih, the 11th son of Emperor Shen Tsung (A.D. 1068–1085). *b* (below) Part seven of the same poem.

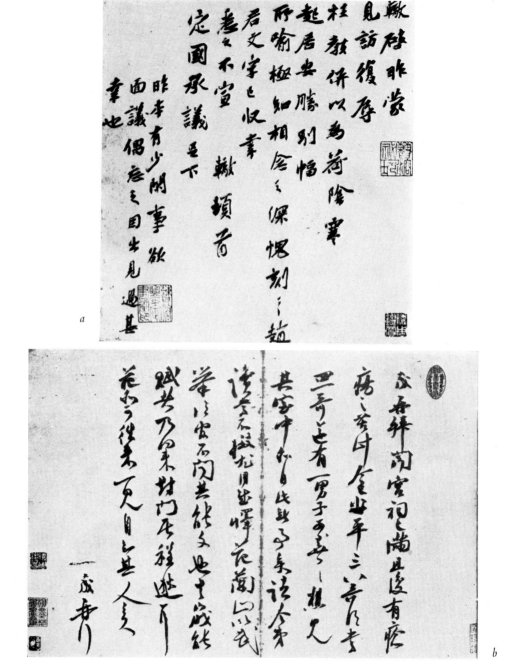

6.13. Sung Dynasty. *a* Su Ch'e's personal letter to Wang Kung (A.D. 1039–1112) younger brother of Su Shih, became a Chin-Shih in 1057, served as Deputy Premier under Emperor Cheh Tsung. Posthumously was given—by Emperor Hwei Tsung—the title Wen Ting. *b* Personal letter by Chang Chin-Chen (A.D. 1092–1159). Born on K'ai-Feng, topped the list of Chin-Shih 1132, vice minister of Rites, southern Sung Dynasty. Posthumous title: Wen-Chung.

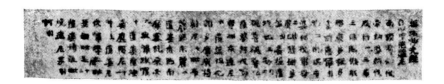

6.14*a*. The earliest preserved printing; Japanese Buddhist charms, in the Sanskrit language and in Chinese characters (*c.* A.D. 770).

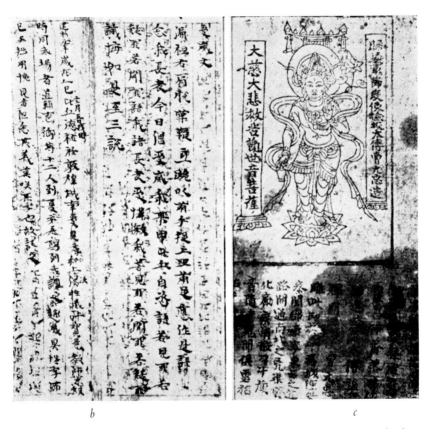

      b   *c*

6.14. *b* Earliest example of a Chinese dated colophon (Vinaya text, *Prātimokṣa* by Sarvāstivādin, dated 10.1.406); *c* printed and hand-coloured Chinese prayer-sheet dated 947; it gives the name (Lei Yen-mei) of the first known printer (or rather blockmaker). Both documents were found at the 'Caves of the Thousand Buddhas' and are preserved in the British Museum.

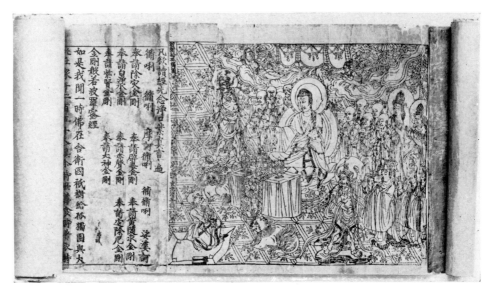

6.15a. The earliest preserved book: the *Diamond Sutra* in Chinese, A.D. 868 (British Museum).

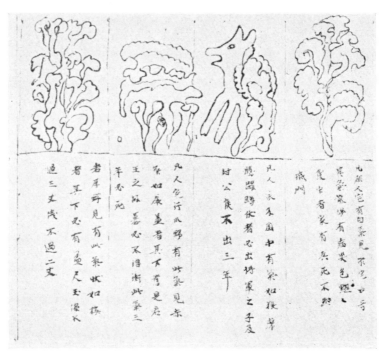

6.15b. Chinese Taoist text on divination from vapours.

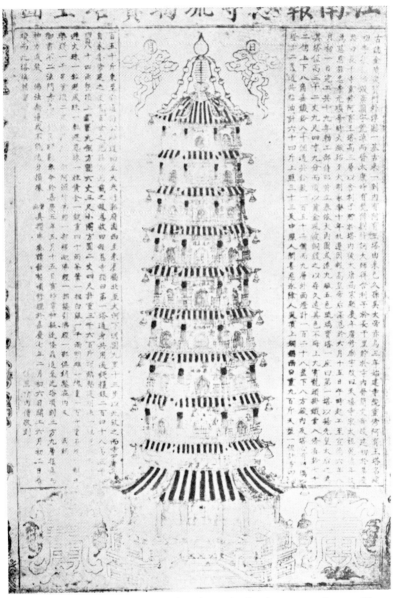

6.16. Page from a Chinese book (The John Rylands Library, Manchester, *Chin. No.* 465).

6.17. *a* Mahāprajñaparamitasûtra. Chap. 110, printed at Fêng-hua, A.D. 1162. (University Library, Cambridge). *b* Jade book: Diamond Sūtra, A.D. 1732 (Chester Beatty Library, Dublin).

6.17 *b* Jade Book: *Dirmond Sutra*, A.D. 1732 (Chester Beatty Library, Dublin).

6.18a. 1, *Jên*, man, person, human. 2, *Nü*, girl, woman, female. 3, *Tzu*, child, son, posterity. 4 (composed of symbols 2 and 3), *Hao*, good, well, fond of, very. 5, *Kuo*, kingdom or country surrounded with boundaries. 6, *Chung*, centre, middle, inside. 7, *Ta* or *da*, great, noble, very. 8, *Ying*, superior used for Eng(land). 9, *I* (*ee*), one. 10, *Erh*, two. 11, *San*, three. 12, *Szu*, four. 13, *Wu*, 'five.' 14, *Lu*, six. 15, *Chi*, 'seven. 16, *Pa*, eight. 17, *Chiu*, nine. 18, *Shih*, ten.

6.18. Modern Chinese characters.

6.18b. 1. (2+1), *Nü-jên*, female + person = woman. 2. (6+5), *Chung-kuo*, middle + kingdom = China. 3. (8+5), *Ying-kuo*, Ying (England) + kingdom = England. 4. (8+5+1), *Ying-kuo-jên*, English + kingdom + man = Englishman.

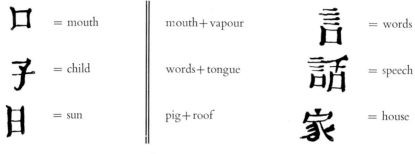

口 = mouth	mouth + vapour	言 = words
子 = child	words + tongue	話 = speech
日 = sun	pig + roof	家 = house

a

'fang' square	方 square	pig + roof + woman	= to marry
place	坊 square + earth	woman + broom + storm	= wife
spinning	紡 square + silk	woman + roof	= peace
fragrant	芳 square + herbs	2 women + roof	= discord
enquire	訪 square + words	3 women	= intrigue
hinder	妨 square + woman	women + mouth + crooked	= dangerous
		word + mouth + mountain	= slander

b   *c*

6.19. *a*, *b* and *c* Modern Chinese characters.

92

一 one (i)	仁 perfect virtue (jen)	字 characters (tzŭ)	反 to turn over, to turn back (fan)
十 ten (shih)	河 river (ho)	思 to think (szŭ)	店 inn, shop (tien)
中 centre (chung)	栢 cypress (pai)	要 important must (yao)	眉 eyebrow (mei)
女 woman, daughter (niü)	銀 silver (yin)	買 to buy (mai)	虐 harsh cruel (nüeh)
本 root, origin (pen)	輪 wheel (lun)	集 to gather (chi)	差 different (ch'a)
武 military, violent (wu)	近 near (chin)	回 to return (hui)	門 the bolt used to bar a door (shuan)
式 fashion, rule (shih)	廸 to bring forward, to direct (ti)	因 because (yin)	閃 to flash (shan)
飛 to fly (fei)	建 to build to establish (chien)	固 firm, strong (ku)	問 to ask (wen)
或 or (huo)	逼 to annoy to press (pi)	圓 round (yuan)	開 to open (k'ai)
成 success (ch'eng)	避 to shun to avoid (pi)	團 (a) mass, to coil (tuan)	鬭 to flight (tou)

6.20. Modern Chinese characters: simple, and compounds of two elements.

93

衍 (yen) to overflow to spread out

漪 (i) the ripples on water

樹 (shu) tree

謝 (hsieh) to thank

鐵 (tie) iron

稟 (ping) to inform

賣 (mai) to sell

器 (ch'i) vessel

算 (suan) to reckon, to calculate

靈 (ling) spirit, efficacious

咒 (chou) to curse, incantations

智 (chih) wisdom

豎 (shu) to set up

賢 (hsien) virtuous

瞽 (ku) blind

品 (p'in) conduct

森 (shen) overgrown, dark

晶 (ching) crystal, bright

焱 (yen) flames

鑫 (hsin) used as names

盟 (meng) oath, alliance

盤 (p'an) plate, dish

契 (ch'i) contract, to notch

染 (jan) to dye, to infect

點 (tien) dot, spot

符 (fu) to agree with, to tally

筋 (chin) sinews

萌 (meng) the budding of plants

莊 (chuang) sedate

箱 (hsiang) box, chest

6.21. Modern Chinese compound characters—three elements.

94

7.1a. *Codex Dresden*. Portion of divinatory almanac (4 *Ahau*, 12 *Lamat*, 7 *Cib*, 2 *Kan*, 10 *Eb*, 5 *Ahau*, 13 *Lamat*, South, God B, fire god, maize god, drought).

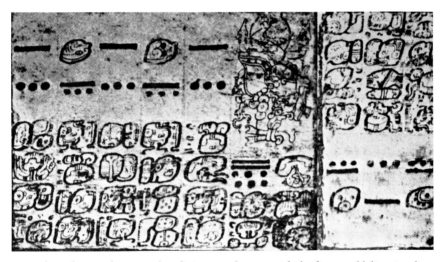

7.1b. *Codex Dresden*. Complete divinatory almanac with the four world directional colours: red, white, black, and yellow, and glyphs of various offerings to be made to the gods. (Explanation by J. Eric S. Thompson.)

Fig. 7.2. *Codex Paris* (infra red photo of p. 4, the best preserved page of the manuscript). Represents events connected with the Maya *katun* (twenty-year period) 11 *Ahau*. (Explanation by J. Eric S. Thompson.)

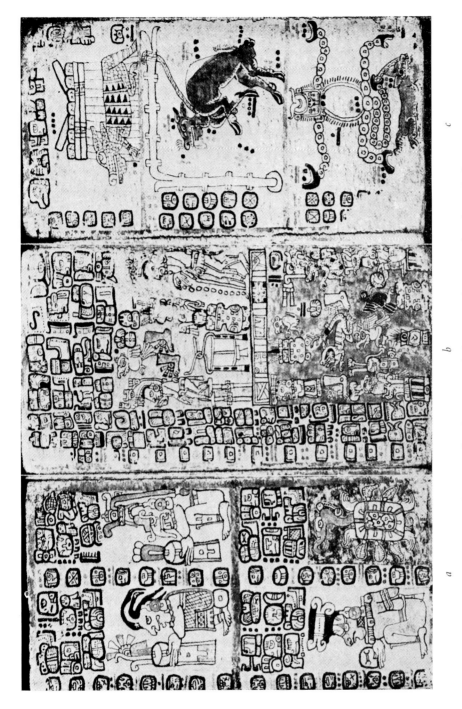

a

b

c

7.3. *Codex Tro-Cortesiano. a*, page 72 (page 38 of *Codex Cortesiano*). *b*, page 36 (page 21 of *Codex Tro*), showing New Year ceremonies for the *Kan* years, and including the unusual feature of a man walking on stilts and also a man sowing; *c*, page 48 (page 9 of *Codex Tro*), showing an *armadillo* in a dead-fall trap and a deer caught in a noose trap, and also the scorpion god. Each picture illustrates a divinatory almanac, presumably for hunters (Explanation by J. Eric S. Thompson).

97

a *b*

c

7.4. *a*, *b* Maya Stelae. *c* Maya altar.

7.5a. Maya 'hieroglyphs'. One of the few surviving texts in wood, from Tikal.

7.5b. Maya 'hieroglyphs'. Text from the left side of the cross at Palanque.

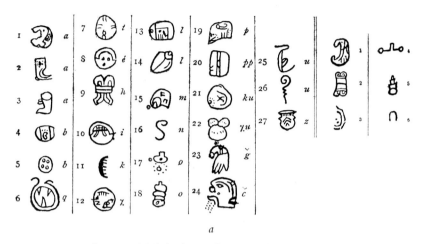

a

7.6*a*. The Maya 'alphabet' according to Bishop Diego de Landa.

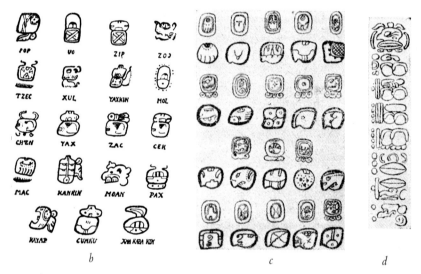

b	*c*	*d*

7.6. *b* Maya symbols of the months, according to the Dresden codex. *c* Maya symbols of the days, according to monuments (upper part) and manuscripts (lower part). *d* The highest number found in a Maya inscription: 1,841,639,800 days, corresponding to over 5,100,000 years.

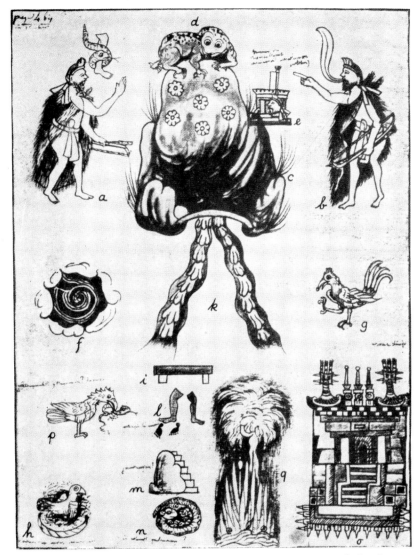

7.7. Page from an Aztec manuscript. Arrival of the Toltecs at Tlachiualtepec. *a*, Icxicouatl; *b*, Quetzalteueyeac at *c*, Tlachiualtepec, *e*, the seat of Aquiach-Amapane (K. Th. Preuss and E. Mengin, *Die Mexikanische Bilderhandschrift Historia Tolteca-Chichimeca*, Berlin, 1937, pl. IV).

7.8a. Portion of *Codex Zouche* (*Nuttall*) (British Museum).

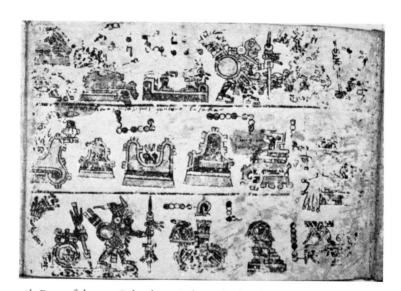

7.8b. Page of the pre-Columbian *Codex Colombino* (National Anthropological Museum, Mexico).

7.9. Post-Conquest *Codex Fernandez Leal* (National Anthropological Museum, Mexico), shows a *volador*; the frame on which the fliers sit—owing to ignorance of perspective—is shown vertical instead of horizontal. (Explanation by Dr. Bodil Christensen).

7.10*a*. The migrations of the Aztecs, as represented in native manuscripts.

7.10*b*. The Ten Commandments in Aztec post-Conquest manuscripts.

7.10*c*. The First Article of the Catholic dogma, in Aztec post-Conquest manuscripts.

7.10*d*. Year 1 of the Flint-knife, corresponding to A.D. 1168.

7.10*e*. The place-names Tepeyacac, Tepetitlan, and Qauhnauc; (1) *tepe(.tl)*, mountain+ *yaca(.tli)*, nose = Tepeyacac, On-the-Mountain-nose. (2) *tepe(.tl)*, mountain+*tlan(.tli)*, tooth, denture = Tipetitlan, Between-the-Mountains. (3) *qua(i.tl)*, tree, forest+ *nau(a.tl)*, mouth = Qauhnauc, On-the-Trees.

7.10*f*. A suitor, named One House, brings presents to Nine Wind and Ten Eagle, the parents of princess Six Monkey, living at a place called Cloud-Belching-Mountain; Six Monkey turns her back on the wooer (H. G. Spinden, *Indian Manuscripts of Southern Mexico*, Washington, 1935, p. 436).

7.11*a*. Mexican symbols representing the twenty days.
7.11*b*. 'Paper' manufacture in modern Mexico: from San Pablito, Sierra Norte de Pueblo.

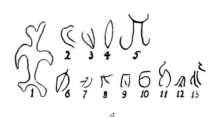

a

b

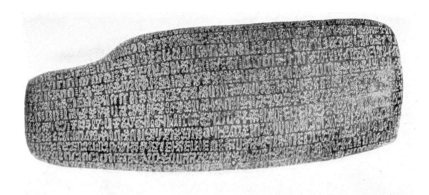

c

8.1. Easter Island writing. *a* Signatures of the native chiefs on the treaties with the Spaniards in 1770. *b–c* Specimens of *kohau-rongo-rongo* tablets.

8.2. Obverse and reverse of an Easter Island Tablet (Courtesy Smithsonian Institution, catal. no. 129773).

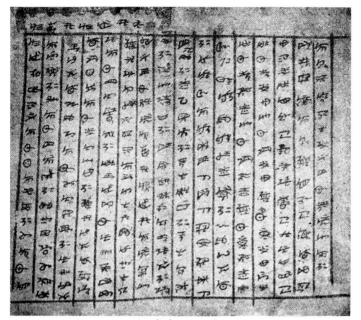

9.1a. Lo-lo horizontal script.

9.1b. Lo-lo vertical script.

9.1c. Lo-lo printed book, edited by Prince Len.

4 3 3 1

Kàng-siang-ying

Kiao-kyo

Yei-Ming-cheu

Local variant characters
The characters for 1, 'sun', 2, 'rain',
3, 'wind', and 4, 'mountain'.

a

b

c

d

sky earth moon father mother person heart foot tiger dragon door to make the same name family hand tree

e

I
1 2 3 4 5 6 7 8 9 10 11 12 13 14 15 16 17 18

II
1 2 3 4 5 6 7 8 9 10 11 12 13 14 15

f

9.2. *a* Lo-lo script: local variant characters. *b* The five known ideograms of
the Khitan script. *c* Niu-chih 'little' script. *d* Niu-chih 'national' character.
e Ideograms of the Yao script. *f* Miao-tzu ideograms.

a

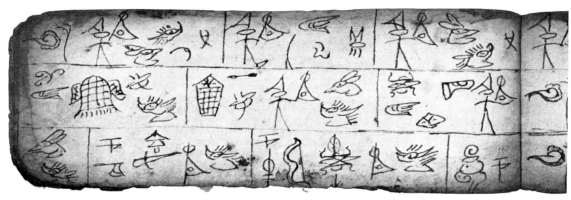

b

c

9.3. *a* First page of a Mo-so manuscript. *b*, *c*, Na-Khi book (Alphabet Museum, Tel-Aviv).

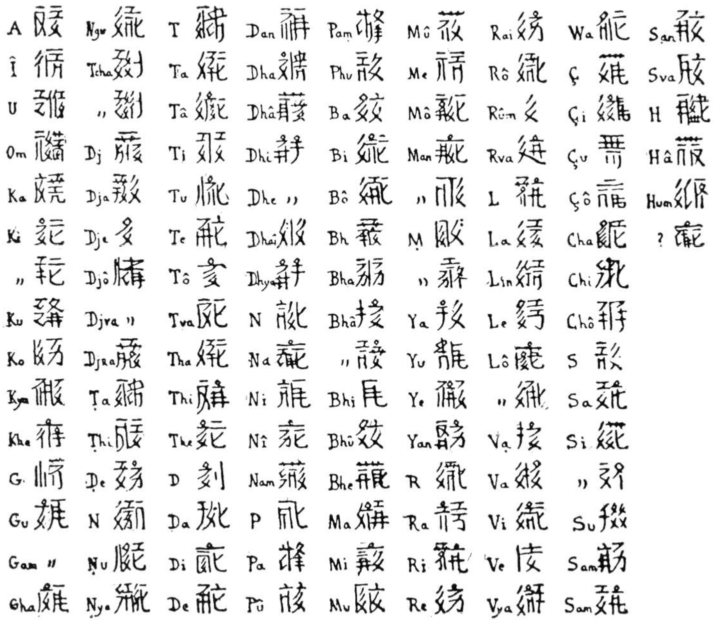

Si-Hia or Hsi-hsia syllabary chart with Tangut characters and romanized syllable labels arranged in columns.

Column 1: A, î, U, Om, Ka, Ki, ,,, Ku, Ko, Kṃ, Khe, G., Gu, Gam, Gha

Column 2: Ngu, Tcha, ,,, Dj, Dja, Dje, Djo, Djva, Djæa, Ṭa, Thi, De, N, Nu, Nyo

Column 3: T, Ta, Ta, Ti, Tu, Te, To, Tva, Tha, Thi, Tu, D, Da, Di, De

Column 4: Dan, Dha, Dhâ, Dhi, Dhe, Dhâi, Dhya, N, Na, Ni, Nî, Nam, P, Pa, Pû

Column 5: Pam, Phu, Ba, Bi, Bô, Bh, Bhâ, Bhâ, ,,, Bhi, Bhû, Bhe, Ma, Mi, Mu

Column 6: Mô, Me, Mô, Man, ,,, M, ,,, Ya, Yu, Ye, Yan, R, Ma, Mi, Mu

Column 7: Rai, Rô, Rṃ, Rva, L, La, Lin, Le, Lô, ,,, Va, Va, Vi, Ve, Vya

Column 8: Wa, Ç, Çi, Çu, Çô, Cha, Chi, Chô, S, Sa, Si, ,,, Su, Sam, Sam

Column 9: San, Sva, H, Hâ, Hum, ?

9.4. Si-Hia or Hsi-hsia syllabary.

9.5 and 9.6. Chinese Si-Hia (Hsi-hsia) glossary.

9.6. Si-Hia glossary.

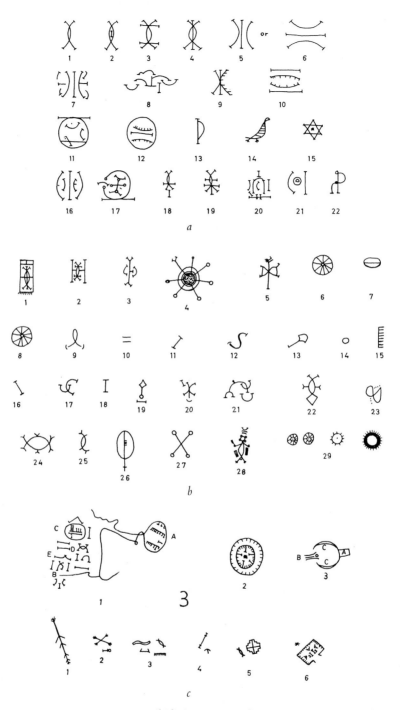

9.7. Nsibidi signs or records.

a. 1, Married love. 2, Married love, with pillow. 3, Married love with pillows for head and feet (a sign of wealth). 4, Married love with pillow. 5 and 6, Quarrel between husband and wife (a pillow is between them). 7, Violent quarrel between husband and wife. 8, One who causes a disturbance between husband and wife. 9, A woman with six children and a husband, and a pillow. 10, A man with two wives and their children, with the roof-tree of their house. 11. A house in which are three women and a man. 12, Two women with many children in the house with their husband. 13, A woman with child. 14, The same. 15, (shield of David), Ardent love. 16, Two women on each side of a house; one on each side has a child. 17, Two women who live in the same house have palaver every time they meet; a third woman is entering by the door. 18, A man comes to a woman who has a husband and asks her to live with him. 19, Three men who sought the same married woman. 20, A man committed adultery with a woman who lives apart from her husband; he has to pay compensation to the woman's family and to her husband. 21, A woman goes to bathe in the river at a ford, while her husband watches to see that no one shoots her. 22, fire.

b. 1, A man and a woman sleeping together on a native bed; it was very hot, so they put their arms outside, the short strokes at the bottom are the legs of the bed. 2, A boy kept a girl as his friend until they grew up. He then married her, and they lived together and made their bed with a pillow for the head and feet. 3, A man and his friend went into the town to get two girls; one of them got a girl and took her home with him; the other could not find one, and therefore they parted and went different ways. 4 and 5, A man's heart; he stands with his arms spread out to show that he knows more about Egbo than any other man; the dots represent the blood in the heart. 6, Young boys sitting in a Nsibidi house. 7, A palaver house.

An episode. 8, The young boys were sitting in the Nsibidi house. 9, there were two young women who sold their favours for money, 10, and they had two boys whom they used to send out to get the men to come to them, or to get money from them; 11, one of the boys took 12, a chewing stick, 13, a bottle of *tombo* and 14, a native glass; to 15, the young men sitting on the *ekfrat* stick; these young men sent 16, their boy to bring 17, a bag containing rods; 18, the boy took the bag of rods to the two men, who in turn took them to the women; 19, the young men sent their boy (with the sign of the comet) to meet them that night; 20, one of the young men met one of the women in an open place, where they rested to their mutual satisfaction and content; 21, the next day, the young man found the woman with a different man, and knew she was unfaithful.

22, Two young girls carrying water pots on their heads. 23, Large stone for grinding up medicine. 24, The sign of love: a man and woman sleeping together. 25, A sick boy and girl sleeping together. 26, Rat trap set to catch the rat which ate the corn in the house. 27, Two sticks crossed before the door of an Egbo house. 28, Husband and wife love each other ardently: they like to put their arms round one another (shown by extended hands); they are rich (having three pillows and a table on each side); the wife holds a comb. 29, Some representations of the Nsibidi house.

c. 1. A record of an *ikpe* or judgment case. The lines round and twisting mean that the case was a difficult one which the people of the town could not judge by themselves, so they sent to the surrounding towns to call the wise men from them, and the case was tried by them (*a*) and decided; it was a case of adultery (*b*); the court was held under a tree (*c*); (*d*), the party who won the case; (*e*) a man who thumbs as a sign of contempt.

2. The record of a trial by the Nsibidi club, drawn on a small calabash: the circles show the court-house, with verandah, round which, are the inner walls, the towns-folk are standing; also the executioners are represented (T-signs).

3. A stranger (B enters a town; he walks up the main street between two rows of houses (C–C) till he comes to Egbo House (A). As a consequence of the comet (4) lately seen, property (5, 6, 7) is strewn about in disorder, the Head Chief is dead and his body has been set in an armchair (8); before his house there is a seat. In the Egbo House (9), the townspeople have collected to decide between the two claimants to the office of Head Chief now vacant.

PHON. VALUE	MEANING	SYMBOL	PHON. VALUE	MEANING	SYMBOL	PHON. VALUE	MEANING	SYMBOL
si	BIRD		pe	CULLENDER		ngüê	LEOPARD	
baka	PLATE		nyam	HORSE		memfi	GOAT	
kuo	LADDER		wuo	STONE		men-gob	COCK	
nôd	BODY		tu	HEAD		nyu	HAIR	
mon	CHILD		ndàb	THREAD		kuob	PALM-GROVE	
nuê	SNAKE		li	EYE		kom	RAZOR	
sie	DITCH					ndab	HOUSE	
tüt	EAR		mi	FACE		tâm	MUD	

9.8a. Symbols of the Bamun ideographic script.

Actual value	Word	Meaning	1907	1911	1916	1918
F, fa, 8	Fama	Eight				
F, fè	Fè	Burn & work				
F, fo	Fom	King				
F, fou	Fou	Measure				
G, ga	Ngè	(Chose-faite)				
G, go, 10	Ngom	Ten				

9.8b. Development of Bamun characters.

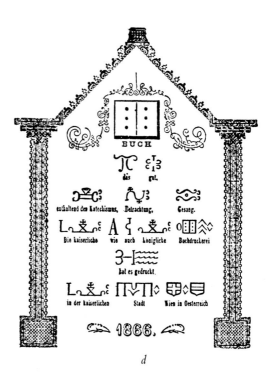

9.9. *a* Native pictographic writing of Paucartambo (Peru). *b* Minhassa ideographic script. *c* Aymarà ideographic script. *d* Micmac ideographic script.

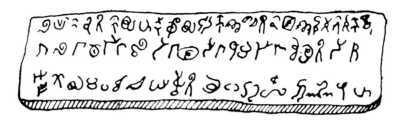

9.10a. Chukcha inscribed tablet.

Father	Mother	Son	Reindeer herd	On the river	Small, little
Rich	Poor	Good	Bad	I	My, mine,
Our	Food, to eat,	To live	To be	There	No
Only	Also	Various	kinds of	Fishes	Plate
Light	Tea-pot	Milk	Tobacco-pipe	Cigarette	

9.10b. Chukcha ideograms.

118

10.1. *a* Bronze tablet inscribed in the pseudo-hieroglyphic syllabary of Byblos (*left*, obverse; *right*, reverse). *b* Pseudo-hieroglyphic inscription on stone (fragment g). *c* Bronze tablet in the script of Byblos (*above*, obverse; *below*, reverse). *d* Spatulae from Byblos with N. Semitic inscriptions and traces of pseudo-hieroglyphic character.

10.2. *Spatulae* inscribed in the pseudo-hieroglyphic syllabary of Byblos (a and e *obverse*, b and d *reverse*).

10.3. Stone inscriptions in the pseudo-hieroglyphic script of Byblos. *a* Fragment h, *b* Stele a, *c* fragment j, *d* 'Linear' pseudo-heiroglyphic on stone.

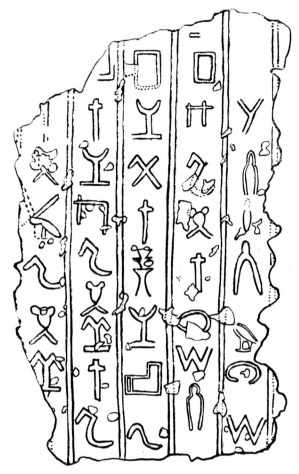

10.4*a*. Stone inscription from Byblos (stele g).

ꜣ-	Y X̄ ✳ ₃ ⊖ X �aᴍ A	ḥ-	ᘒ ᘗ ᔙ	ꜥ-	∩ ⧾ ⅂
b-	⬛ ↘ ⅏ ⅄	y-	⅄ ⬜ A ▢	p-	⟁ ⼖ aᴍ △ ꙷ
g-	W	k-	X ⊡ ⸜ Ꝏ	ṣ-	ᘔ ⊡
d-	ⵛ ⵁ	l-	⅃ Y̆ ᕪ ⅄ ꞇ	q-	⅄ W
h-	⼦	m-	⅃ X̌ X̆ ꭥ	r-	ᘐ ⅄ ꭙ ⴵ
w-	⊓ ⅀ ꝑ T >	n-	ᘔ ᕋ ◠ ⅏	š-	⼿ ⣌ X
z-	Ŧ ⅃ ꝺ ᘗ	s,ś-	O ᘔ	t-	┼ Y ⵱ ⋀ ᖡ

10.4*b*. The pseudo-hieroglyphic syllabary of Byblos according to Dhorme.

122

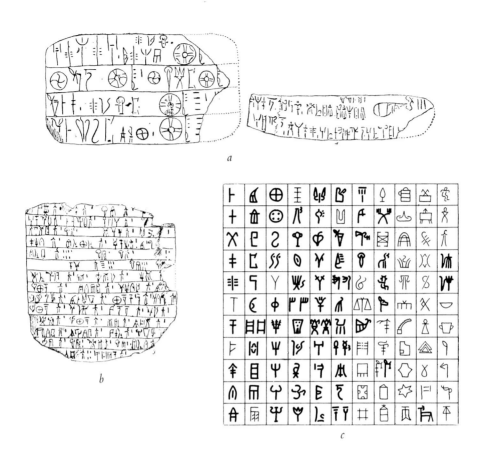

10.5. *a* and *b* Inscriptions in Linear B. *c* Symbols of Linear B drawn by the late Michael Ventris, before his decipherment.

10.6a. Tablets inscribed in Linear B. (Museum of Classical Archaeology, Cambridge).

a ⼐ a2 ⼙	e ⼓	i ⼢	o ⼻	u ⼥
ai ⼽				
ja ⼾	je ⼿		jo ⽀	
wa ⽁	we ⽂	wi ⽃	wo ⽄	
da ⽅ de ⽆		di ⽇	do ⽈	da2 ⽉
ka ⊕	ke ⽊	ki ⽋	ko ⽌	ku ⽍
ma ⽎	me ⽏	mi ⽐	mo ⽑	
na ⽒	ne ⽓	ni ⽔	no ⽕	nu|⽖ nu2? ⽗
pa ‡pa2? ⽘	pe ⽙	pi ⽚	po ⽛	pu ⽜
	qe ⊙	qi ⽝	qo ⽞ qo2? ⽟	
ra ⽠ ra2 ⽡	re ⽢	ri ⽣	ro ⽤ ro2 ⽥	ru ⽦
sa ⽧	se ⽨	si ⽩	so ⽪	
ta ⽫ ta2? ⽬	te ⽭ pte ⽮	ti ⽯	to ⽰	tu ⽱
	z?e ⽲		z?o ⽳ z?o2 ⽴	

10.6b. Experimental syllabic grid for Linear B., by Ventris and Chadwick (J.H.S. 1953, p. 86).

124

LINEAR B (MYCENAEAN) SYLLABARY

a (8)		e (38)		i (28)		o (61)		u (10)		a₂ (25)		ai (43)			
da (1)		de (45)		di (7)		do (14)		du (51)		dwe (71)		dwo (90)			
ja (57)		je (46)				jo (36)									
ka (77)		ke (44)		ki (67)		ko (70)		ku (81)							
ma (80)		me (13)		mi (73)		mo (15)		mu (23)							
na (6)		ne (24)		ni (30)		no (52)		nu (55)		nwa (48)					
pa (3)		pe (72)		pi (39)		po (11)		pu (50)		pte (62)		pu₂ (29)			
qa (16)		qe (78)		qi (21)		qo (32)									
ra (60)		re (27)		ri (53)		ro (2)		ru (26)		ra₂ (76)		ra₃ (33)		ro₂ (68)	
sa (31)		se (9)		si (41)		so (12)		su (58)							
ta (59)		te (4)		ti (37)		to (5)		tu (69)		ta (66)					
wa (54)		we (75)		wi (40)		wo (42)									
za (17)		ze (74)				zo (20)									

UNCERTAIN PHONETIC VALUE

18	19	22	34	35	47	49	56
63	64	65	79	82	83		
	84	85	86	87	88	89	

10.7. The Mycenaean syllabary as deciphered by Ventris and Chadwick.

NUMBER	KNOSSOS	PYLOS	MYCENAE	THEBES	PHONETIC VALUE	NUMBER	KNOSSOS	PYLOS
1					da	31		
2					ro	32		
3					pa	33		
4					te	34		
5					to	35		
6					na	36		
7					di	37		
8					a	38		
9					se	39		
10					u	40		
11					po	41		
12					so	42		
13					me	43		
14					do	44		
15					mo	45		
16					qa	46		
17					za	47		
18					?	48		
19					?	49		
20					zo	50		
21					qi	51		
22					?	52		
23					mu	53		
24					ne	54		
25					a_2	55		
26					ru	56		
27					re	57		
28					i	58		
29					pu_2	59		
30					ni	60		

10.8. Linear B symbols from Knossos, Pylos, Mycenae and Thebes.

MYCENAE	THEBES	PHONETIC VALUE	NUMBER	KNOSSOS	PYLOS	MYCENAE	THEBES	PHONETIC VALUE
		sa	61					o
		qo	62					pte
		ra_3	63					?
		?	64					?
		?	65					(j u)?
		jo	66					ta_2
		ti	67					ki
		e	68					ro_2
		pi	69					tu
		wi	70					ko
		si	71					dwe
		wo	72					pe
		a	73					mi
		ke	74					ze
		de	75					we
		je	76					ra_2
		?	77					ka
		nwa	78					qe
		?	79					(z u)?
		pu	80					ma
		du	81					ku
		no	82					?
		ri	83					?
		wa	84					?
		nu	85					?
		?(pa_3)	86					?
		ja	87					?
		su	88					?
		ta	89					?
		ra	90					dwo

10.9. Linear B symbols from Knossos, Pylos, Mycenae and Thebes.

CYPRIOTE SYLLABARY

Vowels	a	e	i	o	u
Vowels					
y + Vowel					
f̱/w̱ + "					
ṟ + "					
ḻ + "					
m̱ + "					
ṉ + "					
p̱ + "					
ṯ + "					
ḵ + "					
s̱ + "					
ẕ + "					
kh + "					

a

	A	E	I	O	U
Θ H					
J					
K		?		
L					
M					
N					
P					
Q					
R					
S					
T					
W					
X	?				
Z					

1. = FINAL S.
2. = (PROBABLY) ME̅.
3. = (POSSIBLY) WE AS WELL AS LE.
4. = (POSSIBLY) MA AS WELL AS ME.
5. = CLAY-BALL CHARACTER.

c

b

10.10. *a* Cypriote syllabary. *b* Cypro-Minoan or Cypro-Mycenaean symbols. *c* Suggestion for decipherment of Cypro-Minoan.

JAPANESE SYLLABARIES

PHONETIC VALUE	KATA KANA	HIRA GANA	PHONETIC VALUE	KATA KANA	HIRA GANA	PHONETIC VALUE	KATA KANA	HIRA GANA	PHONETIC VALUE	KATA KANA	HIRA GANA
i	イ	い	wa	ワ	わ	w(i)	ヰ	ゐ	sa	サ	さ
ro	ロ	ろ	ka	カ	か	no	ノ	の	ki	キ	き
fa (ha)	ハ	は	yo	ヨ	よ	o	オ	お	yu	ユ	ゆ
ni	ニ	に	ta	タ	た	ku	ク	く	me	メ	め
fo (ho)	ホ	ほ	re	レ	れ	ya	ヤ	や	mi	ミ	み
fe (he)	ヘ	へ	so	ソ	そ	ma	マ	ま	si (shi)	シ	し
to	ト	と	tu (tsu)	ツ	つ	ke	ケ	け	w(e)	ヱ	ゑ
ti (chi)	チ	ち	ne	ネ	ね	fu	フ	ふ	fi (hi)	ヒ	ひ
ri	リ	り	na	ナ	な	ko	コ	こ	mo	モ	も
nu	ヌ	ぬ	ra	ラ	ら	e	エ	ゑ	se	セ	せ
ru	ル	る	mu	ム	む	te	テ	て	su	ス	す
(w)o	ヲ	を	u	ウ	う	a	ア	あ	n	ン	ん

10.11. Japanese syllabaries.

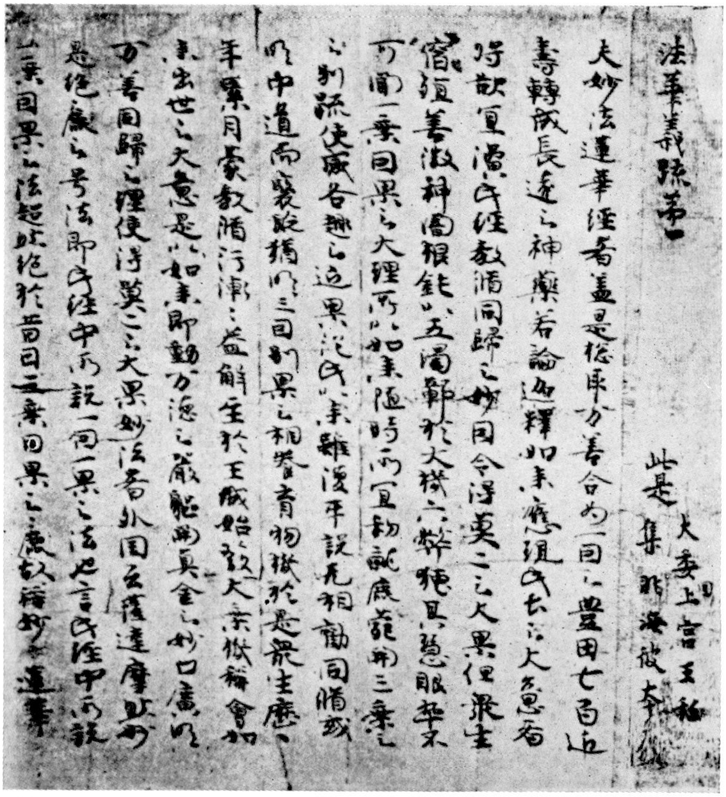

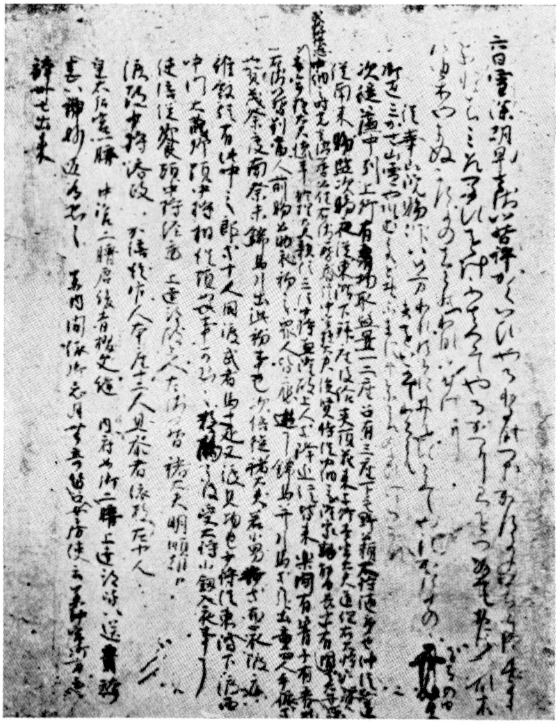

10.12a. (above) Earliest extant work written by a Japanese: *Commentary* on a Buddhist *sūtra* written in Chinese, Shotoku Taishi (or Prince Shotoku) A.D. 573–622. 12b. (left) Earliest extant Japanese manuscript of which both the date and the name of the writer are known: *Diary* by Fujiwara Michinaga (961–1095). The portion shown here is written in pure Japanese, in *Kana* script, and dated 6.2.1004 A.D., according to the lunar calendar.

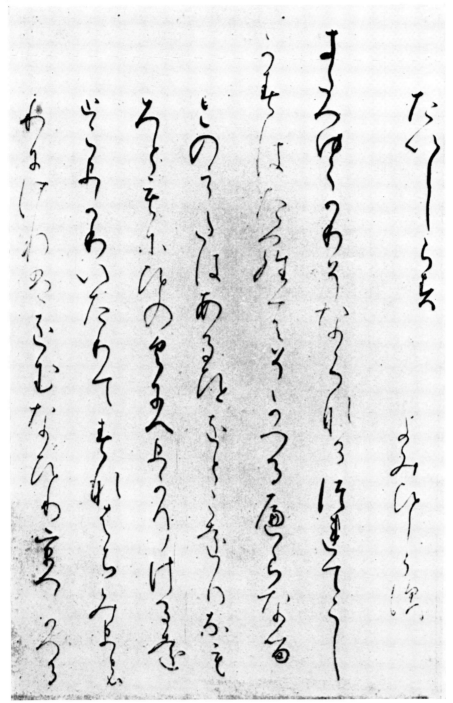

10.13. Hiragana calligraphy: Ki No Tsurayuki (Died A.D. 946), Poems from *Koninshu*, Book 9.

a	e	i	o	u
ga	ge	gi	go	gu
ha	he	hi	ho	hu
la	le	li	lo	lu
ma	me	mi	mo	mu
na	ne	ni	no	nu
gwa	gwe	gwi	gwo	gwu
sa	se	si	so	su
da	de	di	do	du
dla	dle	dli	dlo	dlu
dza	dze	dzi	dzo	dzu
wa	we	wi	wo	wu
ya	ye	yi	yo	yu
ö	gö	hö	lö	nö
gwö	sö	dö	dlö	dzö
wö	yö	ka	hna	nah
s	ta	te	ti	tla

10.14. Cherokee syllabary.

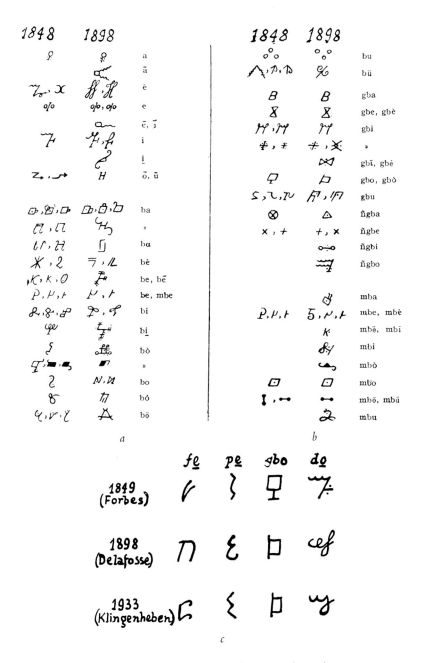

10.15. *a* and *b* The Vai syllabary. *c* Development of Vai characters.

tu, ta, ti su, sa, si du, da, di u, a, i bu, ba, bi mu, ma, mi wu, wa, wi ku, ka, ki

kpe, nga ho, ha, he nu, na, ni fu, fa, fi yu, ya, yi ju, ja, ji lu, la, li

ndô, njô, mba, vi, nyô, mê, nya, ngô, gba, tê, lo, hi, heⁿ, pê, pu, wo, kô, mbe, huⁿa, wô

yê, sô, fe, vô, ko, fê, kpu, lê, mbê, gbo, gbô, tô, pi, ndô, pô, ke

he, kê, mo, gbê, kpa, tê, ndi, ndê, fo, huⁿ, ge, bo, ve, le, hei, ngu, pe

le, vê, nga, mbô, yê, kpe, gbe, ngô, mbô, tô, bô, pô, fâ, e, pa, nye, do, be

ngua, wê, ndu, gbi, ndi, mbu, vo, ngo, nde, we, ne, se, ngê, wô, je, po

kua, wei, mbo, yô, ho, we, bo, ei, sô, ì, njô, fô, kpi, î, haⁿ, nda, hou

jê, gô, hi, gi, mua, lô, nja, vu, be, njê, gbu, o, nge, mbi, vô, jô

va, gu, gua, guei, vi, eⁿ, ngua, ô, nyi, dô, ê, sê, be, jo, ga, kpo

nju mue bê bu hu go nge ra nyu no

10.16. Mende syllabary.

134

Plain Cree

a da ka ma na ra sa sla cha ya ta ba
(ta) (pa)

Tinné

a ba da ga ka la ma na sa ga ka tha tsa kia pla

Cree Vocalization

a e i o o da de di do ka ke ki ma me mi mo

Final consonants

aspirate s Cree
Tinné

Eastern Cree

Tinné

Ojibway

Eskimo

	a	*e*	*o*	*à*
Vowels	▽	△	▷	◁
p + vowel	V	∧	>	<
t + vowel	U	∩	⊃	⊂
k + vowel	9	ρ	d	b
j + vowel	⌐	⌐	∪	⌐
m + vowel	⌐	Γ	⌐	L
n + vowel	⌐	σ	⌐	⌐
s + vowel	ˊ	ˊ	ˊ	ˊ
l + vowel	⊃	⊂	⊃	⊂
y + vowel	ˊ	ˊ	ˊ	ˊ
v + vowel	V	∧	>	<
gh + vowel	⌣	⌢	ρ	ˊ

Eskimo
(Baffin Land dialect)

10.17. Native Canadian syllabaries and writing specimens.

135

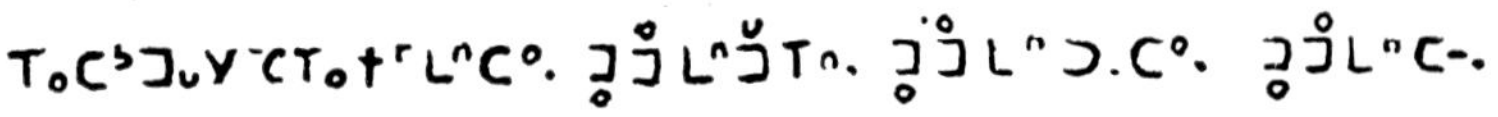

Т₀Ꮯᵇᒐᵤᐰ ᑕᎢₒᵻᒋᐸᏟº. ᒍᒍᏞᒍᎢᶰ. ᒍᒍᏞᒋ.Ꮯº. ᒍᒍᏞᶰᏟᵎᵎ.

Hwa Miao

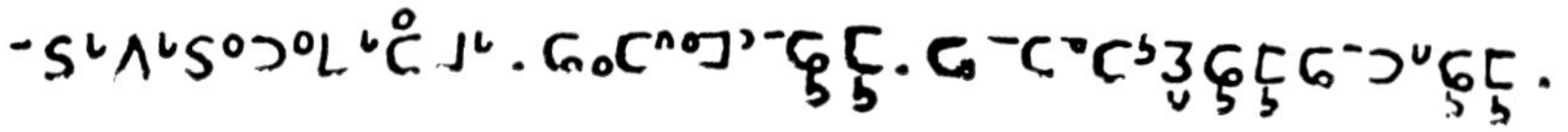

⁻ᏚᵇᐱᵇᏚₒᒍₒᏞᵇᏟᵘ ᒍᵘ. ᏀₒᏟᶰᒍᵎᵎᵛᏳᏞ. ᏀᵎᏟᵎᏟᵇ�McᏀᏳᏀᵎᒍᵛᏳᏞ.

Kopu

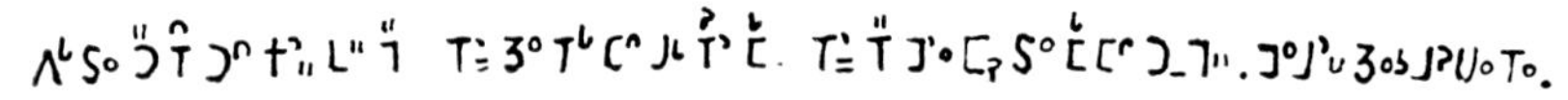

ᐱᵇᏚₒᵞᎢᒍᶰᵻᵎᏞᵎᵎᵞ ᏆᵎᵌᵒᎢᵇᏟᶜᒐᵻᵻᏋ. ᎢᵎᎢ ᏆᵎᏋᏚᵒᏋᏟᵎᒍᵎᵎᵎ.ᒍᵎᒍᵛᵤᵌₒᵇᒍᵎᏌₒᎢₒ.

Laka

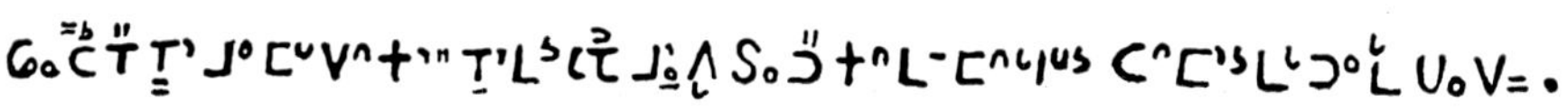

ᏀₒᏋᎢᎢᎢᵎᒍᵒᏟᵛᏙᶺᵻᵎᵎ ᎢᵎᏞᵇᏋᎢ ᒍᵖᐱ ᏚₒᵌᵻᶰᏞᵎᏟᶺᵎᵎᵘᵎ ᏟᶺᏟᵇᏞᵇᒍᵎᏞ ᑌₒᏙᵎ.

Nosu

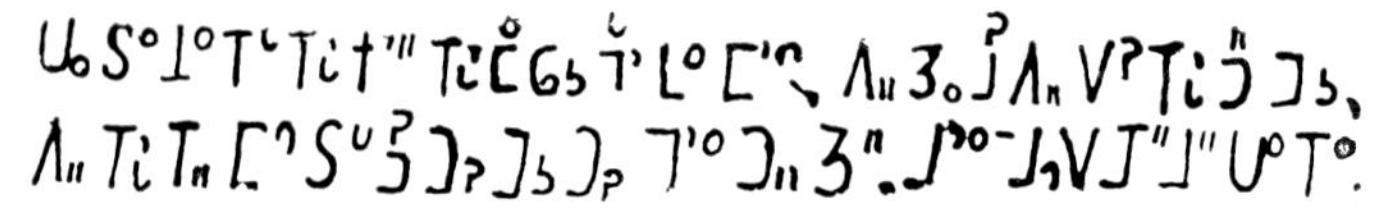

ᑌᵇᏚᵒᵎᵒᎢᵇᎢᵻᵻᵎᵎᵎ ᎢᵎᏋᏀᵇᎢᵎᏞᵒᏟᵎᵎ ᐱᵎᵌₒᒍᐱᵎ ᏙᵖᎢᵎᵌ ᒍᵇ,
ᐱᵎᎢᵻᎢᵎᏟᵎᏚᵛᵌᒍᵖᒍᵇᒍᵖ Ꭲᵒᒍᵎᵌᵎᵎ.ᒍᵖᵒᵌᵥᏙᒍᵎᵎᵎᑌᵖᎢº.

Lisu

ꞮꞮA: M ʌ̀—MꞮ=YꞮ. TꝞ. ᒍꓵ⎯ M Ꮮ: ꓸ0 TꝞ. M: ꓒꞮ:
YEFꞮ SꞮ.=ꞮꞮᵀ: ꓒꞮ; ꞮꞮ: P M SꝞ; MY M7 FꞮ⎯ BE=

Hwa Lisu

VE Ǝ SU—NDU N�6U ꓳꓵ BE, BE Nꓵ Ǝ xI

ᒪᏳ SE, ꛭᎫ Ǝ A—BU, Ꮐꓵ—Rꓵ ME—ME,

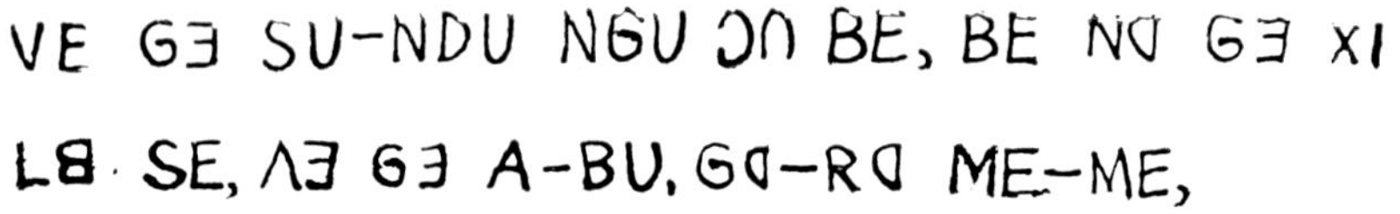

Lo-lo

10.18. Pollard and allied systems, of South Western China.

a

			CONSONANTS +								Closed Syllables
a	aa	ä	o	oa	oo	oi	ö	u	ü	ui	
		bä		boa *(2 symbols)*			bö				bag
	da1				doo			du			
		gä			goo						
								ku	kü		
		lä					lö				lüh
ma (2symbols)		mä		moa	moo	moi					
		mmä									
na					noo						
		pä						pu		pui	
	raa	rä	ro					ru	rü		
		shä		soa							
		tä			too						tüt
va				voa							
		wä									warr
nga		ngä									
chra				chroa							
							shrö		shrü		
gkaa		chä									sthah
											uh

b

10.19. Woleai syllabary.

a. symbols.

b. phonetic values.

10.20. Specimens of Caroline writing *a* on the arms and legs of a man; *b* on a food bowl.

10.21. Page from a Caroline manuscript.

NO.	SYMBOL	PHON. VALUE	NO.	SYMBOL	PHON. VALUE
1		a	22		n(u)
2		b(a)	23		p(a)
3		č(a)	24		r(a)
4		d(a)	25		r(u)
5		d(i)	26		s(a)
6		d(u)	27		š(a)
7		f(a)	28		t(a)
8		g(a)	29		t(u)
9		g(u)	30		ṭ(a)
10		h(a)	31		u
11		ḫ(a)	32		v(a)
12		i	33		v(i)
13		j(a)	34		y(a)
14		j(i)	35		z(a
15		k(a)	36		tr(a)
16		k(u)	37		ḫšāyaϑia "king"
17		l(a)	38		dahyu "country" (two forms)
18		m(a)			
19		m(i)	39		Awra - Mazda (divine name)
20		m(u)	40		bumi "earth"
21		n(a)	41		word-divider

11.1. Early Persian character (*See* also 1.16*b* and 17).

11.2. Meroitic writing. *a* The Meroitic scripts. *b* Comparison of Meroitic hieroglyphic letters with Egyptian hieroglyphs. *c–d* Meroitic inscriptions.

Table a

Hierogl.	Derived North–Semitic Letters	Differentiated

(columns of hieroglyphic and North-Semitic letter forms)

Table b

Egyptian Phon. Value	Hierogl.	Hieratic	Semitic Letters	Semitic Phon. Value
'(a)				'
b				b
ḳ(g)				g
ṭ(d)				d
h				h
f				w
z				z
x(kh)				ḥ
o(th)				ṭ
i				y
k				k
l				l
m				m
n				n
s				s
ʻa				ʻ
p				p
t'(ts)				ṣ
q				q
r				r
sh				sh
t				t

12.1. Origin of the alphabet. *a* Halévy's Egyptian Hieroglyphic theory, *b* Taylor's Egyptian Hieratic theory.

Meaning	Name	Semitic	Cretan Linear	Cretan Hierogl.
ox	aleph			
house	beth			
door	daleth			
hook	waw			
fence	he			
fence	heth			
hand	yod			
palm of hand	kaph			
fish	nun			
mouth	pe			
head	resh			
tooth	shin			
eye	'ayin			
mark	taw			

Phon. Value	Semitic	Cretan Linear	Cretan Hierogl.
g			
z			
ṭ			
l			
s			
q			
ṣ			

Egypt	Crete	N.-S. Alph.	Modern Hebrew

12.2. a (*above left*) Sir Arthur Evans Cretan theory: Derivation of North Semitic letters of known meaning and b (*left*) letters of uncertain meaning. c (*above*) Grumach's Egyptian–Cretan theory.

143

b

KEY	PREHISTORIC LINEAR	PALAEO-SINAITIC	PHOENIC.

Phonetic Value	g	h	z	s	'	sh
N. Sem. Letters						
Cuneiform Letters						

c

a

12.3. *a* Gaster's prehistoric-geometric theory. *b* Gardiner's identification of Ba'alat. *c* Ugarit signs resembling N. Semitic letters.

EGYPT HIER.	SINAI	SOUTH-SEMITIC	NORTH-SEMITIC	MEANING IN SEMITIC	SINAITIC SYMBOLS	MEANING IN SEMITIC	HEBREW
				ox		ox ח ל א	א
		ה ט		house		house בית	ב
						nose-ring	ג
						fish דג	ד (Cowley)
				hook nail			ה ? (Sayce)
							ו ? (Gardiner)
							ז ? (Cowley)
				hand			ח ? (Sayce)
				bent hand			ט
		ךךל				goad	י
				water		water מים	כ
		ר		fish			ל
				snake		snake נחש	מ
		◊ o		eye		eye עין	נ
		o		mouth			ס
						bow קשת	ע
				head		head ראש	פ
		ذذز		tooth		tooth שן	צ
		+ +		mark		cross תו	ק
						determinative of goddess	ר
							ש
							ת

12.4. Sinaitic theory of Gardiner, with Cowley's and Sayce's additions.

	Modern Hebrew	South Arabic	Se'irite-Sinaitic	Canaanite-Phoenician	Ras Shamra Cuneiform
1	א	𐩱			
2	ב				
3	ג	ד			
4	ד				
5	ה	YY			
6	ו	Φ			
7	ז	X	= (?)		
8	ח	ΨΨ 丩			
9	ט	♀			
10	כ	∧			
11	ל				
12	מ				
13	נ				
14	ס	X			
15	ע	○			
16	פ	◇			
17	צ				
18	ק	♦			
19	ר				
20	ש				
21	ת	X	+	X	

12.5. The relation of the Early Sinaitic (Se'irite-Sinaitic) script to the South Semitic (South Arabic), North Semitic (Canaanite–Phœnician) and Ugarit (Ras Shamra) alphabets, according to Martin Sprengling.

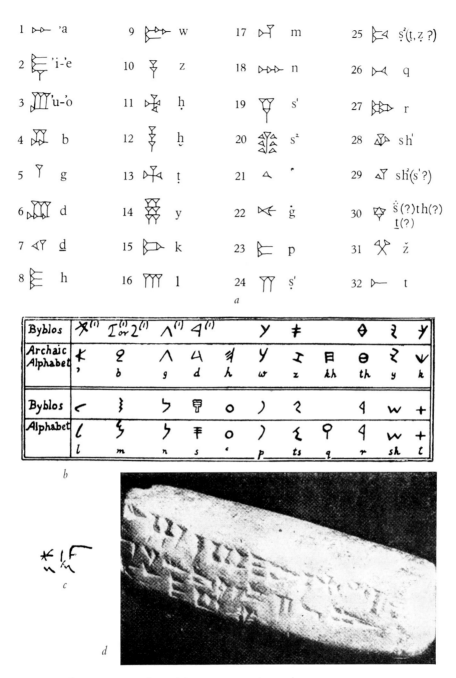

12.6. *a* The Ugarit cuneiform alphabet (15th–13th century B.C.). *b* Dunand's theory of the derivation of the Alphabet from the pseudo-hieroglyphic script of Byblos (1) 'Linear' variety of the same script. *c* Alphabet 'incunabula' according to Dunand. *d* Ugaritic ABC tablet.

147

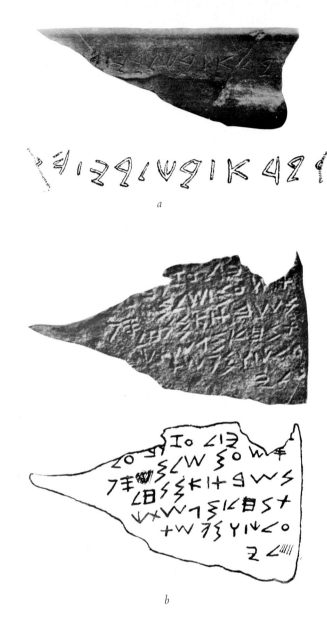

12.7. Early North Semitic inscriptions. *a* Abdo fragment, photograph and transcription. *b* Asdrubal spatula, photograph and transcription.

12.8a. Shafatba'al Inscription, photograph.

12.8b. Shafatba'al Inscription, transcribed.

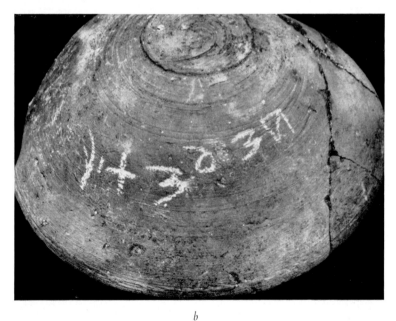

12.9. *a* Early Canaanite inscriptions, 1, Gezer Potsherd; 2, Shechem Plaque; 3, Lachish Dagger; 4, Tell el-Hesy; 5, Tell el-'Ajjul; 6, Beth Shemesh Ostracon (obverse above, reverse below); 7, 8, inscriptions from Lachish; 9, signs painted or engraved in the foundations of the Temple of Jerusalem; 10, 11, different drawings of some Lachish inscriptions. *b* Lachish Bowl No. 1 (transcription in 9*a*[8] above).

b

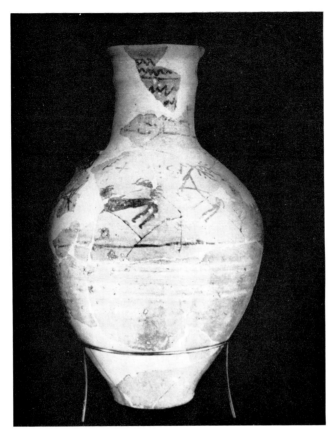

12.10*a*. Lachish ewer (transcription shown in 12.9*a*^{7}).

12.10*b*. Inscription from Lachish (transcription shown in 12.9*a*^{11}).

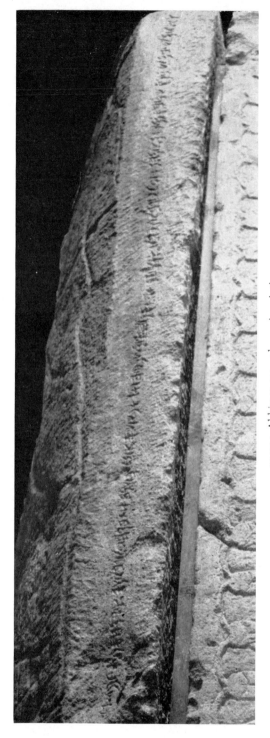

12.11a. Akhiram sarcophagus inscription.

12.11b. Transcription from Akhiram sarcophagus.

12.11c. Akhiram grafitto.

12.11d. Abiba'al inscription.

PHON. VALUE	ʿABDÔ	SHAFATBAʿAL	ASDRUBAL	AHIRAM	YEHIMILK	RUEISSEH	ABIBAʿAL	ELIBAʿAL	MEŠAʿ
ʾ									
b									
g									
d									
h									
w									
z									
ḥ									
ṭ									
y									
k									
l									
m									
n									
s									
ʿ									
p									
ṣ									
q									
r									
š									
t									

12.12. Early development of the North Semitic alphabet according to Maurice Dunand.

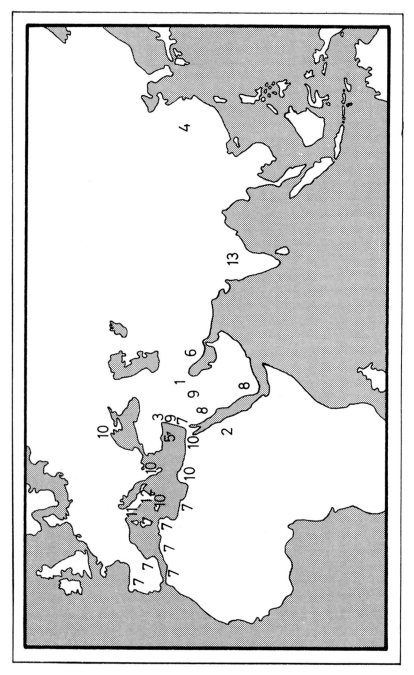

Map. 2. Early Development of alphabet *c.* 1000–1 B.C.

1 Cuneiform Scripts	6 Persian Semi-alphabetic Cuneiform Script	11 Etruscan Alphabet
2 Egyptian Scripts	7 Canaanite Alphabetic Branch	12 Latin Alphabet
3 Hittite Hieroglyphics	8 S.-Semitic Alphabetic Branch	13 Indian Branch
4 Chinese Scripts	9 Aramaic Alphabetic Branch	
5 Cyprus Syllabary	10 Greek Alphabet	

Phon. Value	Sabaean	Lihyanian	Thamudene	Safaitic	Early Ethiopic
ʾ					
b					
g					
ḏ					
d					
h					
w					
z					
ḥ					
ḫ					
ẓ					
ṭ					
y					
k					
l					
m					
n					
s					
g̱					
ʿ					
p					
ḍ					
ṣ					
q					
r					
š					
ṯ					
ṭ					

13.1. The South Semitic Alphabets.

a

d

13.2. *a*, *b* Sabaean inscriptions. *c* Minaean inscription. *d* Himyaritic inscription.

b

c

Original	Ethiopic	ሰ	ፐ	፟	ከ	ዘ	ደ	ጠ
Letter	Phon. Value	sa	ta	na	ka	za	da	ṭa
Derived	Amharic	ሸ	ች	ኘ	ኽ	ዠ	ጀ	ጨ
Letter	Phon. Value	sha	cha	ña	kh'a	ja or zha	dja	ṭcha

a

j

13.3. *a* Derivation of modern Abyssinian additional letters. *b, c* South Semitic inscription from Ethiopia. *d* to *h* Thamudene inscriptions. *i* The earliest, still unvocalized Ethiopic inscription from Matara, Eritrea. *j* Page from an Ethiopic gospel, 1675–6 (British Museum Or. 510, f. 51a).

Consonant +

	a	*û*	*î*	*â*	*ê*	*e**	*ô*
h	ሀ	ሁ	ሂ	ሃ	ሄ	ህ	ሆ
l	ለ	ሉ	ሊ	ላ	ሌ	ል	ሎ
ḥ	ሐ	ሑ	ሒ	ሓ	ሔ	ሕ	ሖ
m	መ	ሙ	ሚ	ማ	ሜ	ም	ሞ
sh	ሠ	ሡ	ሢ	ሣ	ሤ	ሥ	ሦ
r	ረ	ሩ	ሪ	ራ	ሬ	ር	ሮ
s	ሰ	ሱ	ሲ	ሳ	ሴ	ስ	ሶ
q	ቀ	ቁ	ቂ	ቃ	ቄ	ቅ	ቆ
b	በ	ቡ	ቢ	ባ	ቤ	ብ	ቦ
t	ተ	ቱ	ቲ	ታ	ቴ	ት	ቶ
kh	ኀ	ኁ	ኂ	ኃ	ኄ	ኅ	ኆ
n	ነ	ኑ	ኒ	ና	ኔ	ን	ኖ
'a	አ	ኡ	ኢ	ኣ	ኤ	እ	ኦ
k	ከ	ኩ	ኪ	ካ	ኬ	ክ	ኮ
w	ወ	ዉ	ዊ	ዋ	ዌ	ው	ዎ
'	ዐ	ዑ	ዒ	ዓ	ዔ	ዕ	ዖ
z	ዘ	ዙ	ዚ	ዛ	ዜ	ዝ	ዞ
y	የ	ዩ	ዪ	ያ	ዬ	ይ	ዮ
d	ደ	ዱ	ዲ	ዳ	ዴ	ድ	ዶ
g	ገ	ጉ	ጊ	ጋ	ጌ	ግ	ጎ
t	ጠ	ጡ	ጢ	ጣ	ጤ	ጥ	ጦ
p	ጰ	ጱ	ጲ	ጳ	ጴ	ጵ	ጶ
s	ጸ	ጹ	ጺ	ጻ	ጼ	ጽ	ጾ
ḍ	ፀ	ፁ	ፂ	ፃ	ፄ	ፅ	ፆ
ḟ	ፈ	ፉ	ፊ	ፋ	ፌ	ፍ	ፎ
p	ፐ	ፑ	ፒ	ፓ	ፔ	ፕ	ፖ

13.4. The Ethiopic character (the form marked * also expresses the pure consonant).

ጸሉተ፡ባሕታዊ፡ሰበ፡ይቲክኧ፡ወደጊሉ። ።
ወይክቡ፡ትድመ፡እግዚእብሔር፡ስለሷ። ።
የስ ስምባኒ፡እግዚኡ፡ጸሉትየ፨
ወደብጸሕ፡ትድሚክ፡ገጻርየ፨
ወኢትሚዋ፡ገጸ ክ፡እምኒየ። ።
በዕለት፡መንደቢየ፡እጸምዕ፡እዝነክ፡ኃቢየ። ።
እመ፡ዕለተ፡እጼውዓ ክ፡ፋጡነ፡ስምባኒ፨
እስመ፡ኃልቀ፡ክመ፡ጢስ፡መዋዕልየ፨
ወነትጸ፡ክመ፡ሣዕር፡እዕጹም ትየ ፨
ተቀሠፍኩ፡ወየብሰ፡ክመ፡ሣዕር፡ልብየ፨
እስመ፡ተረስዓኒ፡በሲዓ፡እክል፨
እምቃለ፡ገጻርየ፡ወጠግፃ፡ሥጋየ፡ዲበ፡እኧጸምትየ፨
ወኮንኩ፡ክመ፡እዴገ፡መረብ፡ዘገደም ፨
ወኮንኩ፡ክመ፡ጉጋ፡ወሕተ፡ቢት፡ሊሊት፨
ተጋህኩ፡ወክንኩ፡ክመ፡ዖፍ፡ባሕታዊ፡ወስተ፡ናሕስ፨
ወሠሉ፡እሜሬ፡ይጺዕሉኒ፡ጸላእትየ፨
ወእስኒ፡ይስዱኒ፡ይሰክታዩ፡ላዕሊየ፨
እስመ፡ሐመደ፡ክመ፡እክል፡ተማሕኩ ፨

13.5. Ethiopic manuscript: psalms, 17th cent. (Chester Beatty MS. 908).

159

LETTER-NAME	PHON. VALUE	NORTH-SEMITIC	EARLY PHOEN-ICIAN	LATE PHOEN-ICIAN	NEO-PUNIC
aleph	ʼ	K	ⱡ	ⱡ	X
beth	b	g	⟨	⟨	9 ʼ
gimel	g	⟩	Λ	Λ	Λ
daleth	d	△	△	◁	◁ ʼ
he	h	⧻	⧻	⧻	ⴹ
waw	w	Y	Y	Ч	ⴹ
zain	z	I	I	ⴽ	ⴽ
heth	ḥ	⊟	⊟	ⴴⴴ	ʼⴽⴽ ʼⴽⴽ ⴽⴽⴽ
teth	ṭ	⊕	⊗	⊙	⊖
yod	y(i)	ⴣ	ⴴ	ⴴ ⴼ	ⴴ
kaph	k	Ⴟ	Ⴟ	⅂⅂	⅄
lamed	l	⟨	⟨	ⴽ	⁄
mem	m	ⱬ	ⱳ	Ⴟ ⱬ	×
nun	n	ⱬ	ⱴ	ⱬ	J
samek	s	ⱦ	ⱦ	ⱦ	Ⱶ
ʼain	ʻ	O	o	o	O
pe	p (ph)	ⴺⴺ	ⴺ	ⴺ	ⴺ
sade	ṣ	ⴽ	ⴽⴲ	ⴽ	ⴽ
qoph	q	φ	φ	ⴲ	ⴲ
reš	r	ⴹ	ⴹ	ⴴ	9ⴴ ʼ
šin	sh-s	w	w	ⱱ ⱴ	ⴼ
taw	t	+	×	ⴻⴼ	ⴼⴼ

14.1. Origin and development of the Phoenician alphabet.

	GEZER	MONUMENTAL	CURSIVE	BOOK-HAND	COIN-SCRIPT	SAMARITAN	MOD.-HEBREW
1							א
2							ב
3							ג
4							ד
5							ה
6							ו
7							ז
8							ח
9							ט
10							י
11							כ
12							ל
13							מ
14							נ
15							ס
16							ע
17							פ
18							צ
19							ק
20							ר
21							ש
22							ת

14.2. Development of early Hebrew alphabet.

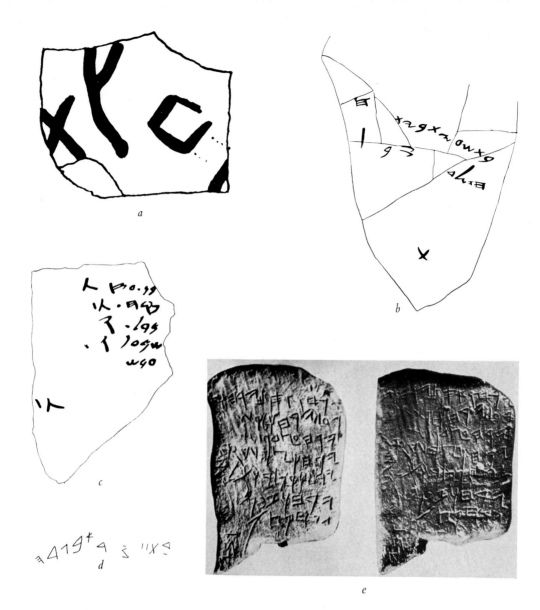

14.3. Early Hebrew alphabet. *a* 'Incunabula' (?) from Lachish. *b, c* Samarian ostraca. *d* Earliest Hebrew ABC. *e* Gezer calendar.

14.4*a*. Seal of Jereboam.

14.4*b*. Seal of Hananyahu son of 'Akhbor.

14.4*c*. Siloam inscription.

14.4*d*. Tomb inscription from Siloam (British Museum).

14.5. Early Hebrew royal and private jar handle, stamps and weights.

14.6. Early Hebrew ostracon from Metsad Khasha-vyahu; photograph and transcription.

אל אדני . יאוש ישמע .
יהוה , את אדני . ש[מ]עת של
ם . עת . כים עת כים מי . עבד
ך . כלב . כי . זכר . אדני . את .
[ע]בדה . יבכר . יהוה . את . א
[? ?]י דבר . אשר לא . ידעתה

c

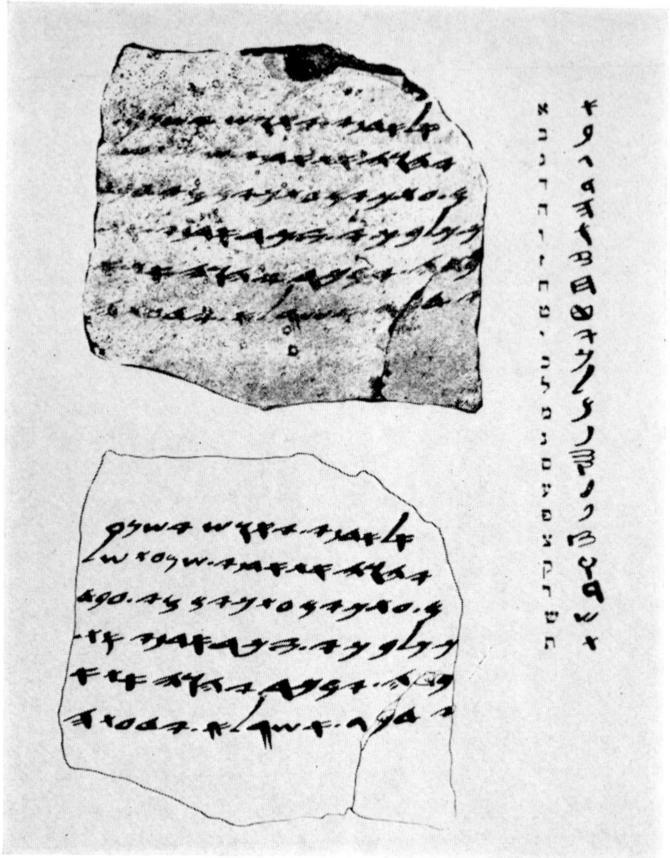

a

b

d

14.7. Lachish letter. *a* photograph; *b* transcription; *c* transliteration into modern Hebrew; *d* style of writing.

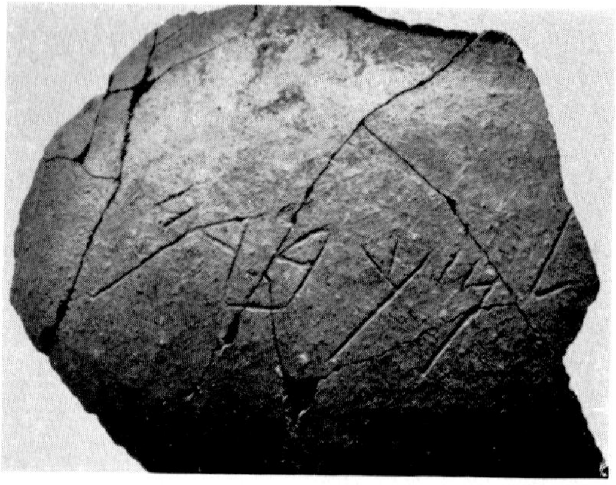

e

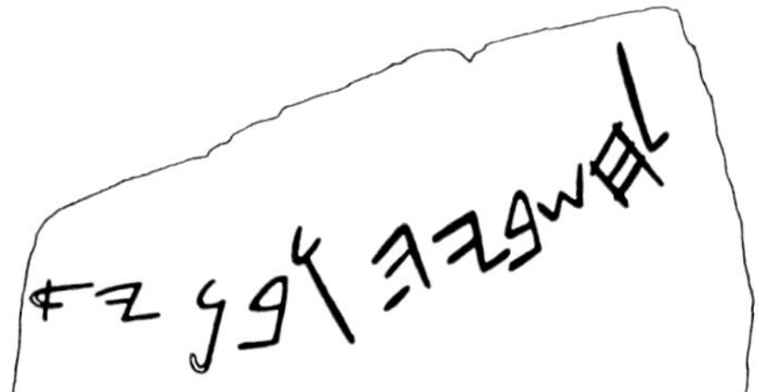

f

14.7. *e*, *f* Hazor inscription; photograph and transcription.

	I	II	III	IV	V	VI
א						
ב						
ג						
ד						
ה						
ו						
ז						
ח						
ט						
י						
כ						
ל						
מ						
נ						
ס						
ע						
פ						
צ						
ק						
ר						
ש						
ת						

14.8. *a* (left) Early Hebrew cursive alphabet, as it appears in Lachish letters 1–6. *b* (below) Pottery vessel inscription from Lachish: liquid measure, reading from right to left, *bt lmlk* = 'bath of the king' = Royal bath.

Leviticus 19: 31-33

Leviticus 20: 20-23

14.9*a.* Early Hebrew fragments from *Leviticus.*

Leviticus 21: 24-25   *Lev. 22: 4-5*

a

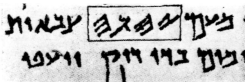
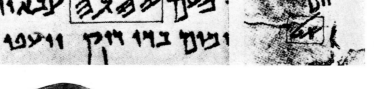

b

14.9. *b* Portion of a Dead Sea scroll, written in Square Hebrew character: within squares, *left*, Tetragrammaton (Hebrew divine name) and *right*, 'el (= God), both in early Hebrew script. *c* Coin of the small autonomous state of Judah, inscribed in early Hebrew script.

c

14.10. *a* Earliest Samaritan inscription. *b* Samaritan pentateuch written in 622 (A.H.) = A.D. 1225 (Chester Beatty MS. 751).

14.11. *a* Samaritan Pentateuch, Deuteronomy (Alphabet Museum, Tel-Aviv).
b Modern Samaritan character: beginning of Genesis.

14.12. Copper plate (inscribed in modern Samaritan character) presented to the second President of Israel by the Samaritan community of Holon.

14.13. *a* Jewish coins and Ammonite seal (centre). *b* Script from Maccabean and Bar-Kochba coins.

a

b

Coins of Year Four	Silver Shekels Year-Two-Three	Maccab. Coins	Phon. Value	
𐤀	𐤅	𐤀 𐤀	א	ʾ
𐤁	𐤁	𐤁 𐤁	ב	b
𐤂	𐤂	𐤂 𐤂	ג	g
𐤅	𐤅	𐤅 𐤅	ו	w
𐤉	𐤉	𐤉 𐤉	י	y
𐤇	𐤇	𐤇 𐤇	ח	ḥ
𐤋	𐤋	𐤋 𐤋	ל	l
𐤍	𐤍	𐤍 𐤍	נ	n
𐤑	𐤑		צ	ṣ
𐤏	𐤏		ע	ʿ
𐤓	𐤓	𐤓 𐤓	ר	r
𐤔	𐤔	𐤔 𐤔	ש	š
𐤕	𐤕	𐤕 𐤕	ת	t
𐤑𐤅𐤉𐤍	𐤑𐤅𐤉𐤍		ציון	ṣyon
𐤔𐤍𐤕	𐤔𐤍𐤕		שנות	šnt
𐤇𐤑𐤉	𐤇𐤑𐤉		חצי	ḥṣi

172

14.14. The Mesha' Stone.

Phon. Value	Punic or Carthagin	Libyan		Iberian		
		Ancient	Tifinagh	North-	South-	Turdetan
ʾ						(ʎ)
b						
g						(?)
d				×	×	
ḥ						
w						
ḫ						
ḥ						
ṭ						
y						
k						
l						
m						(?)
n						
s						
ʿ						
p						
ṣ						
q						
r						
š						
t						
ca(z)						
ce						
du						

14.15. Descendants of Phoenician alphabet.

14.16. *a* (left) Yehaw-milk inscription, c. 5th–4th century B.C. (Beirut Museum). *b* (below) Kharaib inscription (Beirut Museum).

14.17. Karatepe, with the Phoenician, Hittite and other inscriptions engraved on the row of stones shown on the right: see also 5.7.

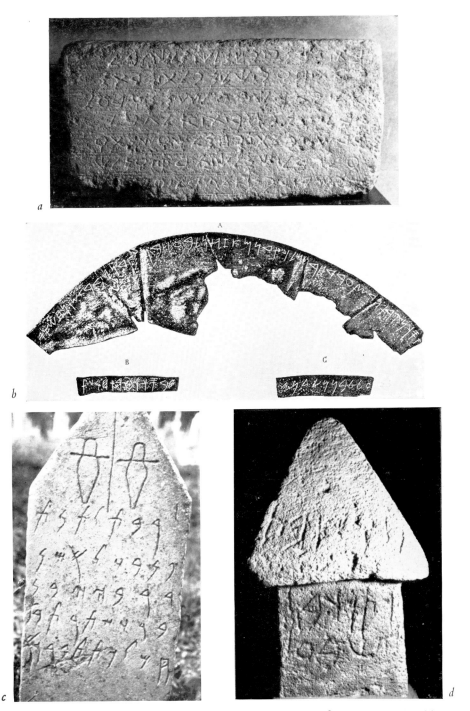

14.18. *a* Kharaib inscription. *b* Cypro-Phoenician inscription of c. 735 B.C. *c* Tunisian tombstone, Bardo Museum. *d* Sardinian tombstone.

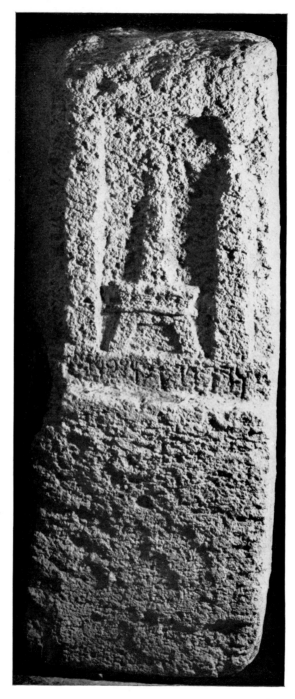

14.19. Early Phoenician inscription found in 1838 at La Marmora (Nora), Sardinia.

178

14.20. *a* Another early inscription from Nora. *b* Early Phoenician inscription on gold from Sulcis, now at Cagliari, Sardinia.

a

b

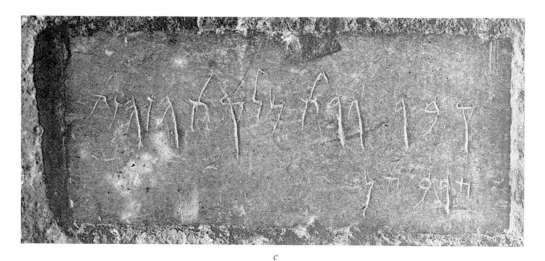

c

d

e

14.21. *a* Part of a Phoenician *stele* from Sidon. *b* Part of a Sidonian inscription from Piraeus (96 B.C.). *c–e*, Punic inscriptions fromdinia Sarand Tunisia.

b

a

14.22. Neo-Punic inscriptions, *a* Salambo inscription, *b* Latin–neo-Punic bilingual inscription.

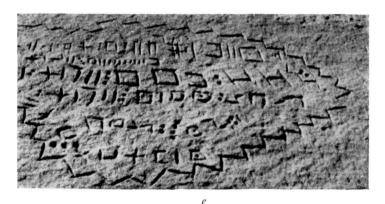

14.23. *a* Punic inscription from North Africa. *b* Punic inscription from Gozo, Malta (200–100 B.C.) *c*, *d* Neo-Punic inscriptions.

14.23. *e*, *f*, *g* Libyan inscriptions.

182

Letter	Phon. Value	Letter	Phon. Value	Letter	Phon. Value	Letter	Phon. Value	Letter	Phon. Value
ᚹ	a	Ψ	m	⟨	ds tz	✳	bo po	⊙	gu ku
↳	e	ᚿ	n	⟩	ds tz	◻	bu pu	X	da ta
ᛝ	i	Y	nn	T	z	Λ	ga ka	◇	de te
H	o	◁	r	I	ba pa	⟨	gue ke	Ψ	di ti
↑	u	⟡	rr	⟨	be pe	ʃ	gui ki	Ш	do to
M	l	M	sx	Γ	bi pi	⟆	go ko	△	du tu

14.24. *a* The Iberian alphabet. *b* Iberian stone inscription. *c* Iberian pottery inscription.

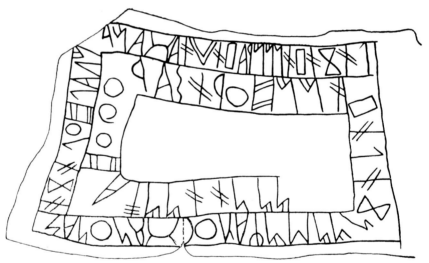

‡⧓‡1O⧓1ΛΝ٩Μ٩ΑΠΑ‡Ψ‡□ΛΥΝΝ٩‡O‡⧓‡1
□‡1‡⧓ΥΝΝΜΝΦΑΥOΠΑΥOΥΑΥ
ΝΝΒO⋔⧓ΖΑΒOCOBΑ‡٩OBΜΝΝ

l e c o e b u e n i i r a b u e d u e a b e a i r i c a a l t i o l e c o e

n a n o n a b e k e o n a c u i s i i n c o e l e b u

e i i t i o r e m a r o t e o t i a s i i e e n i i

14.25. Turdetan inscription on stone from Bensafrim near Lagos, S.W. Portugal preserved in the Municipal Museum of Figueira da Foz (Courtesy of Manuel-Gomez Moreno). Top to bottom; photograph, transcriptions, transliteration.

PHONETIC VALUE	EARLY ARAMAIC			PALMYRENE	NABATAEAN
	8th. CENT. B. C.	6th. CENT. B. C.	4th. CENT. B. C.		
ʾ					
b					
g					
d					
h					
w					
z					
ḥ					
ṭ					
y					
k					
l					
m					
n					
s					
ʿ					
p					
ṣ					
q					
r					
š(sh)					
t					

15.1. Aramaic, Palmyrene and Nabataean alphabets.

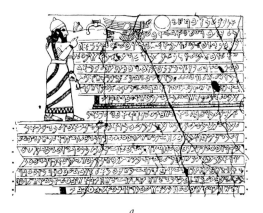

a

b

c

15.2. Royal Early Aramaic inscriptions (9th and 8th centuries B.C.). *a* Canaanite–Aramaic inscription of Kilamuwa, son of Khaya (?), king of Ya'di. *b* Zakir, king of Hamath and La'sh. *c* Bar-Rekub, king of Samal. [Samal was a small state of considerable importance at that time—it is now the Kurdish hamlet of Zenjirli.] *d* Earliest royal inscription: the stele of the Aramaean king Ben Hadad.

d

15.3. *a* Aramaic papyrus from Elephantine, a Jewish military colony in Egypt
(5th century B.C.). *b* Rock inscription
from Cilicia (5th century B.C.).

15.3*c*. Aramaic letter written on leather, 5th century B.C. (Bodleian Library,
Oxford).

15.4. Aramaic papyrus of the 5th century B.C., from Egypt (Brooklyn Museum).

The table on the left (a):

MODERN HEBREW	660-50 B C	600-550 B C	515-4 B C	494-3 B C	PHON. VALUE
א	(letter)	(letter)	(letter)	(letter)	'
ה	(letter)	(letter) ?	(letter)	(letter)	h
ט	(letter)	(letter) ?	(letter)	(letter)	ṭ
י	(letter)	(letter)	(letter)	(letter)	y
כ	(letter)	(letter)	(letter)	(letter)	k
מ	(letter)	(letter)	(letter)	(letter)	m
ס	(letter)	(letter)	(letter)	(letter)	s
ע	(letter)	(letter) ?	(letter)	(letter)	ʿ
ק	(letter)	(letter)	(letter)	(letter)	q
ש	(letter)	(letter)	(letter)	(letter)	š

The table on the right (b):

	V. CENT.	III. CENT.	PAP. NASH	HERODIAN	DURA
א	(letters)	(letters)	(letters)	א (א)	(letters)
ה	(letters)	(letters)	(letters)	ה (ה)	ה
כ	(letter)	(letters)	(letters)	כ (ך)	כ ך ך
ל	(letters)	(letters)	(letters)	ל (ל)	ל
מ	(letters)	(letters)	(letters)	מ (ם)	ם ם ם
נ	(letters)	(letters)	(letters)	(letters)	נ
צ	(letter)	(letters)	(letters)	(צ)	צ
ק	(letter)	(letters)	(letters)	(ק)	ק
ת	(letter)	(letters)	(letters)	ת (ת)	ת

a The most characteristic letters used from the middle of the 7th century B.C. to the early 5th century B.C., according to Prof. W. F. Albright.

b Comparative table of selected characters, from the 5th century B.C. to 3rd century A.D.

15.5. Development of Cursive Aramaic script.

15.6b Greek–Aramaic bilingual, from Armazi. (Courtesy, Acad. George Tseret'eli).

15.6a. Armazi Aramaic inscription No. 1.

	SQUARE HEBREW (MONUMENTAL)		MEDIEVAL FORMAL STYLES			RABBINIC STYLES			CURSIVE STYLES			CONTEMPORARY	
												CURSIVE	PRINT
1	‡	א	א	א	ﬡ		ש	ﬡ	ץ	ﬣ	ץ	k	IC K	א
2	ﬗ	ב	ב	ב	ﬔ		ﬖ	ב	כ	ﬗ	ﬕ	ﬖ	ﬡ	ב
3	ﬖ		ﬔ	ﬕ	ﬗ		ﬡ	ﬗ	ﬕ	ﬖ	ﬗ	ﬡ	ﬔ	ﬕ
4	ﬔ	ﬗ	ﬗ	ﬗ	ﬗ		ﬗ	ﬗ	ﬗ	ﬖ	ﬡ	ﬖ	ﬗ	ﬗ
5	ﬡ	ﬡ	ﬡ	ﬡ	ﬡ		ﬡ	ﬡ	ﬡ	ﬡ	ﬡ	ﬡ	ﬗ	ﬡ
6	?	ﬡ	ﬡ	ﬡ	ﬡ		ﬡ	ﬡ	ﬡ	ﬡ	ﬡ	ﬡ	ﬡ	ﬡ
7	ﬡ	ﬡ	ﬡ	ﬡ	ﬡ		ﬡ	ﬡ	ﬡ	ﬡ	ﬡ	ﬡ	ﬡ	ﬡ
8	H	ﬡ	ﬡ	ﬡ	ﬡ		ﬡ	ﬡ	ﬡ	ﬡ	ﬡ	ﬡ	ﬡ	ﬡ
9	ﬡ	ﬡ	ﬡ	ﬡ	ﬡ		ﬡ	ﬡ	ﬡ	ﬡ	ﬡ	ﬡ	ﬡ	ﬡ
10	ﬡ	ﬡ	ﬡ	ﬡ	ﬡ		ﬡ	ﬡ	ﬡ	ﬡ	ﬡ	ﬡ	ﬡ	ﬡ
11	ﬡ	ﬡ	ﬡ	ﬡ	ﬡ		ﬡ	ﬡ	ﬡ	ﬡ	ﬡ	ﬡ	ﬡ	ﬡ
12	ﬡ	ﬡ	ﬡ	ﬡ	ﬡ		ﬡ	ﬡ	ﬡ	ﬡ	ﬡ	ﬡ	ﬡ	ﬡ
13	ﬡ	ﬡ	ﬡ	ﬡ	ﬡ		ﬡ	ﬡ	ﬡ	ﬡ	ﬡ	ﬡ	ﬡ	ﬡ
14	ﬡ	ﬡ	ﬡ	ﬡ	ﬡ		ﬡ	ﬡ	ﬡ	ﬡ	ﬡ	ﬡ	ﬡ	ﬡ
15	ﬡ	ﬡ	ﬡ	ﬡ	ﬡ		ﬡ	ﬡ	ﬡ	ﬡ	ﬡ	ﬡ	ﬡ	ﬡ
16	ﬡ	ﬡ	ﬡ	ﬡ	ﬡ		ﬡ	ﬡ	ﬡ	ﬡ	ﬡ	ﬡ	ﬡ	ﬡ
17	ﬡ	ﬡ	ﬡ	ﬡ	ﬡ		ﬡ	ﬡ	ﬡ	ﬡ	ﬡ	ﬡ	ﬡ	ﬡ
18	ﬡ	ﬡ	ﬡ	ﬡ	ﬡ		ﬡ	ﬡ	ﬡ	ﬡ	ﬡ	ﬡ	ﬡ	ﬡ
19	ﬡ	ﬡ	ﬡ	ﬡ	ﬡ		ﬡ	ﬡ	ﬡ	ﬡ	ﬡ	ﬡ	ﬡ	ﬡ
20	ﬡ	ﬡ	ﬡ	ﬡ	ﬡ		ﬡ	ﬡ	ﬡ	ﬡ	ﬡ	ﬡ	ﬡ	ﬡ
21	F	ﬡ	ﬡ	ﬡ	ﬡ		ﬡ	ﬡ	ﬡ	ﬡ	ﬡ	ﬡ	ﬡ	ﬡ
22	ﬡ	ﬡ	ﬡ	ﬡ	ﬡ		ﬡ	ﬡ	ﬡ	ﬡ	ﬡ	ﬡ	ﬡ	ﬡ

* FINAL LETTERS

15.7. Main styles of the [square] Hebrew alphabet.

Phon. Value	Eleph. Pap.	Louvre Pap.	Edfu Ostr.	4Q Sam.b	4Q Jer.a	4Q XII a	Nash Pap.	1Q Is.a	Man. Disc.
ʾ									
b									
g									
d									
h									
w									
z									
ḥ									
ṭ									
y									
k									
l									
m									
n									
s									
ʿ									
p									
ṣ									
q									
r									
s									
t									

* Final Letters

15.8

1 Q Is.[b]	Hab. Comm.	Hod.	IV Q Dent.[j]	Běnê Hězîr	Kedron	Uzziah Slab	Queen Sara (Helena)	Ossuary Inscriptions	Mod. Hebr.

15.8 and 9. Early development of the Square Hebrew alphabet, based partly on various Dead Sea scrolls, and partly on ancient papyri and funerary inscriptions.

a   b

וה ד׳ רוחמא דלאלערמה ועוריחזורת לעין רוחנן
טרוחחל ך ריב אעונ ולעורי טעות
ס מטו חוור

c

d

e

15.10. *a* Sepulchral inscription from 'Araq el-Emir. Late 6th or early 5th century B.C. *b* The 'Gezer boundary'. First half of the 1st century B.C. *c* Early Square Hebrew tomb inscription. *d* Uzziah plaque. *e* Chufutkale (Crimea) sepulchral inscription. *f* Jericho synagogue inscription. *g* Toledo synagogue inscription.

f

g

15.11. *a* Nash papyrus. *b* Dead Sea Scrolls: Manual of discipline. *c* Dead Sea Scrolls: Isaiah A.

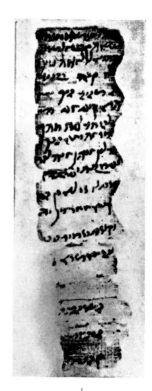

a   *b*

c

15.12. *a* Dead Sea Scrolls: Isaiah B. *b* Marriage contract, written in a hitherto unknown
Hebrew cursive script, from Muraba'at. *c* Dead Sea Scrolls: Children of Light and
Children of Darkness.

משמעון בן כוסבה לישע 1

בן גלו[גלה ולאנשי הברך 2

שלו[ם] מעיד אני עלי־תשמים 3

יפק[ד] מן הגללאים שהצלכם 4

כל אדם שאני נתן־כבלים 5

ברגלכם כמה שעקיבא[וא] 6

לבן עפלול 7

ו[ש]מעון 8

b

1 From Simeon ben Kosba to Jeshua
2 ben Ga[l]gola and the men of the fortress,
3 Gree[tings]. I call Heaven to witness against me <that if>
4 of the Galileans, who are at your place, there should be missing
5 (even) a single one, I will put fetters
6 on your feet, as Akiba <did>
7 to Ben Aflul.
8 [Si]m̄eon b̄[en Kosba]

c

15.13. *a* Photograph of letter from Simon Bar-Kochba (2nd century A.D.). *b* transliteration into modern Hebrew. *c* Tentative translation into English. *d* Papyrus letter from the administrators of Bēth Māshkhô, found at Muraba'at.

15.14. *a* Incantation text on a bowl from Babylonia, attributed to 8th century A.D. *b* Divorce letter (*get*) of the year 1128 (Cairo Genizah). *c* Legal Document of the year 1137, from Léon (Spain). *d* Italian cursive hands of the 16th century: signatures of 3 Italian rabbis (Codex Livorno No. 27).

15.15. *a* Hebrew papyrus book (University Library, Cambridge). *b* Formal Hebrew alphabet: Leningrad pentateuch (Codex 85), dated to 1132 (from Jerusalem). *c* Apparently the oldest Hebrew Bible in Vellum codex form, late 9th or early 10th century. (British Museum, Or. 4445).

15.16. Hebrew Bible of Tiflis (Genesis 5, 28 to 6, 12) with Massoretic annotation assuming the form of decoration of the pages.

15.17. Titled Bible, Model Codex of the Pentateuch (formerly Gaster Collection No. 85, now in the Brit. Mus.).

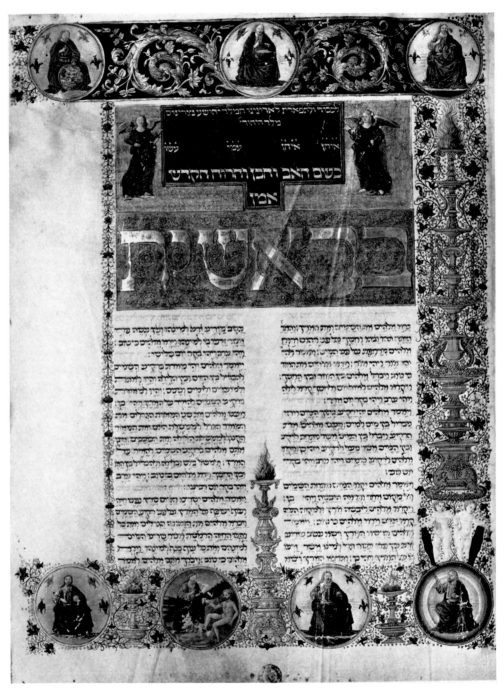

15.18. Beginning of a beautifully illuminated Hebrew Bible produced by Francesco d'Antonio del Cherico (worked from about 1455 to 1485), Laurentian Library, Florence, MS. Plut. 1,31.

בָּרָא אֱלֹהִים אֵת הַשָּׁמַיִם וְאֵת הָאָרֶץ וְהָאָרֶץ
הָיְתָה תֹהוּ וָבֹהוּ וְחֹשֶׁךְ עַל פְּנֵי תְהוֹם וְרוּחַ א
אֱלֹהִים מְרַחֶפֶת עַל פְּנֵי הַמָּיִם וַיֹּאמֶר אֱלֹהִים
יְהִי אוֹר וַיְהִי אוֹר וַיַּרְא אֱלֹהִים אֶת הָאוֹר כִּי
טוֹב וַיַּבְדֵּל אֱלֹהִים בֵּין הָאוֹר וּבֵין הַחֹשֶׁךְ וַיִּק
רָא אֱלֹהִים לָאוֹר יוֹם וְלַחֹשֶׁךְ קָרָא לָיְלָה
וַיְהִי עֶרֶב וַיְהִי בֹקֶר יוֹם אֶחָד :

וַיֹּאמֶר אֱלֹהִים יְהִי רָקִיעַ בְּתוֹךְ הַמָּיִם
וִיהִי מַבְדִּיל בֵּין מַיִם לָמָיִם וַיַּעַשׂ אֱלֹהִים אֶת
הָרָקִיעַ וַיַּבְדֵּל בֵּין הַמַּיִם אֲשֶׁר מִתַּחַת לָרָקִיעַ
וּבֵין הַמַּיִם אֲשֶׁר מֵעַל לָרָקִיעַ וַיְהִי כֵן וַיִּקְרָא
אֱלֹהִים לָרָקִיעַ שָׁמָיִם וַיְהִי עֶרֶב וַיְהִי בֹקֶר יוֹם
שֵׁנִי :

וַיֹּאמֶר אֱלֹהִים
יִקָּווּ הַמַּיִם מִתַּחַת הַשָּׁמַיִם אֶל מָקוֹם אֶחָד וְ
תֵּרָאֶה הַיַּבָּשָׁה וַיְהִי כֵן וַיִּקְרָא אֱלֹהִים לַיַּבָּשָׁה
אֶרֶץ וּלְמִקְוֵה הַמַּיִם קָרָא יַמִּים וַיַּרְא אֱלֹהִים
כִּי טוֹב וַיֹּאמֶר אֱלֹהִים תַּדְשֵׁא הָאָרֶץ דֶּשֶׁא
עֵשֶׂב מַזְרִיעַ זֶרַע עֵץ פְּרִי עֹשֶׂה פְּרִי לְמִינוֹ א
אֲשֶׁר זַרְעוֹ בוֹ עַל הָאָרֶץ וַיְהִי כֵן וַתּוֹצֵא הָאָרֶץ
דֶּשֶׁא עֵשֶׂב מַזְרִיעַ זֶרַע לְמִינֵהוּ וְעֵץ עֹשֶׂה פְּרִי
אֲשֶׁר זַרְעוֹ בוֹ לְמִינֵהוּ וַיַּרְא אֱלֹהִים כִּי טוֹב
וַיְהִי עֶרֶב וַיְהִי בֹקֶר יוֹם שְׁלִישִׁי :

וַיֹּאמֶר אֱלֹהִים
יְהִי מְאֹרֹת בִּרְקִיעַ הַשָּׁמַיִם לְהַבְדִּיל בֵּין הַיּוֹם
וּבֵין הַלָּיְלָה וְהָיוּ לְאֹתֹת וּלְמוֹעֲדִים וּלְיָמִים

15.19. Earliest extant incunabula of Hebrew Bible, by Joshua Saloman, Soncino, 1488.
(Biblioteca Palatina, Parma).

כו וַיֵּלֶךְ וְשֵׁרְתוּ לַיהוָֹה אֱלֹהֵינוּ וְגַם־מִקְנֵנוּ יֵלֵךְ עִמָּנוּ לֹא
תִשָּׁאֵר פַּרְסָה כִּי מִמֶּנּוּ נִקַּח לַעֲבֹד אֶת־יְהוָֹה אֱלֹהֵינוּ
כז וַאֲנַחְנוּ לֹא־נֵדַע מַה־נַּעֲבֹד אֶת־יְהוָֹה עַד־בֹּאֵנוּ שָׁמָּה: וַיְחַזֵּק
כח יְהוָֹה אֶת־לֵב פַּרְעֹה וְלֹא אָבָה לְשַׁלְּחָם: וַיֹּאמֶר־לוֹ פַרְעֹה
לֵךְ מֵעָלָי הִשָּׁמֶר לְךָ אַל־תֹּסֶף רְאוֹת פָּנַי כִּי בְּיוֹם
כט רְאֹתְךָ פָנַי תָּמוּת: וַיֹּאמֶר מֹשֶׁה כֵּן דִּבַּרְתָּ לֹא־אֹסִף עוֹד
רְאוֹת פָּנֶיךָ: ס

א וַיֹּאמֶר יְהוָֹה אֶל־מֹשֶׁה עוֹד נֶגַע אֶחָד אָבִיא עַל־פַּרְעֹה
וְעַל־מִצְרַיִם אַחֲרֵי־כֵן יְשַׁלַּח אֶתְכֶם מִזֶּה כְּשַׁלְּחוֹ כָּלָה
ב גָּרֵשׁ יְגָרֵשׁ אֶתְכֶם מִזֶּה: דַּבֶּר־נָא בְּאָזְנֵי הָעָם וְיִשְׁאֲלוּ
אִישׁ מֵאֵת רֵעֵהוּ וְאִשָּׁה מֵאֵת רְעוּתָהּ כְּלֵי־כֶסֶף וּכְלֵי
ג זָהָב: וַיִּתֵּן יְהוָֹה אֶת־חֵן הָעָם בְּעֵינֵי מִצְרַיִם גַּם הָאִישׁ
מֹשֶׁה גָּדוֹל מְאֹד בְּאֶרֶץ מִצְרַיִם בְּעֵינֵי עַבְדֵי־פַרְעֹה וּבְעֵינֵי
ד הָעָם: ס וַיֹּאמֶר מֹשֶׁה כֹּה אָמַר יְהוָֹה כַּחֲצֹת הַלַּיְלָה אֲנִי
ה יוֹצֵא בְּתוֹךְ מִצְרָיִם: וּמֵת כָּל־בְּכוֹר בְּאֶרֶץ מִצְרַיִם אֲשֶׁר
מִבְּכוֹר פַּרְעֹה הַיֹּשֵׁב עַל־כִּסְאוֹ עַד בְּכוֹר הַשִּׁפְחָה אֲשֶׁר
ו אַחַר הָרֵחָיִם וְכֹל בְּכוֹר בְּהֵמָה: וְהָיְתָה צְעָקָה גְדֹלָה
בְּכָל־אֶרֶץ מִצְרָיִם אֲשֶׁר כָּמֹהוּ לֹא נִהְיָתָה וְכָמֹהוּ לֹא
ז תֹסִף: וּלְכֹל בְּנֵי יִשְׂרָאֵל לֹא יֶחֱרַץ־כֶּלֶב לְשֹׁנוֹ לְמֵאִישׁ
וְעַד־בְּהֵמָה לְמַעַן תֵּדְעוּן אֲשֶׁר יַפְלֶה יְהוָֹה בֵּין מִצְרַיִם
ח וּבֵין יִשְׂרָאֵל: וְיָרְדוּ כָל־עֲבָדֶיךָ אֵלֶּה אֵלַי וְהִשְׁתַּחֲווּ־לִי
לֵאמֹר צֵא אַתָּה וְכָל־הָעָם אֲשֶׁר־בְּרַגְלֶיךָ וְאַחֲרֵי־כֵן אֵצֵא
ט וַיֵּצֵא מֵעִם־פַּרְעֹה בָּחֳרִי־אָף: ס וַיֹּאמֶר יְהוָֹה אֶל־מֹשֶׁה
לֹא־יִשְׁמַע אֲלֵיכֶם פַּרְעֹה לְמַעַן רְבוֹת מוֹפְתַי בְּאֶרֶץ
י מִצְרָיִם: וּמֹשֶׁה וְאַהֲרֹן עָשׂוּ אֶת־כָּל־הַמֹּפְתִים הָאֵלֶּה
לִפְנֵי פַרְעֹה וַיְחַזֵּק יְהוָֹה אֶת־לֵב פַּרְעֹה וְלֹא־שִׁלַּח אֶת־
בְּנֵי־יִשְׂרָאֵל מֵאַרְצוֹ: ס

a

הוֹפֵר הַשֶּׁקֶט בִּגְבוּלֵנוּ הַדְּרוֹמִי. הִסְמַנּוּ
מוּקְשִׁים, וְאַף מִסְתַּנְּנִים חָדְרוּ, מֵעֵבֶר
לַגְּבוּל. נִרְאָה, כִּי מִתְחַדְּשׁוֹת פְּעֻלּוֹת
הָרֶצַח הַמִּצְרִיּוֹת.

הָאַחֲרָיוּת הַמְּלֵאָה לַהֲפִיכָתָהּ־מֵחָדָשׁ
שֶׁל רְצוּעַת־עַזָּה לְקֵן מְרַצְּחִים מֻטֶּלֶת
בְּכָל חֻמְרָתָהּ עַל מוֹסְדוֹת או"ם וְעַל
כֹּחַ־הַחֵרוּם שֶׁלּוֹ, שֶׁחוֹבָתָם הִיא לִמְנֹעַ
אֶת חִדּוּשָׁם שֶׁל מַעֲשֵׂי־הָאֵיבָה הַמִּצְ־
רַיִּים, לִשְׁמֹר עַל הַשֶּׁקֶט וְהַבִּטָּחוֹן בַּגְּ־
בוּל. רוֹדְנֵי מִצְרַיִם נָחַל כַּמָּה כִּשְׁלוֹנוֹת
מְדִינִיִּים בַּתְּקוּפָה הָאַחֲרוֹנָה, וְנִרְאֶה, כִּי
הוּא שׁוֹאֵף "לְתַקֵּן אֶת מַזָּלוֹ" עַל־יְדֵי
חִדּוּשׁ הַהִתְנַקְּשֻׁיּוֹת הָרַצְחָנִיּוֹת בְּחַיֵּיהֶם
שֶׁל חַקְלָאִים וְאֶזְרָחִים יִשְׂרְאֵלִים. מִמֶּ־
שֶׁלֶת יִשְׂרָאֵל הֵבִיאָה אֶת הַתַּקְרִית
הַחֲמוּרָה לִידִיעַת מוֹעֶצֶת־הַבִּטָּחוֹן.
מִמּוֹסְדוֹת או"ם וְהַגּוֹרְמִים הַקּוֹבְעִים
בָּהֶם תִּתָּבַע הָאַחֲרָיוּת לַמַּצָּב שֶׁנּוֹצַר
וְלַסַּכָּנָת הַנִּשְׁקָפוֹת מִמֶּנּוּ לִשְׁלוֹם הָאֵ־
זוֹר.

בְּרִיטַנְיָה וְיַרְדֵּן

פְּנִיַּת יַרְדֵּן לִבְרִיטַנְיָה בְּבַקָּשַׁת סִיּוּעַ
כַּסְפִּי הִיא עוֹד עֵדוּת אַחַת לְהִתְפָּרְקוּ־
תָהּ שֶׁל הַלִּיגָה הָעַרְבִית כְּגוֹרֵם "אַנְטִי־
אִימְפֶּרְיָאלִיסְטִי", כּוֹתֵב "דָּבָר" בְּמַ־
אֲמַר הָרָאשִׁי מִיּוֹם ו'. סַמְלֵי הַדָּבָר
לַמַּצָּב שֶׁנּוֹצַר בָּאֵזוֹר, כִּי פְּנִים רַבַּת־
עָמְמוֹן לְלוֹנְדּוֹן בָּאָה יוֹם אוֹ יוֹמַיִם לִפְנֵי
פְּנוֹת הַכֹּחוֹת הַבְּרִיטִיִּים מִן הַבַּסִּיס הַגָּ־
דוֹל בְּמַפְרַק. קָרוֹב לְוַדַּאי, כִּי קָשֶׁת
הָעֶזְרָה לֹא תִמָּנַע אֶת הַמֶּלֶךְ חֻסֵין
מֵקְּשׁוֹא בַּחֲגִיגוֹת הַפִּנּוּי נְאוּם "אַנְטִי־
אִימְפֶּרְיָאלִיסְטִי". שֶׁיְּפָאֵר אֶת הַמַּאֲבָק
לְצַמְאֻמוֹת אֲשֶׁר נִפְתַּח עִם הַדָּחָתוֹ שֶׁל
גֶּנֶרָל גְלָב...

לֹא נְכַחֵשׁ. מִצְיוֹ הָעַתֵּק, כִּי אָנוּ חוֹ־

b

c

15.20. Hebrew character: *a* Vocalised modern Hebrew Bible. *b* Vocalized modern Hebrew for children. *c* Yiddish letter, 1818.

PHONETIC VALUE	NABATAEAN	NEO-SINAITIC	EARLY ARABIC	A.D. 8th CENTURY	KUFIC	EARLY NASKHI	MAGHRIBI	QARMATHIAN	MODERN NASKHI
'									
b									
g (ǧ)									
d (ḏ)									
h									
w									
z									
ḥ (ḫ)									
ṭ (ẓ)									
y									
k									
l									
m									
n									
s									
' (ġ)									
(p) f									
ṣ (ḍ)									
q									
r									
sh – š									
t (ṯ)									

ARABIC ADDITIONAL LETTERS	PERSIAN	...	PUSHTU	...
	URDU	APART FROM PERSIAN ADDITIONAL LETTERS	MALAY	...

15.21. Development of the Arabic alphabet.

15.22. *a* Important Nabataean inscriptions from Petra. *b, c* Minor Nabataean inscriptions. *d–f* Neo-Sinaitic inscriptions.

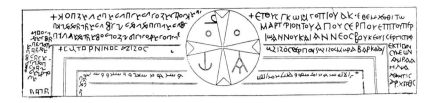

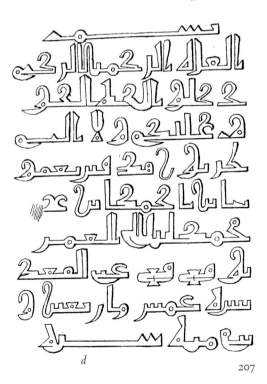

15.23. *a* Earliest extant Arabic inscription: Greek-Syraic-Arabic trilingual, A.D. 512. *b* Comparison of *left*, Kufic and *right*, Qarmathian scripts. *Koran*, Sura 3, 1–2. *c* Modern Kufic character. *d* Sepulchral epigraphic in Kufic character dated 445 A.H. [A.H. = in the year of the Hegira (*English* flight). The Moslem era, A.H., is reckoned from Mohammed's flight from Mecca to Medina in A.D. 622].

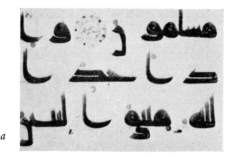

فَوْتُ الْغَنِيِّ فِي الْعِزِّ مِثْلَ حَيَاتِهِ وَعَيْشُهُ فِي الذُّلِّ عَيْنُ مَمَاتِهِ   *d*

فوت الغني في العز مثل حياته وعيشه في الذل عين مماته   *e*

فوات الغني في العز مثل عيشه في الذل عين ممات تقلم ذلك العمل في   *f*

فَوْتُ الْغَنِيِّ فِي الْعِزِّ مِثْلُ حَيَاتِهِ وَعَيْشُهُ فِي الذُّلِّ عَيْنُ مَمَاتِهِ   *g*

فوت الغني في العز مثل حياته وعيشه في الذل عين مماته   *h*

فوت الغني في العز مثل حياته وعيشه في الذل عين مماته   *i*

  j

فوت الغني في العز مثل حياته وعيشه في الذل عين مماته   *k*

  l

15.24. *a* Earliest dated Kufic manuscript in England, bearing the dedication of Amadjur, Governor of Damascus, A.D. 870–7. (University Library, Cambridge, *Add. M.S.* 1116). *b* Koran Sura 24, verses 32–6. 8th century Kufic on vellum. (British Museum, Dr. 2165, f. 676). *c* Oldest dated Christian Arabic manuscript: *Treatise on Christian Theology* A.D. 876, attributed to Theodorus Abū Kurrah, bishop of Harran (British Museum, *Or. MS.* 4950). *d* to *l* Varieties of Naskhi script.

d Naskhi current hand
e Diwani
f Naskhi-Djerisi
g Thuluth
h Ryq'a
i Ta'liq current hand
j Kalemi-Rasd
k Djeri
l Syakat

15.25. Page of a very elegant copy of the Koran, by a copyist who names himself, Husain Fakhkhâr. The pages measure 13¼ by 8½ inches, and some are entirely gilt, or written on a dyed ground, or ornamented with gold, blue, etc. The text is written in *Naskhi*, but the first, middle and last lines are written in large *Thuluth* (Courtesy S. C. Sutton, Librarian, India Office Library. No. 32A).

15.26. Copy of the Koran, probably early 10th century. (In a private collection at Izmir: Courtesy Glyn Meredith-Owens.)

15.27b. Koran with glosses, in Kanembu, N. Nigeria. (Courtesy Glyn Meredith-Owens.)

15.27.a. A medical encyclopaedia, A.D. 1085. The second earliest dated Persian MS. (Courtesy Glyn Meredith-Owens.)

15.28. Old Ottoman Naskhi: opening of the Koran with the ex-libris of the poet (Courtesy Glyn Meredith-Owens).

212

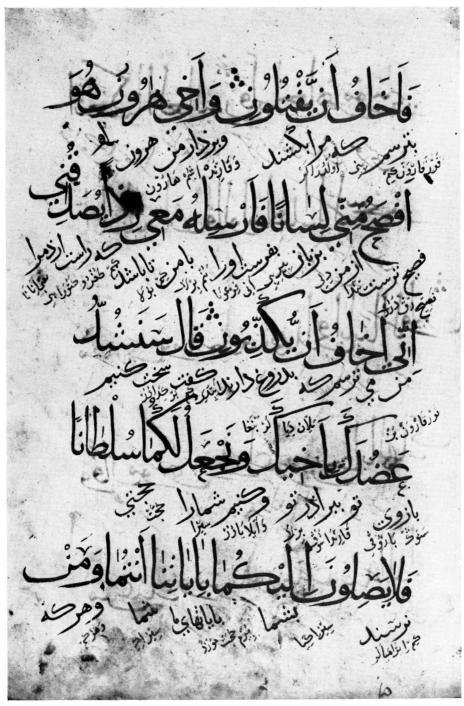

15.29. Old Ottoman translation of the Koran (Courtesy Glyn Meredith-Owens).

213

15.30. Luxurious 16th century Persian MS., ornamented in gold (Rylands Persian MS. 35; courtesy, Librarian John Rylands Library).

15.31. Çaģatay or Old Uzbek MS. Dīvān of Mīr 'Alī Shīr Nevā'ī (Courtesy Glyn Meredith-Owens).

15.32a. Urdu: *Amwaj-i-khūdi*, A.D. 1667
(India Office Library, *Hindust.* B.2.)

15.32b. Malay: *Shair jaran Tamas*, c.
1800 (India Office Library, *Malay*,
D.6).

15.32c. Sindhi: Shab-i-Mi'rāj, A.D. 1807
(India Office Library, *Sindhi* 14).

15.32d. Pashtu: *Qissah-i-Bahramgor*, A.D.
1750 (India Office Library, *Pash.* B.28).

کرنل جناب ڈاکٹر درینگر صاحب ۔

مجھے یہ معلوم کرکے بڑی

مسرت ہوئی کہ حرف تہجی اور رسم الخط پر آپ کی کتاب

زیر طبع ہے ۔ آپ کی خواہش کے مطابق یہ چند سطور اردو

طرز تحریر کے نمونے کے طور پر روانہ کی گئی ہیں ۔ امید ہے

یہ آپ کی اغراض کیلئے کافی ہوں گی

مخلص نیاز گزار

سعید احمد

15.33*a*. Arabic adapted to a non-Semitic language: letter written in Urdu.

بُوَانَ دَ كِتَابِ دِ رِنغَ

نِفُرَاجِ كُكُتُنُكَ بَرُوَهِي نَدَاعَ اِلَ اِبُغُو

نَابُ كِتَكَ كِتَابُ شَكَ شَحَرُوفِ

كُوَ نِعَيْنَ عَلُنْدِ يَتَشِ يَكُسُوَ حِيْلَ

نَتَمَاءِ مَأَنْدِ يْتَشِ هَيَ يَتَمِيْزَ مَكُسُدِ يْ يَدَكَ

مُكُوَنِلِ وَاكَ

سعيد بن هلال البو علي

۳۱ نُقَمْبَرْ ۱۹٤۷ مر

15.33*b*. Arabic adapted to a non-Semitic language: letter written in Swahili.

217

Phon. Value	Palmyrene	Syriac					Christ. Palestin. or Palestin Syriac	Mand.	Manichaean
		Early Syriac	Estrang	West-Syrian or Serta	East-Syrian or Nest.	Jacob.			
'									('ā)
b									
g									
d									
h									
w									(v, û ô)
z									(ž) (ǰ ǧ)
ḥ									
ṭ									
y									(j, î, ê)
k									(kh)
l									(l)
m									
n									
s									
‘									
p									(ph)
ṣ									(č) (ǧ)
q									
r									
sh									
t									

15.34. Various offshoots of the Aramaic alphabet.

218

b

c

15.35. *a* Latin–Palmyrene inscription discovered in a Roman camp at South Shields near Newcastle, and the transcription of the Palmyrene text. *b, c* Palmyrene inscriptions.

a

15.35*d*. Palmyrene inscription in the background of a stone carving (Fitzwilliam Museum, Cambridge).

a

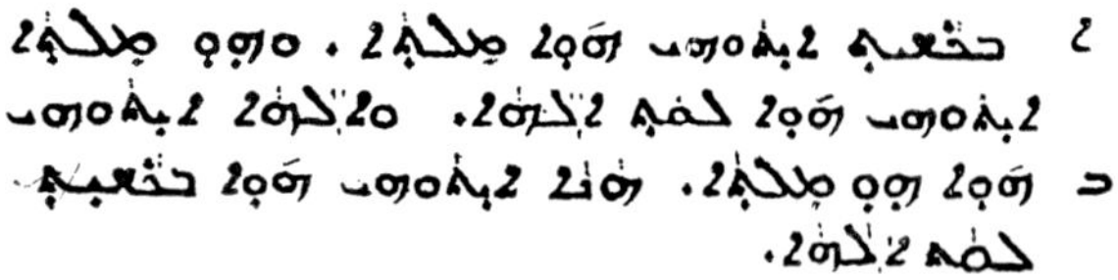

b

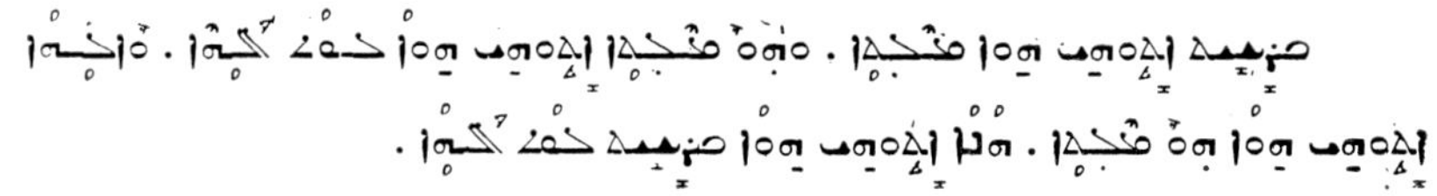

c

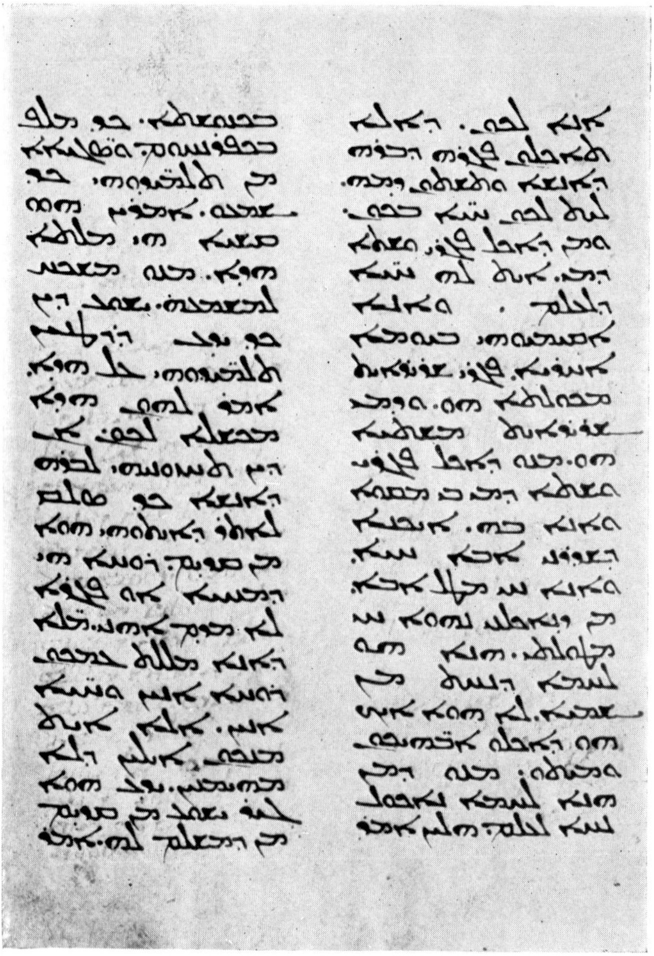

15.36. Syriac inscriptions and manuscripts: *a* Early Syriac, from Edessa, attributed to 4th century A.D. *b* Printed Nestorian script (St. John's Gospel 1, 1–2). *c* Jacobite script. *d* Curetonian Gospels, 5th century A.D. (British Museum).

d

15.37. Rabbūlā Gospels, folio 6r. Written and illuminated by the monk Rabbūlā in A.D. 586 at the monastery of St. John at Zagba in Mesopotamia. Laurentian Library, Florence (Cod Plut. 1.56).

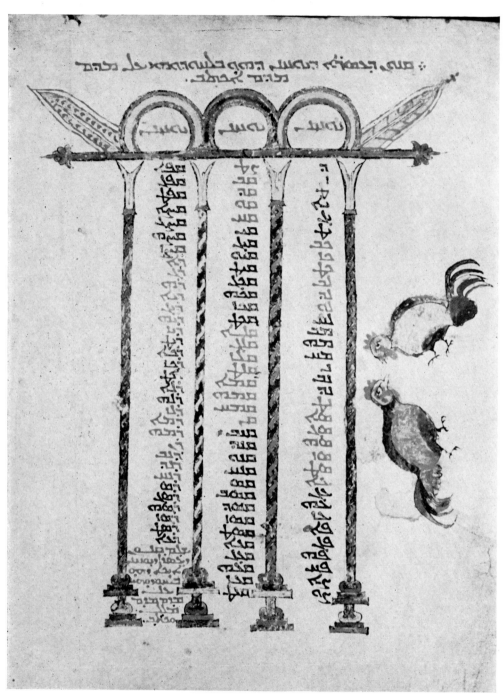

15.38. Illuminated Syriac MS.: courtesy Sir Chester Beatty. (MS. 16.)

222

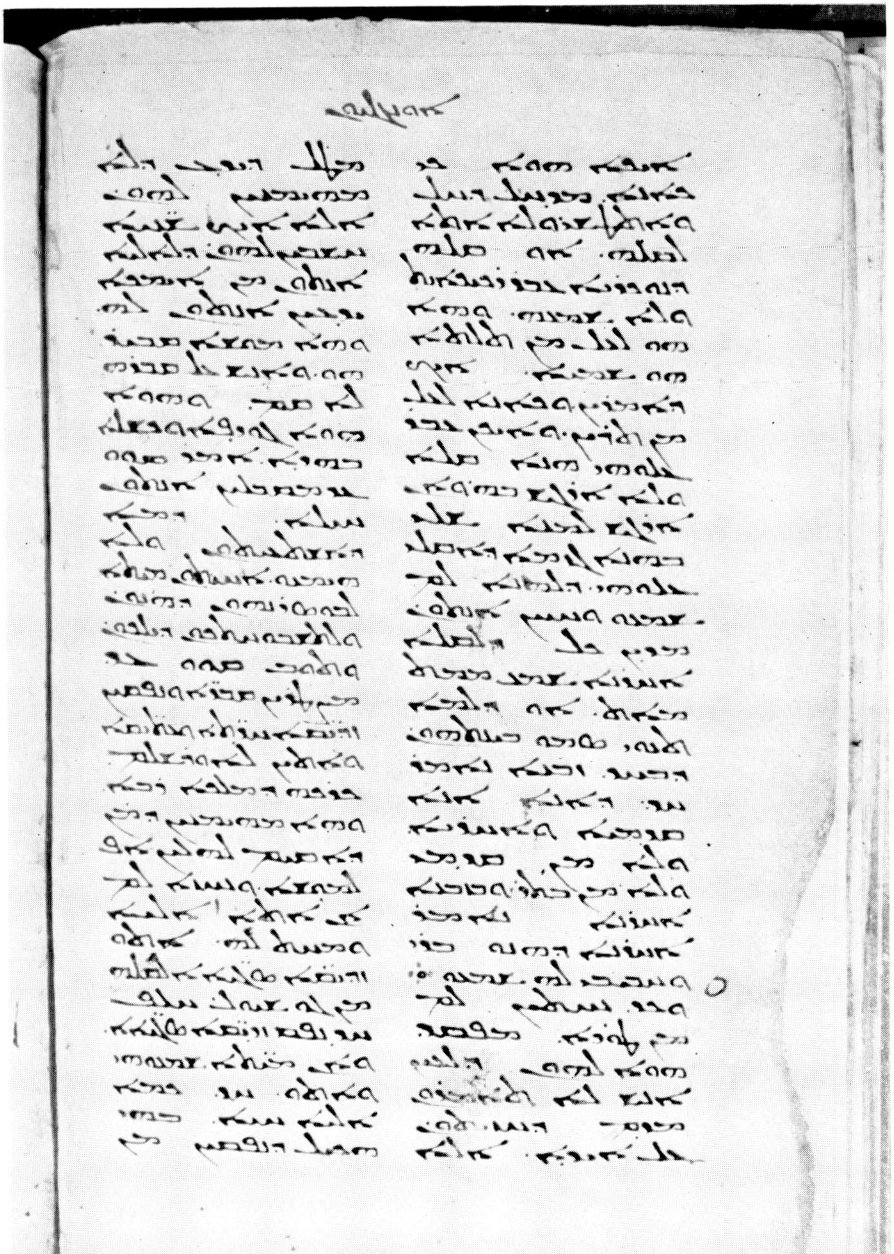

15.39. Syriac Codex: courtesy, Sir Chester Beatty. (MS 17.)

223

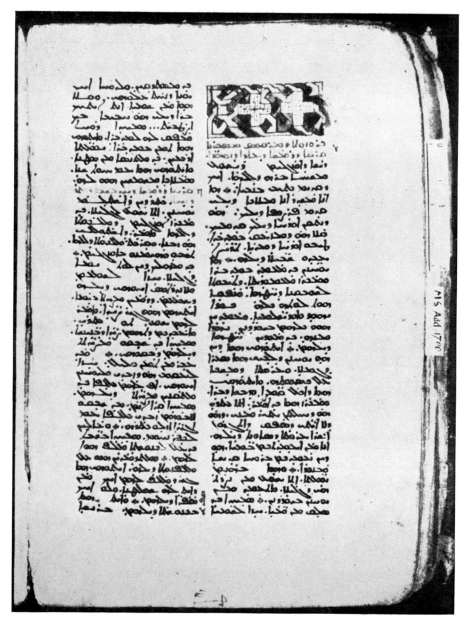

15.40. Harqleian version of the New Testament. Written in a neat regular Jacobite cursive hand, it contains 216 leaves of vellum, each measuring 9½ by 6½ inches. It is dated A.Gr 1481, corresponding to A.D. 1170. (University Library, Cambridge, *Add. MS.* 1700.)

15.41. Nestorian book, written by a secluded monk, completed in the year 892. It contains meditations, prayers, sermons, Christian chronology, and so on. (Courtesy, Rev. A. E. Goodman.)

ʾa b p t s ġ c ḥ ẋ d z r z z s s

s d(z) t z č g f w̄ q k g l m n w h y

15.42a. Yezidi cryptic alphabet.

b

c

ʾ b t ġ ḥ ḥ d r s š ḍ gʿ f

q k l m n w h y i u o a e

d

15.42. *b* Yezidi specimen from *Kitab-al-Jalweh*. *c* Yezidi specimen from *Miskhaf Resh*. *d* Somali alphabet.

Chā zernah, khudā-si khuri bui-kha
« What say-if, God-by his son-on
chhes-luh lya-khan kun mi shi, do-
faith-sort making all not die, that-
patse khong-lah hrtane. duk-pi
from him-to faithful being-ones-of
khson-luk thop-tuk, zere, khuri bu chik-bu mins; ditse khosi mi-
living-short receive, saiying, his son only-one gave; thus him-by men-
yul-po-lah rgas.
land-to liked ».

e

15.42e. Balti script. Specimen from St. John's Gospel, 3, 16, with transliteration and translation into English, according to G. A. Grierson.

226

1 a	2 am	3 ā	4 i	5 u	6 um	7 r̥	8 e	9 o	10 ka	11 ka	12 kā	13 kr̥	14 ko
15 ḱa	16 ḱum	17 ḱe	18 kha	19 khi	20 khu	21 ga	22 gu	23 gaṃ	24 ǵa	25 ǵu	26 ḡaṃ	27 gha	28 ghe
29 ca	30 ca	31 caṃ	32 ci	33 ce	34 co	35 cha	36 chi	37 chaṃ	38 cha	39 ćha	40 ćhaṃ	41 ćhu	42 ćhum
43 ja	44 ja	45 jaṃ	46 jā	47 ji	48 ja	49 ji	50 jha	51 jha	52 jhu	53 ña	54 ñi	55 ñi	56 ñe
57 ta	58 taṃ	59 tuṃ	60 ṭha	61 ṭhaṃ	62 thu	63 tha	64 thi	65 tho	66 ḍa	67 ḍa	68 ḍa	69 ḍi	70 ḍem
71 ḍha	72 ḍha	73 ḍhi	74 ṇa	75 ta	76 taṃ	77 ti	78 te	79 tai	80 tā	81 taḥ	82 tha	83 thā	84 tha
85 da	86 da	87 du	88 de	89 do	90 dha	91 dhaṃ	92 dhik	93 dhiḥ	94 na	95 ni	96 ni	97 na	98 ne
99 pa	100 pi	101 puṃ	102 pū	103 pha	104 pha	105 phu	106 ba	107 bim	108 bu	109 bha	110 bhi	111 bhu	112 bhom
113 ma	114 mā	115 maṃ	116 mu	117 mr̥	118 me	119 me	120 mo	121 ya	122 yaṃ	123 yi	124 yu	125 ya	126 yo
127 ra	128 raṃ	129 ru	130 ret	131 ro	132 roṃ	133 la	134 le	135 va	136 viṃ	137 vi	138 vu	139 vo	140 vr̥
141 va	142 vu	143 ve	144 ba	145 baṃ	146 bamñ(?)	147 bi	148 bu	149 be	150 bai	151 ba	152 ba	153 bam	154 bo
155 ba	156 baṃ	157 bim	158 bu	159 bu	160 bom	161 ba	162 bi	163 ha	164 hā	165 hi	166 hu	167 ha	168 ho
169 kha	170 khrā	171 kma	172 kra	173 kra	174 kva	175 khva	176 ḱtṣi	177 gtsi	178 gra	179 ǵnu	180 ghra	181 ṅka	182 ṅga
183 cma	184 cva	185 jhbo	186 jhmo	187 ñǵe	188 tma	189 tya	190 tra	191 tva	192 tsa	193 tsma	194 dra	195 dryu	196 dvi
197 dhya	198 ng	199 nǵe	200 pte	201 pgu	202 pǵu	203 pǵe	204 pre	205 prá	206 pru	207 pro	208 mge	209 mya	210 mṣo
211 rta	212 rtha	213 rdha	214 rmi	215 rya	216 rura	217 rṣa	218 rsu	219 lpa	220 lpi	221 lpi	222 lme	223 lme	224 lve
225 vyā	226 brā	227 bru	228 brr	229 bvaṃ	230 ṣṭha	231 ṣǵa	232 ṣǵe	233 ṣṭa	234 ṣḍhi	235 ṣṭa	236 ṣrá	237 ṣva	238 ṣpa
239 sta	240 stra	241 sthi	242 sthai	243 spa	244 opa	245 opu	246 oma	247 oya	248 ora	249 ova	250 ñsa	251 ñsam	252 ñse
253 1	254 1	255 1	256 2	257 2	258 3	259 3	260 3	261 4	262 4	263 10	264 20	265 100	266 1,000

16.1. The Kharoshthi character according to E. J. Rapson.

16.2. *a* Kharoshthi inscription. *b* Kharoshthi book on wood, found at Niya (Ruin 24, 7), Eastern Turkestan, by Sir Aurel Stein's expedition of 1906–8.

Table 16.3a — Pahlavi alphabets compared with the Sogdian and Aramaic scripts. Columns: S (Sogdian), 1 (phonetic value), 2 (Elephantine Aramaic), 3 (Pahlavik), 4 (Avromán), 5 (Parsik), 6 (Avesta), 7 (phonetic value).

S	1	2	3	4	5	6	7
	'						a
	b						b
	g						g
	d						d
	h						h
	w						w-u
	z						z
	ḥ						ḥ
	y						y-i
	k						k
	l						l-r
	m						m
	n						n
	s						s
	ʿ						ʿ
	p						f-p
	ṣ						ǰ-ž
	q						q
	r						r-?
	š						š
	t						t

16.3a. Pahlavi alphabets compared with the Sogdian and Aramaic scripts. S, Sogdian, 1, phonetic value, 2, Elephantine Aramaic, 3, Pahlavik, 4, Avromán, 5, Parsik, 6, Avesta, 7, phonetic value.

Table 16.3b — Avesta alphabet (phonetic values):

a	i	c	l	z
ā	ī	t	m	š
ã	u	d	n	ž
å	ū	th	n'	s
e	ty	dh	y	ž
ē	k	d	r	y
ə	h	p	v	h
ō	g	f	uv	h'
o	gh	b	w	hᵛ
ō	ǧ	w	s	n, m

16.3b. Avesta alphabet.

16.3c. Parchment Document from Avromán, Kurdistán, found with Greek deeds dated B.C. 88 and 22/21. The earliest specimen of Pahlavi (Middle Persian): some words are actually Aramaic but were read as Persian, just as we write e.g. = *exempli gratia* and say 'for example'.

229

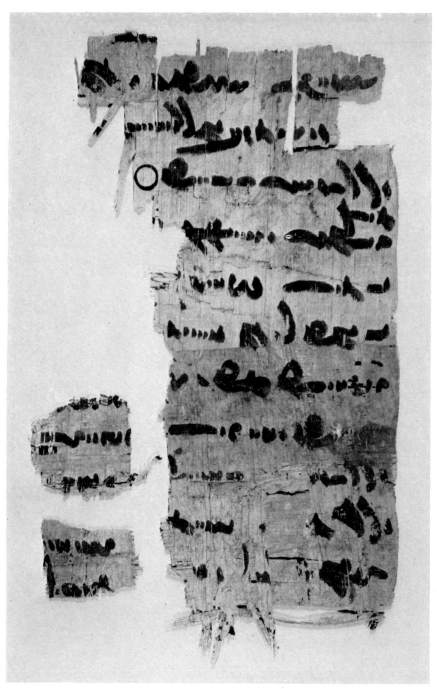

16.4. Pahlavi papyrus (Brooklyn Museum, 351452-A).

16.5. Iranian manuscripts

a Cursive eastern Pahlavi.

b Khordan Avesta, A.D. 1723 (India Office Library, Z & P. 21)

c Pazand: Strikand Gumani Vigar, A.D. 1737 (India Office Library, Z & P. 23)

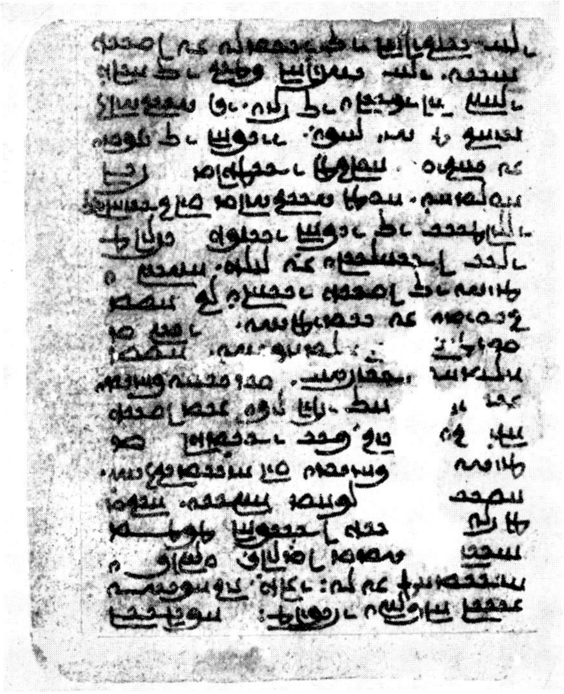

a

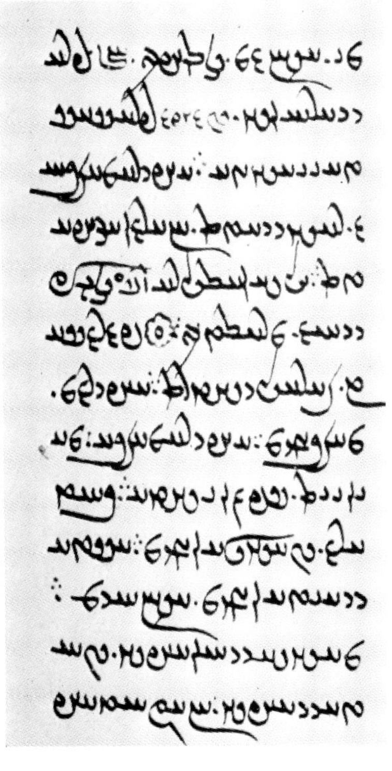

b

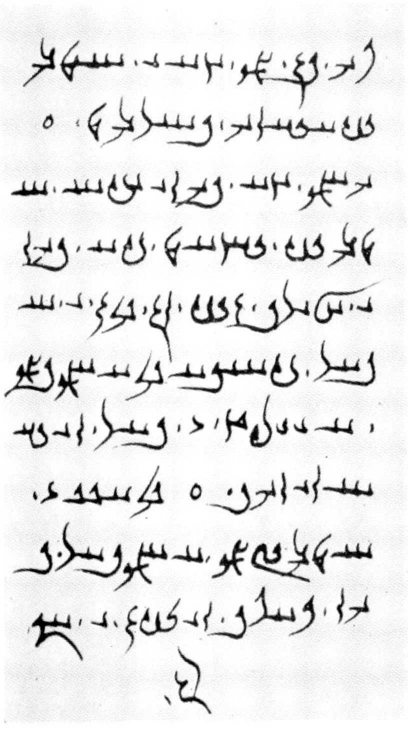

c

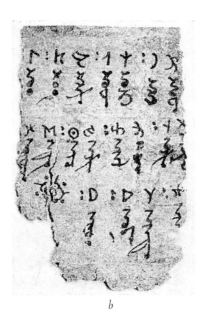

16.6. Specimens of *a* Mani-
chaean writing. *b* Kök Turki
runes and *c* Sogdian writing.

16.7. The Sogdian and Uighur alphabets compared with the Aramaic script.
(1) *Palmyrene* alphabet (2) phonetic values (3) *Sogdian* initial signs (4) medial signs
(5) final signs (6) phonetic values (7) *Uighur* initial signs (8) medial signs (9) final
signs of the script employed in Eastern Turkestan (10) *Qutadghu* initial signs (11) final
signs (12) phonetic value.

Orkhon	Yenisei	Phon. Value	Orkhon	Yenisei	Phon. Value	Orkhon	Yenisei	Phon. Value
		$a\ \ddot{a}$			d^6			r^7
		$y\ \iota$			d^7			l^6
		$o\ u$			p			l^7
		$\ddot{o}\ \ddot{u}$			b^6			$\check{c}$
		k^1			b^7			$i\check{c}$
		k^2			j^6			s^6
		k^3			j^7			s^7
		k^4			i			$\check{s}$
		k^5			$\underset{n}{ng}$			z
		g^6			n^6			$\underline{nd}$
		g^7			n^7			$\underline{n\dot{c}}$
		t^6			m			$\underline{ld}$
		t^7			r^6			

a

Value	RUNES	Kök Turki	Value	Value	RUNES	Kök Turki	Value	Value	RUNES	Kök Turki	Value
f			g'	h			k	t			k
u			š	n			d	b			k'
th			y	i			s	e			lt
a			k	y			ǰ	m			
r				e			a	l			j
			ng	p				ng			b'
g			d'	R			č	o			b'
w			y'	s			v	dh			

b

c

16.8. *a* Kök Turki runes. The figures $^{1-7}$ indicate the shapes of the letters when they precede or follow these vowels ^{1}a, ^{2}y, ^{3}o or u, ^{4}ä, e or i, ^{5}ö or ü, ^{6}a, o, u or y, ^{7}e, i, ä, ö, or ü. *b* Comparison of Germanic with Kök Turki runes. *c* Early Hungarian script.

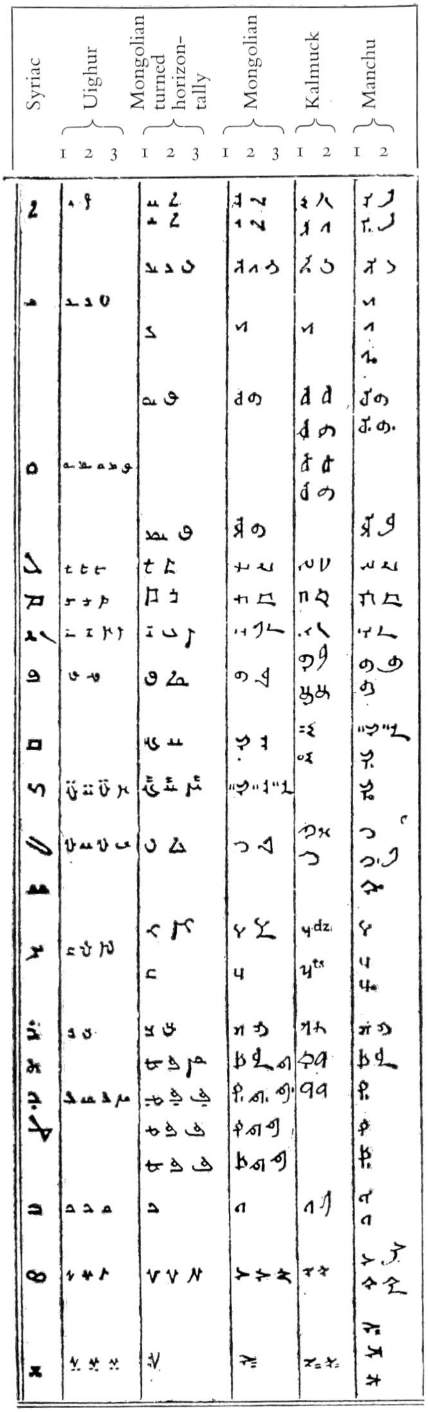

Syriac	Uighur			Mongolian turned horizontally			Mongolian			Kalmuck		Manchu	
	1	2	3	1	2	3	1	2	3	1	2	1	2

a

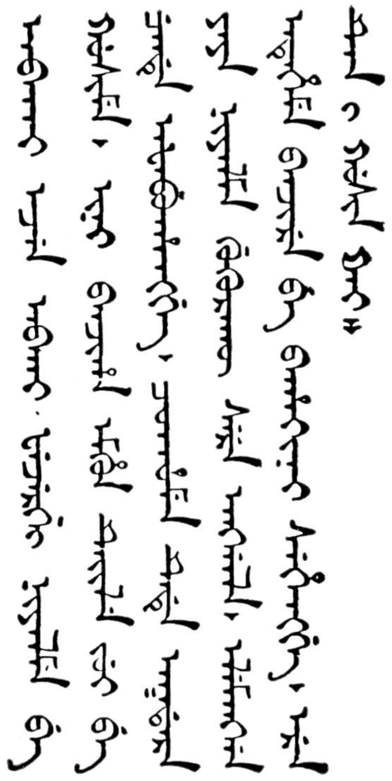

16.9. *a* The Mongolian, Kalmuck and Manchu alphabets compared with the Syriac and Uighur scripts. *b* Portion of The Gospel of St. John, in Manchu.

b

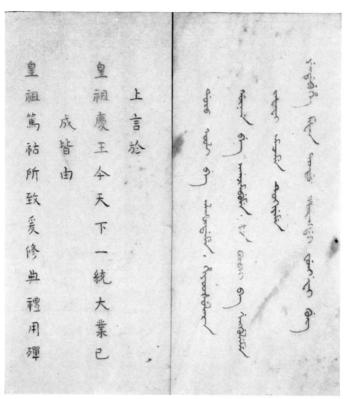

16.10a. Jade book, 1648, *right*, Manchu, and *left*, Chinese: Emperor Fu-Lin (Shuh-Chih) confers posthumous title on ancestor of the 6th generation (Chester Beatty 30).

16.10b. Mongolian, early 18th cent.: translation of Buddhist Sūtra *T'ar-Pa C'en-Po*. (Chester Beatty 29). Courtesy, Sir Chester Beatty.

a

b

a	χa	ba	la	da	tsa	sa	ra
ä	kä	bä	lä	dä	tsä	sä	rä
i	ki	bi	li	di	tsi	si	ri
o	χo	bo	lo	do	tso	so	ro
u	χu	bu	lu	du	tsu	su	ru
ö	kö	bö	lö	dö	tsö	sö	rö
ü	kü	bü	lü	dü	tsü	sü	rü

na	ga	ma	ta	ya	dza	ša
nä	gä	mä	tä	yä	dzä	šä
ni	gi	mi	ti	yi	dzi	ši
no	go	mo	to	yo	dzo	šo
nu	gu	mu	tu	yu	dzu	šu
nö	gö	mö	tö	yö	dzö	šö
nü	gü	mü	tü	yü	dzü	šü

16.11. *a* Uighur book. *b* Mongolian manuscript, *Altasamba*, *c.* 1860 (India Office Library, R.305). *c* Kalmuck syllabic alphabet.

c

237

NO	MAJUSC.	MINUSC.	PHONETIC VALUE	NAMES OF LETTERS
21			y, j, h,	hi
22			n	nu
23			š	ša
24			o	o
25			č̣, č̣, ch	ča
26			p–b	pe
27			ǰ, j, dž	dže
28			ṙ	ṙa
29			s	sē
30			v	vev
31			t–d	tiun
32			r	rē
33			c, t'ˢ	t'so co
34			u, w	hiun
35			p', p', ph	p'iur
36			k, k', x	kē
37			o	ō
38			f	fē
39			&	ev

NO	MAJUSC.	MINUSC.	PHONETIC VALUE	NAMES OF LETTERS
1			a	aïp
2			b–p	bien
3			g–k	gim
4			d–t	da
5			e	eč (yeč')
6			z	za
7			e	ēt'
8			silent ə	ət'
9			t'	t'o
10			ž	že
11			i	ini
12			l	liun
13			ḫ x (Scott. ch)	hē
14			ts	tsa
15			k–g	ken
16			h	ho
17			d – z	dza
18			ł gh	ład
19			č	čē
20			m	men

16.12. The Armenian Alphabet.

238

16.13*b*. Page from 'Arithmetic', by Anania Shirakatsi, 7th century.

16.13*a*. Page from the earliest extant Armenian Gospel, A.D. 887.

16.14. *a* Armenian codex in majuscule script. (Chester Beatty Library, Dublin). *b* Armenian scribe, from an illuminated Gospel-book. (National Library, Paris, *Armén. 18*).

a

b

16.15a. Miniature: The entry into Jerusalem. Matthew 21, 12–16. (Freer Gallery of Art, Washington, D.C.).

16.15b. Armenian manuscript with church melodies, 1352.

16.16b. 15th century manuscript on vellum. (John Rylands Library, *Arm. MS. 3*).

16.16a. Armenian. Title page of *History of Armenians* by Moses Khorewatsi (5th century). Manuscript of the 14th century (Matenadaran, Armenian S.S.R.).

NO.	KHUTSURI MAJUSC.	KHUTSURI MINUSC.	MKHEDRULI	NAMES OF LETTERS	PHON. VALUE	NUM. VALUE
1				an	a	1
2				ban	b	2
3				gan	g (hard)	3
4				don	d	4
5				en	e	5
6				vin	v	6
7				zen	z	7
8				he	h (weak)	8
9				tʼan	tʻ	9
10				in	i (ie, y)	10
11				kan	k	20
12				las	l	30
13				man	m	40
14				nar	n	50
15				hie	i (ie, y)	60
16				on	o	70
17				par	p	80
18				žan	ž (zh)	90
19				rae	r	100
20				san	s (hard)	200
21				tar	t	300
22				un	u	400
23				wi	wi	500
24				pʻar	pʼ (ph)	600
25				kʻan	kʼ (kh)	700
26				ghan	ł (gh)	800
27				kar	ķ (q)	900
28				šin	š (sh)	1,000
29				čin	č	2,000
30				tzan	tz (ŝ)	3,000
31				dzil	dz	4,000
32				tsil	ts, dẑ	5,000
33				tšar	tš, dž	6,000
34				xan	x	7,000
35				xhar	xh, x	8,000
36				džan	dz	9,000
37				hae	h (asp)	10,000
38				hoe	hō, ō	
39				fa	f	
40					ə	

16.17. The Georgian Alphabet.

a

b

c

16.18. Most Ancient Georgian Inscriptions, from Palestine: (a) *c.* A.D. 433; (b) Bolnisi inscription, A.D. 492; (c) 532–555. (d) Inscription of Bakur and Giri-Ormizd.

d

16.19b. Oldest dated Georgian MS. (Sinai MS., A.D. 864). (Courtesy
Acad. George Tseret'eli).

16.19a. Georgian manuscript: Khanmeti palimpsest, 5th–7th centuries A.D.

16.20b. Hymn cycles of Mik'el Modrekili (late 10th century). (a and b Courtesy, Acad. George Tsereťeli).

16.20a. Adishi Four Gospels, A.D. 897.

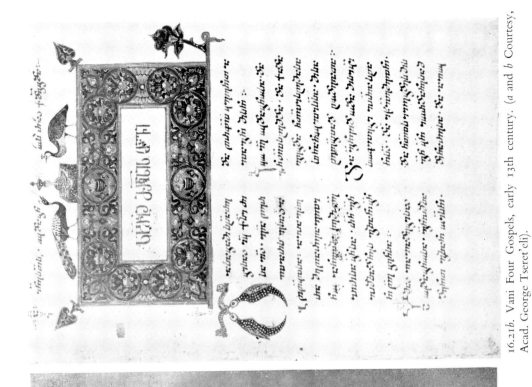

16.21*b*. Vani Four Gospels, early 13th century. (*a* and *b* Courtesy, Acad. George Tseret'eli).

16.21*a*. Page from John Chrysostom, A.D. 969.

16.22b. *Man in Tiger's Skin*, 1680 (*a* and *b* Courtesy, Acad. George Tseret'eli).

16.22a. Patericon of John the Monk, late 11th century.

16.23b. Autograph of poet Ilia Cavcavadse (1837–1909), *The Ghost*. (*a* and *b* Courtsey, Acad. George Tseret'eli).

16.23a. Georgian MS. from Mt. Athos, 1074.

16.24a. Page from Psalms, A.D. 974.

16.24b. Autograph of poet Nikoloz Barat'ashvili, 1817–45. (a and b Courtesy, Acad. George Tseret'eli).

250

16.25b. Modern Verse. (*a* and *b* Courtesy, Acad. George Tseret'eli).

16.25a. Autograph of poet Akaki Tseret'eli, 1840–1915.

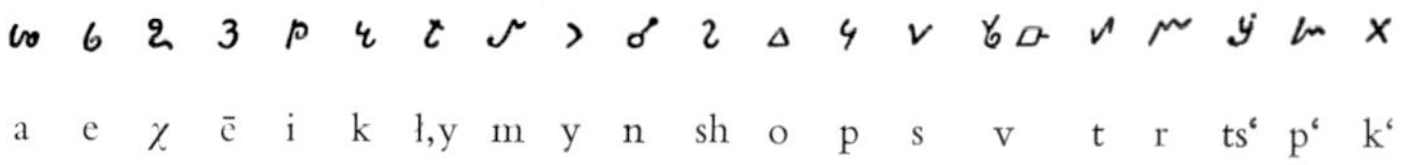

a

16.26. *a* The 'Alban alphabet' according to Karamianz.
b The Alban alphabet together
with miscellaneous Greek,
Syriac, Latin, Georgian, Al-
banian and Coptic alphabets,
contained in a 15th century
Armenian manuscript.

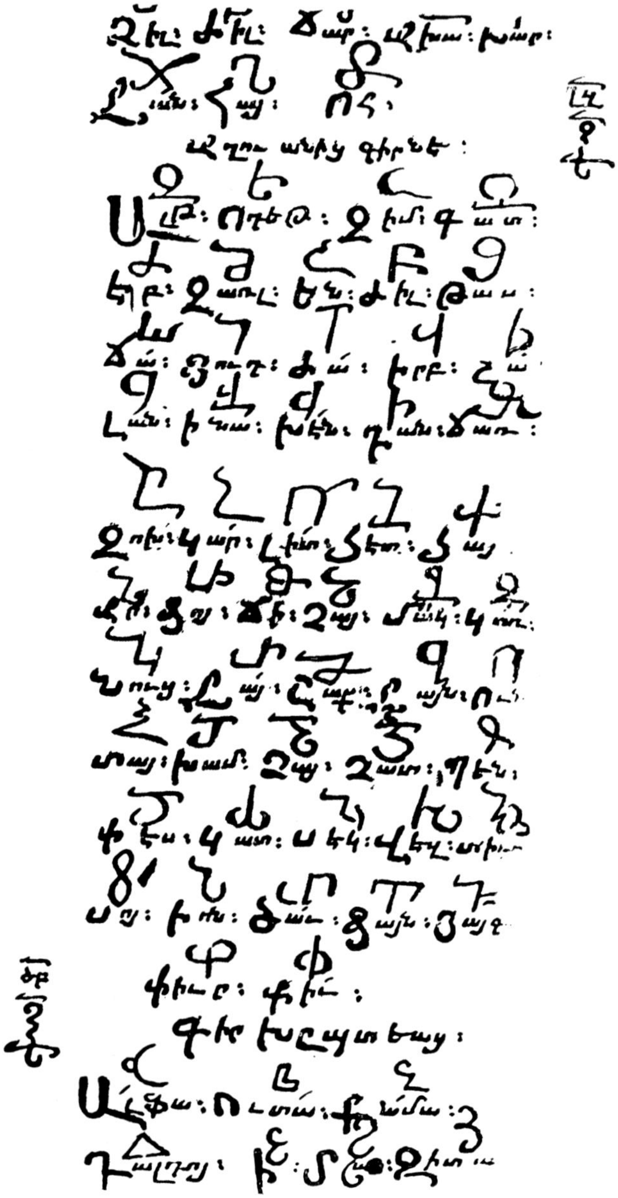

b

PHONETIC VALUE	BRAHMI					NORTH-INDIAN PROTOTYPE & CENTRAL ASIAN VARIETIES					SOUTH-INDIAN PROTOTYPES					EARLY SOUTH-INDIAN					MODERN NORTH INDIAN				
	AŚOKA	BHATT. PRŌLU	ŚUṄGA	KUṢĀṆA	KṢATRAPA	GUPTA	BOWER M.S.	STEIN COLL.	EARLY TIBETAN	KUTILA	TAMIL CAVES	KALIṄGA	SĀTAVAHANA	KADAMBA	PALLAVA	EARLY WEST. CĀLUKYA	EARLY EAST. CĀLUKYA	COLA	PĀṆDYA	LATE WEST. CĀLUKYA	DEVA-NĀGARĪ	GURMUKHI	GUJARATI	SINDHI	MULTANI
a																									
ā																									
i																									
u																									
e																									
o																									
ka																									
kha																									
ga																									
gha																									
ca																									
cha																									
ja																									
jha																									
ña																									
ṭa																									
ṭha																									
ḍa																									
ḍha																									
ṇa																									
ta																									
tha																									
da																									
dha																									
na																									
pa																									
pha																									
ba																									
bha																									
ma																									
ya																									
ra																									
la																									
va																									
śa																									
ṣa																									
sa																									
ha																									

17.1

17.1 and 2. Alphabet Chart: Indian and Further-Indian scripts.

254

MAIN N.-E.-INDIAN			SOUTH-INDIAN						(FURTHER INDIAN) SINHALESE				FURTHER-INDIAN		FURTHER INDIAN									
KRSNA KIRTANA M.S.	BENGALI	ORIYA	VIJAYANAGAR	TELUGU	KANARESE	GRANTHA	TAMIL	VATTELUTTU	VESSAGIRI (A)	MAHARATMALE	VESSAGIRI (B)	MODERN	VŌ-CĀNH	PŪRNAVARMA	MON	PYU	(BURMESE) KYOK CHA	(BURMESE) PALI	(BURMESE) CHA LONH	PATIMOKHA	MODERN SIAMESE	AHOM	ERLANGA	MODERN JAVANESE

a   dha   pa   ma   la   sa

b

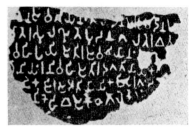

a

c

d

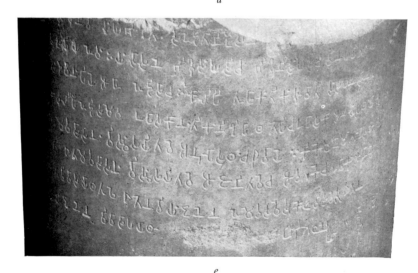

e

17.3. *a* Sohgaura copper plate (4th century B.C.). *b* Eran coin inscription (4th–3rd century B.C.). *c* Mahasthan inscription (4th–3rd century B.C.). *d* Inscription from Sarnath, Benares (Courtesy of A. Master). *e* Asoka inscription from South India.

17.4. Aśoka inscription. The Delhi-Toprā pillar, c. 242 B.C.

a	ai	ca	ḍha	pa	va	-ḥ	ṣa	the
ā	au	cha	ṇa	pha	śa	kä	sä	tho
i	ṛ	ja	ta	ba	ṣa	wa	tha	thai
ī	ka	jha	tha	bha	sa	ṛä	thā	thou
u	kha	ña	da	ma	ha	lä	thi	tho̧
ū	ga	ṭa	dha	ya	-ṃ	pä	thī	tho̧
e	gha	ṭha	na	ṛa	-ḥ	mä	thu	
c	ṅa	ḍa	ṉä	la	-ḥ	śä	thū	

17.5. The Central Asian Slanting Gupta.

a	kh	ṇḍ	bh
ā	g	dh	m
i	gh	n	y
ī	n	nt	r
u	č	th	l
ū	ch	d	v
e	ǧ	dh	ś
ai	ǧh	n	ṣ
o	ñ	p	s
au	ṭ	ph	h
k̥	ṭh	b	kṣ

a

17.6a. Central Asian Cursive Gupta.

c

b

17.6b,c. Specimens of the Central Asian Cursive Gupta.

VOWELS

1	2	3	4	5	6	7	8	9	10	11	12
A	₁Ā	₂Ā	I	₁Ī	₂Ī	U	Ū	Ṛ	E	O	AU

SYLLABLES

13	14	15	16	17	18	19	20	21	22	23	24
ka	kha	ga	gga	gha	ṅga	ca	₁cha	₂cha	ja	ñā	₁ña

25	26	27	28	29	30	31	32	33	34	35	36
ṭa	ṭha	ṭhṭha	ḍa	ṇḍa	ṇa	ta	tta	tha	da	dha	na

37	38	39	40	41	42	43	44	45	46	47	48
pa	pha	ba	₁bha	₂bha	ma	ya	ra	la	va	drai	ṃ

49	50	51	52	53	54	55	56	57	58	59 & 60	
śa	ṣa	sa	ha	rddha	rṣṭa	khā	₁lysa	rvā	mā	tā-ndi	

61	62	63	64	65	66	67	68	69	70	71	72
ṣṭā	hvā	jā	jyā	jā	jā	ttra	₂lysā	ñi	hl	₁lysī	lī

73	74	75	76 (śku)	77	78	79	80	81	82	83	84
jsī	spṛ	du	dū	ṛu	nu	pu	rru	₁rrū	₂rrū̠	rū	

85	86	87	88	89	90	91	92	93	94	95	96
bū	hū	ysmu	gu	śśu	śu	₁tu	₂ttu	pyu'	₁pyū	grū	brū

97	98	99	100	101	102	103	104	105	106	107	108
₁stū	₂ttū̠	rvṛ	kye	kiai	tcei	ysno	khyāu	lo	dāṃ	biṃ	ssiṃ

109	110	111	112	113	114	115	116	117	118	119	120
rtha	ḍḍa	nna	kkra	sde	tva	yyo	dye	ttye	₂pyu	gya	jva

121	122
ryau	crrā

NUMERALS

123	124	125	126	127	128	129	130	131	132	133	134
1	2	3	4	5	6	7	8	9	10	20	30

135	136	137	138	139	140	141	142	143	144		
40	50	60	70	80	90	100	200	300	400		

17.7. Khotanese characters, according to Leumann.

a

མི་ ཞིགལ་ བུ་ གཉིས་ ཡོད་པ་རེད། དེ་དག་ ལས་

ཅུང་བ་ དེས་ རང་གི་ ཕ་ལ་ ཞུས་པ། ཨང་ ཡབ་ ཅེས་ ཁྱེབ་ཁྱེའི་

b

c

d

17.8. Tibetan character *a* Tibetan manuscript (Chester Beatty MS. 28). *b* Specimen of *dbu chan*. *c* Specimen of a current hand; a variety of *dbu med*. *d* Tibetan manuscript (India Office Library).

261

[Lepcha script specimens]

17.9a. Specimens of Lepcha script.

[Lepcha characters with transliterations]

ka	k(la)	kha	ga	gla	ng(a)	cha	chha	ja	nya	t(a)	tya	da
*					*					*		

n(a)	pa	p(la)	pha	fa	fla	ba	bla	ma	mla	m	tsa	tsha
*		*								*		

za	ya	y	r(a)		l(a)		ha	hla	va	sa	sha	wa
			*		*							

â	á	a	i	i	ú	u	e	o	ó

17.9b. The Lepcha character.

Two (or four, when marked *) signs are given for each *akshara*, the first being employed in print, the second being used in current hand. In the *akshara* thus marked *, the final signs are also shown, which are very much abbreviated, and generally consist of little dashes, commas, circles, etc.

[Lepcha manuscript reproduction]

17.9c. Lepcha manuscript, *c.* 1800 (India Office Library).

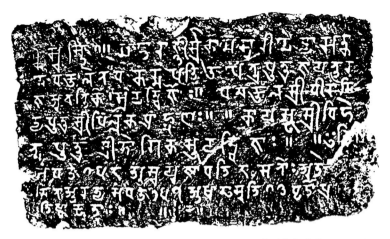

17.10a. Deva-nagari inscription dated A.D. 1064 (published by K. N. Dikshit).

	B.C. 250	A.D. 100	200	400	A.D.	400	500	600	750	800–1200	Present day
a					NORTH						अ आ (west) (east)
					SOUTH						
					TAMIL						அ
ka					NORTH						क
					SOUTH						
					TAMIL						க

17.10b. Evolution of the northern and southern Deva-nagari and Tamil *aksharas* a and ka from the early Brahmi type of *c.* 250 B.C. to the present day (Courtesy, A. Master).

17.10c. Sarada inscription from Hund, 8th century A.D. (Published by R. B. D. Ram Sahri).

263

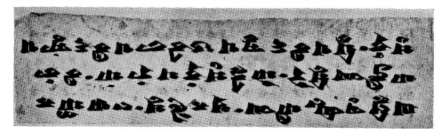

17.11*a*. Kuchean (Indian Office Library).

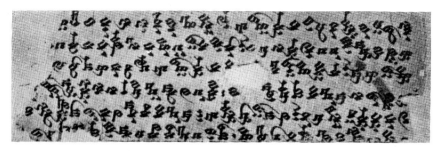

17.11*b*. Khotanese (India Office Library).

17.11*c*. Sanskrit Brahmi (India Office Library).

এতক্ষণ বড় ভাই মাঠে ছেল। যখন সে
বাড়ীর কাছে এল, তখন নাচ গাওনা শুনতে পেলে

a

b

c

d

e

17.12. *a* Bengali script: as employed in print. *b* Bengali script: current hand.
c Oriya script: standard variety (Kalahandi state). *d* Oriya script: Chatisgarhi
(Patna State). *e* Oriya script: Hindustani, used by the Orissa Moslems.

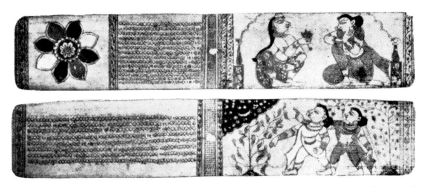

17.12*f*. Oriya 'illuminated' manuscript of palm leaf, *Gītagovinda* by Yayadeva (India
Office Library).

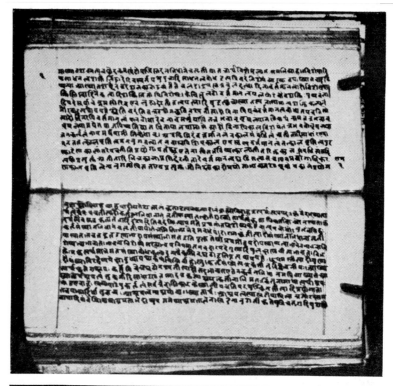

17.13. Sanskrit manuscripts, written in Devānāgarī, Śāradā, and Nepālī scripts: *top*, Devānāgarī (*Alamkaraparisekara*), *c.* 1800 (India Office Library, *E.2042*); *middle*, treatise on ritual in Śāradā script, A.D. 1781 (ibidem, *E.3326 a*); *bottom*, *Pañca Mahāraksa sūtrāni*, in Nepālī script, A.D. 1677 (ibidem, *K.7754*).

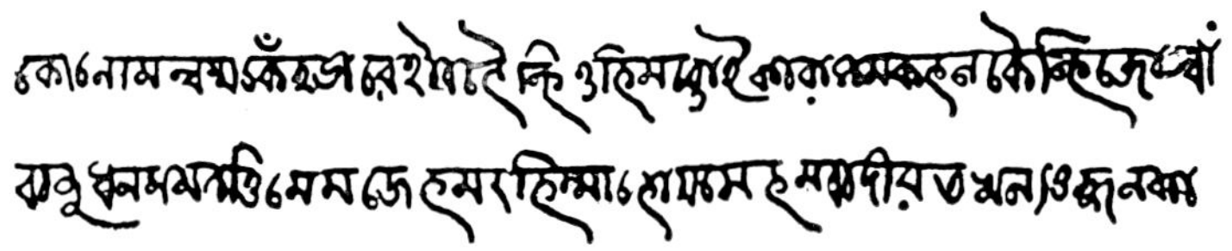

a

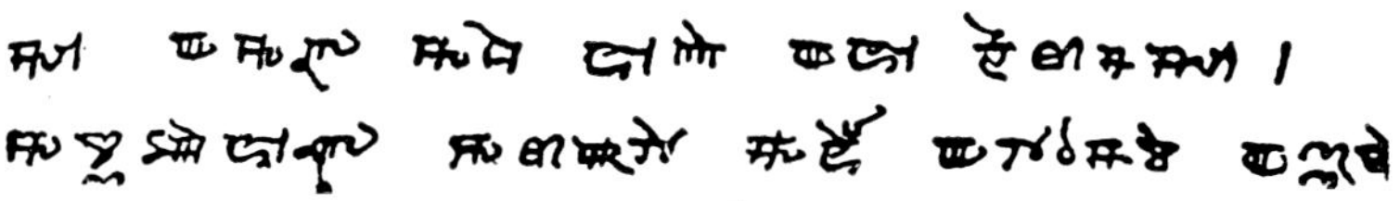

b

17.14. *a* Maithili script. *b* Manipuri script.

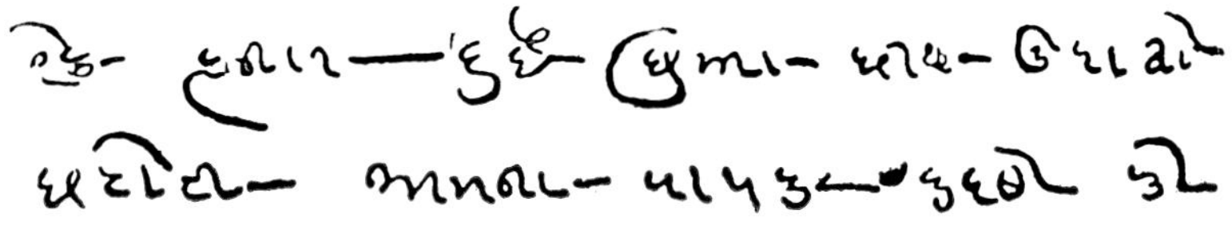

c

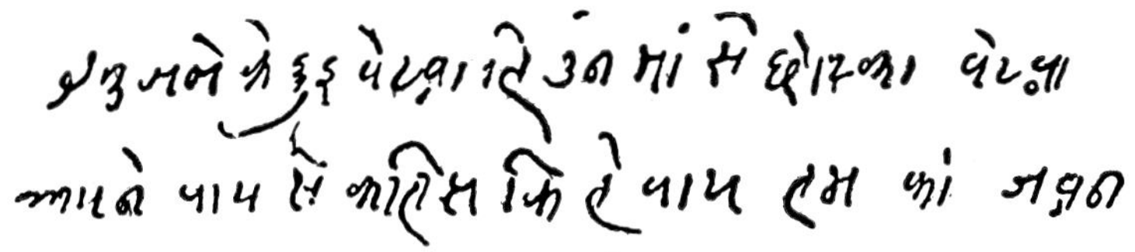

d

17.14. *c* Kaithi script from East Purnea. *d* Kaithi script, Awadhi variant (Eastern Hindi) from Gonda district.

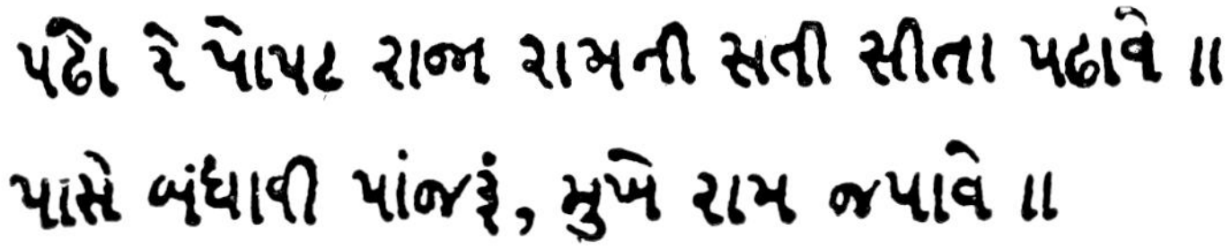

પઢો રે પોપટ રાજા રામની સતી સીતા પઢાવે ॥
પાસે બંધાવી પાંજરૂં, મુખે રામ જપાવે ॥

e

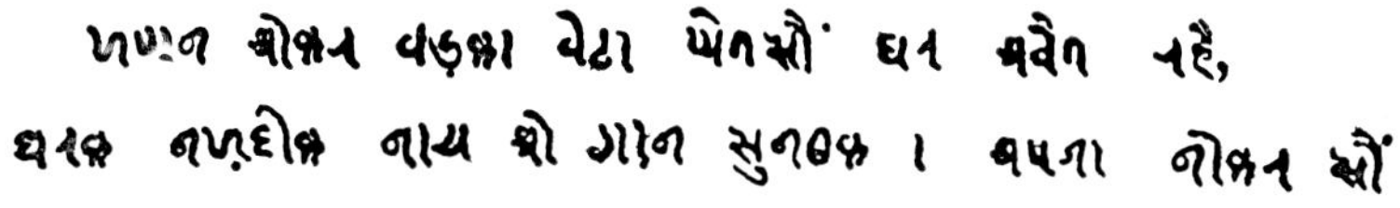

f

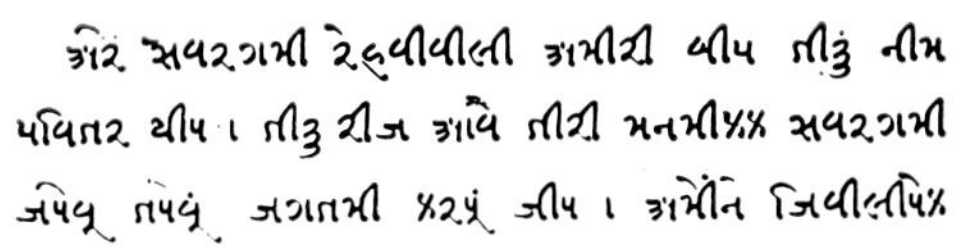

g

17.14. *e, f, g* Specimens of Gujarathi script.

17.15*a*. Marathī manuscript in Modi script, *Notes on Nagpur*, *c.* 1800 (India Office Library, *Mar. B.15*).

17.15*b*. Gurumukhī manuscript, *Janam Sākhī*, 1750 (India Office Library *Panj. B.40*).

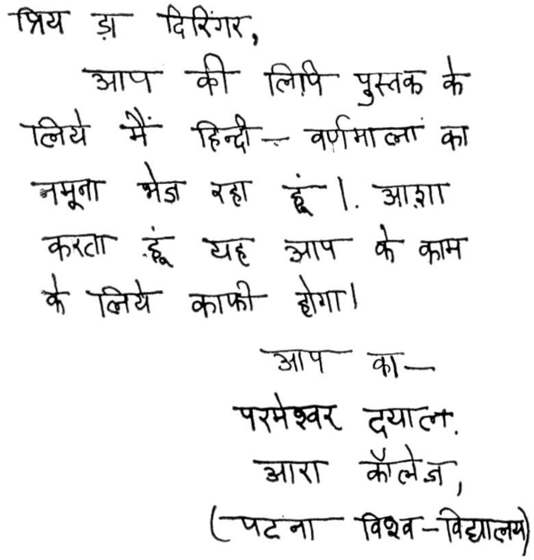

प्रिय ड्रा दिरिंगर,

आप की लिपि पुस्तक के
लिये मैं हिन्दी वर्णमाला का
नमूना भेड रहा हूं। आशा
करता हूं यह आप के काम
के लिये काफी होगा।

आप का

परमेश्वर दयाल.
आरा कॉलेज,
(पटना विश्व-विद्यालय)

17.16a. Modern Indian script: Hindi.

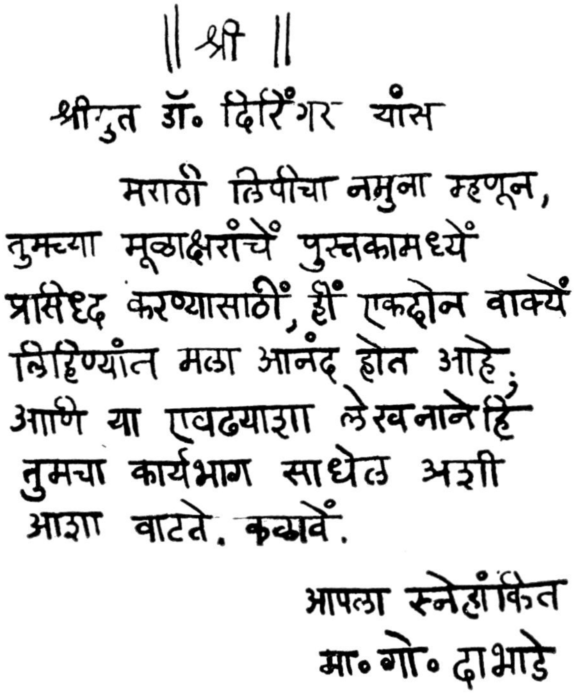

|| श्री ||

श्रीगुत डॉ॰ दिरिंगर यांस

मराठी लिपीचा नमुना म्हणून,
तुमच्या मूळाक्षरांचें पुस्तकामध्यें
प्रासिध्द करण्यासाठीं, हीं एकदोन वाक्यें
लिहिण्यांत मळा आनंद होत आहे,
आणि या एवढयाशा लेखनानेहि
तुमचा कार्यभाग साधेळ अशी
आशा वाटते. कव्ययें.

आपला स्नेहांकित
मा॰ गो॰ ढाभाडे

17.16b. Modern Indian script: Marathi.

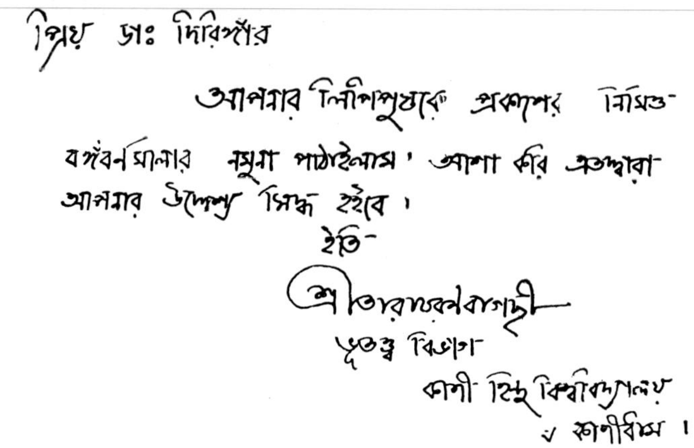

প্রিয় ডাঃ দিরিংগার

আপনার লিপিপুস্তকে প্রকাশের নিমিত্ত
বঙ্গবর্ণমালার নমুনা পাঠাইলাম। আশা করি এতদ্বারা
আপনার উদ্দেশ্য সিদ্ধ হইবে।
ইতি—

শ্রীতারকনাথ...
সংস্কৃত বিভাগ
কাশী হিন্দু বিশ্ববিদ্যালয়
√ কাণীধাম।

17.17*a*. Modern Indian script: Bengali.

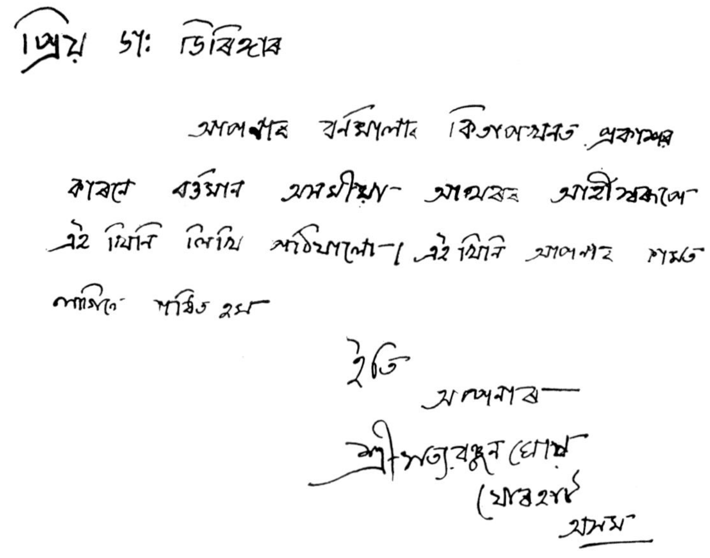

প্রিয় ডাঃ ডিরিংহার

আপনার বর্ণমালার কিছু নমুনা প্রকাশের
কারণে বঙ্গমান সমীপে—আমার আমীসরকলে
এই যিনি লিপি পাঠাইলাম—এই যিনি আপনার পছন্দ
পছন্দ সিদ্ধ হবে

ইতি
আপনার—

শ্রী সত্যব্রত ঘোষ
(ঘোষ)
অসম

17.17*b* Modern Indian script: Assamese.

17.18 Specimens of Bihari scripts. *a*, Maithili. *b*, Southern Maithili. *c*, *d*, Bhojpuri. *e*, Balasore District. *f*, Eastern Masahi. *g*, Midnapore District.

17.19. Bengāli and Kannada manuscripts. (*Above*) Bengāli: *Svarodaya*, *c.* 1780 (India Office Library, *MSS. Ben. F.3*); (*below*) Kannada: *Viveka Chintamanya*, *c.* 1790 (ibidem *MSS. Kan.C.1*).

17.20. *a* Limbū manuscript: alphabet, *c.* 1800 (India Office Library *Hodgson Coll. 87*). *b* Hindī manuscript in Kaithi script: *Santasagara*, 1794 (ibidem. *M.S. Hin. B.*55). *c* Gujarātī manuscript: *Pavagadhano garabo*, 1750 (ibidem, MSS. Guj. 17).

17.21. *a* Modi script. *b, c* Mahajani script. *d* Multani script. *e* Sindhi script.

PHON. VALUE	GUR-MUKHĪ	LANDĀ	ṬĀKRĪ	ŚĀRADĀ	PHON. VALUE	GUR-MUKHĪ	LANDĀ	ṬĀKRĪ	ŚĀRADĀ
ṛa					ṭha				
va					ṭa				
la					ña				
ra					jha				
ya					ja				
ma					cha				
bha					ça				
ba					ṅa				
pha					gha				
pa					ga				
na					kha				
dha					ka				
da					ha				
tha					sa				
ta					ō				
ṇa					'ûrâ'				3 (u)
ḍha					'îrî'				(i)
ḍa					'âirâ'				(a)

17.22. The four main local scripts of north-western India.

17.23a. Sanskrit inscription in 'box-headed' characters, early 6th century A.D. (published by Mirashi in 1935).

17.23b. Part of the earliest Kanarese inscription, from Halmidi. Attributed to 5th century A.D., by A. Master.

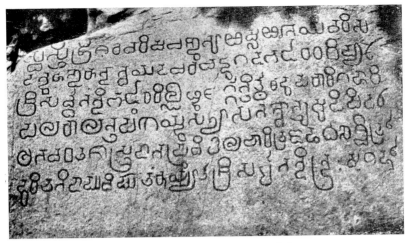

17.24a. Jaina Kanarese from Kopbal.

c

17.24. b Part of a Telugu inscription from Koi-
konda. c Rock inscription in 'Shell' character,
from Ci-Arutön (Java), attributed to the 4th–5th
century A.D. It may be considered to be the early
Grantha lithic style.

b

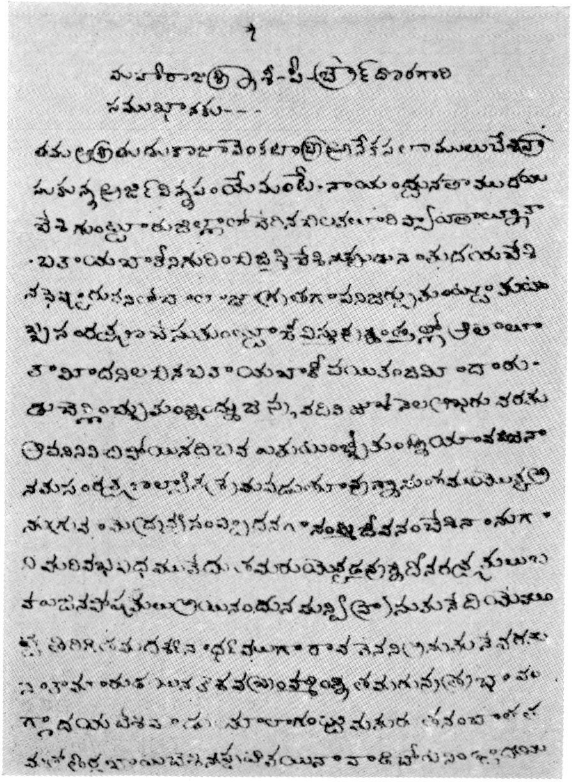

17.25a. Telugu manuscript, *Urzees*, 1820 (India Office Library *Tel. D.6*).

ಇಬ್ಬರು ಹಾದಿಕಾರರು ಕಾಡಿ ಹೊಾಗುತ್ತಿದ್ದರು |
ಆವರಲ್ಲಿ ಒಬ್ಬನಿಗೆ ಹಾದಿಯಲ್ಲಿ ಬಿದ್ದಿರುವ ಹಣದ ಚೀಲವು ಸಿಕ್ಕಿತು |

b

వొక మనుష్యునికి యిద్దరు కుమారులు వుండిరి.——
వారిలో చిన్నవాడు, ఓ తండ్రీ ఆస్తిలో నాకు వచ్చే

c

ಎಕಾ ಗೃಹಸ್ಥಾ಼ಕ ದೊಗ್-ಚಾಣ ಫುತ ಆಶಿಲ್ಲ |
ತಾಂತುಲಿ ಧ್ಯಾಕಿಂ ಸಾನು ಕಪ್ಣಾಗೆಲ್ಯಾ ಬಾಪ್ಸ ಕಡೆ

d

17.25. Modern specimens, *b* Kanarese, *c* Marathi written in Kanarese character, *d* Telugu.

ഒരു മനുഷ്യന്നു രണ്ടു മക്കൾ ഉണ്ടായിരുന്നു.
അതിൽ ഇളയവൻ അപ്പനോടു, അപ്പാ,

a

அவனுடைய மூத்தகுமாரன் வயலிலிருந்தான்.
அவன் திரும்பி வீடுகெருச்சமீபயாய் வருகிறபோது,

b

17.26. *a* Malayalam script. *b* Tamil script.

17.26c. Part of an inscription written in a kind of Vattelutu mixed with Grantha, attributed to the 9th century A.D.

17.26d. Part of a grant to Jews at Kochin, attributed by Burnell to the middle of the 8th century, and by Buehler, to the 10th or 11th century.

PHONETIC VALUE	SINHALESE	BURMESE	THAI	KHMER	
				AKS. CHRI.	AKS. MŪL
a					
ā					
i					
ī					
u					
ū					
e					
o					OR
ya					
ra					
la					
va					
sa					
ha					
ḷa					
ka					
kha					
ga					
gha					
ṅa					

MAIN PĀLI SCRIPTS

17.27. The Main Pāli scripts.

MAIN PĀLI SCRIPTS

PHONETIC VALUE	SINHALESE	BURMESE	THAI	KHMER	
				AKS. CHRI.	AKS. MÜL
ca	එ	၀	จ	ឆ	ឌ
cha	ඡ	ဆ	ฉ	ឆ	ឆ
ja	ජ	ဇ	ช	ជ	ជ
jha	ඣ	ဈ	ฌ	ឈ	ឈ
ña	ඤ	ဉ	ญ	ញ	ញ
ṭa	ට	ဋ	ฏ	ដ	ដ
ṭha	ඨ	ဌ	ฐ	ឋ	ឋ
ḍa	ඩ	ဍ	ฑ	ឌ	ឌ
ḍha	ඪ	ဎ	ฒ	ឍ	ឍ
ṇa	ණ	ဏ	ณ	ណ	ណ
ta	ත	တ	ต	ត	ត
tha	ථ	ထ	ถ	ថ	ថ
da	ද	ဒ	ท	ទ	ទ
dha	ධ	ဓ	ธ	ធ	ធ
na	න	န	น	ន	ន
pa	ප	ပ	ป	ប	ប
pha	ඵ	ဖ	ผ	ផ	ផ
ba	බ	ဗ	พ	ព	ព
bha	භ	ဘ	ภ	ភ	ភ
ma	ම	မ	ม	ម	ម

17.28. The Main Pāli scripts.

PHONETIC VALUE	MALDIVIAN DIVES AKURU	GABULI TANA
h		
th		
ṅ		
r		
b		
l		
k		
a		
w		
m		
ph		
dh		
t		
l		
g		
n		
s		
ḍ		

17.29. *a* Specimen of modern Sinhalese script. *b* Letter written in modern Sinhalese. *c* The Maldivian Dives Akuru and Gabuli Tana.

nī yal baranō' pago'p

18.3*a*. Akhar Srah or Thrah.

18.3*b*. Two lines of the 'Song of Kadhar.'

ni ti–k–u–ḥ k–u–ba–v ri–o–m–n

18.3*c*. Akhar Rik.

nī s–va–t–ti k harĕi adit

18.3*d*. Akhar Atuo'l.

n – i – m t – i – k – u – ḥ k – u – ba – v

18.3*e*. Akhar Yok.

18.1. Specimens of Cham characters.

VOWELS		CONSONANTS		CONSONANTS	
a		ka		pha	
ā		kha		ba	
i		ga		bha	
ï		gha		m o'	
u		ṅ o'		ya	
ū		cha		ra	
ṛo'		chha		la	
ṛō'		ja		va	
ḷo'		jha		s'a	
ḷō'		ñ o'		sa	
e		ta		ha	
ai		tha		ṇa	
o		da		ḍa	
au		dha		ḅa	
am		no'		(ṅ a)	
akh		pa		(ñ a)	
		(na)		(ma)	

18.2. The Cham character as employed in Vietnam.

VOWELS		CONSONANTS		CONSONANTS		CONSONANTS	
a	𝓎	gha	𝓎	dha	𝓎	va	𝓍
i	𝓮	no'	𝓎	no'	𝓎	sa	𝓯
u	𝓮	cha	𝓎	pa	𝓎	ha	𝓯
e	𝓎	chha	𝓎	pha	𝓎	ña	𝓮
ai	𝓮	ja	𝓎	ba	𝓎	ḍa	𝓎
CONSONANTS		jha	𝓎	bha	𝓎	ḅa	𝓎
ka	𝓎	ño'	𝓎	mo'	𝓎	(ña)	𝓮
kha	𝓮	ta	𝓮	ya	𝓎	(ṅa)	𝓮
ga	𝓮	tha	𝓎	ra	𝓯	(na)	𝓮
		da	𝓎	la	𝓮	(ma)	𝓮

18.3. The Cham character as employed in Cambodia.

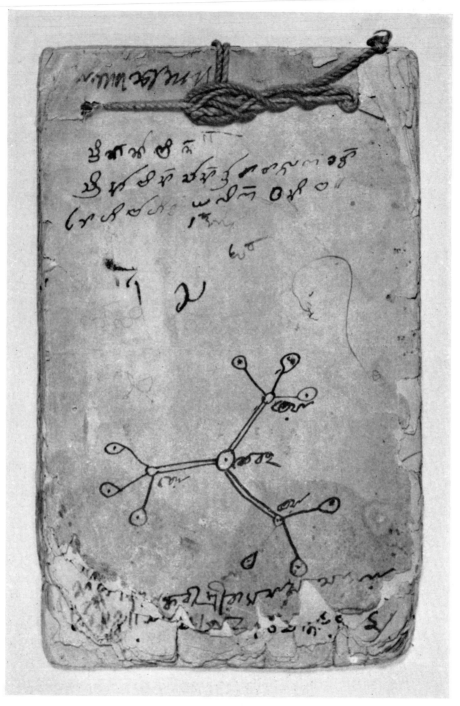

18.4. Title page from a Chakma manuscript (in the author's possession).

18.5. Page from a Chakma manuscript (in the author's possession).

ၜ တ ᨠ. ᨲᨲᨳᨳ ᨠ 3 ဝ ၦ. ၜ ᨳ ᨷ ᠈ ᨸᠬ ᨳ
ၦ ᨯ ᨲ. ᨷ ᨯ ၜ ᨮ ᨴ ᠉. ᠪᠪ. ᨲᨲ ᨯ ᨲ ᨲ

18.6*a*. Chakma.

။ ဒုရိ ॥ ကောင်းကင်ဝယ် နေတော်မူသောကျွန်တော်တို့အဖခ
မည်တော် ॥ ကိုပင်တော်အခည်နာမတော် ရှိသေမြတ်ဦး သိည့်

18.6*b*. Burmese.

ᨠᩮᩢᩛᨽ ᨠ ᨳᩣ ᨷ ᨩ ᨱᩢ ᨾ ᨦ ᩈ ᨿᩢ ᩃᩢ ᨽᩩ ᩁᩥᩢ ᨴᩢ ᨳᩥ ᨩᩥᨻᩢ᩠
ᨾᩩᨩᩢ ᨴ ᨠ ᩁᩥ ᩈᩥ ᨿᩩ ᨻᩩ᩠ ᨷᩢ ᨯᩥᩈ ᩁᩥ ᨿᩥ ᨾ ᨿ ᨦᩣᩢᩣᨦᨳᩥ ᨷᩢ᩠

18.6*c*. Hkün.

ꩬꩳ ꩒ ꩳꩶ ꩱ ꩴꩳꩢ ꩳ ꩬꩳ ꩫ ꩴꩳ ꩭ ꫛ ꩱꩳꩳ ꫛ
ꩱ ꩳ ꩭ ꩱꩳ ꩴꩳ ꩱꩳ ꩴ ꩫꩳ ꩪꩳꩳ ꩭꩳ ꩱꩳ ꩫꩳꩢ ꩴ ꩴꩳꩳ

18.6*d*. Ahom.

॥ ꩬꫜꩰꩪꩮꩫꩰꩠꩭꩧ ꩮꩢꩶꩠꩭꩬꩮ
ꩠꩱꩮꩭꩬꩪꩈꩶꩁꩢꩭꩮꩫꩪꩋꩧ꩜ꩈꩶꩠꩢꩫꩪꩶꩢꩪ
ꩪꩴꩬꩬꩰꩪꩮ ॥ꩬꩰꩪꩮꩬꩮꩈꩶꩠꩈꩳ꩏ꩮ

18.6*e*. Patimokkha.

18.6. Further Indian scripts.

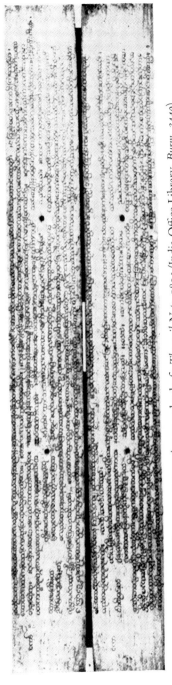

18.7a. Burmese manuscript on palm-leaf; *The evil Nats*, 1805 (India Office Library, *Burn. 3449*).

18.7b. Siamese manuscript; *Thao Sawatthi racha* (ibidem, *Siam. 14*).

18.8*a*. *Manual for the Ordination of a Buddhist Priest:* mother of pearl on wood, written in Burmese Pali. (Cambridge University Library Or. *783*).

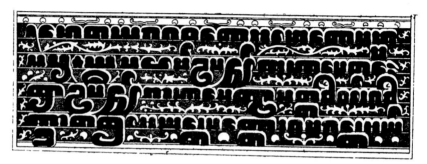

18.8*b*. *Kammuwa*, a sacred Buddhist book. Specimen of Pali script.

18.8*c*. Burmese manuscript on copper (Chester Beatty Library, *MS. 60*).

18.9a. Burmese: last leaf of the Abhui: rājapuṃ manuscript on the lineage of kings. 'Written on the 5th day of the waxing moon of the month of Tabaung 1164 B.E.' (AD 1798)

18.9b. Thai manuscript on cats (Chester Beatty Library, *M.S. 1304*).

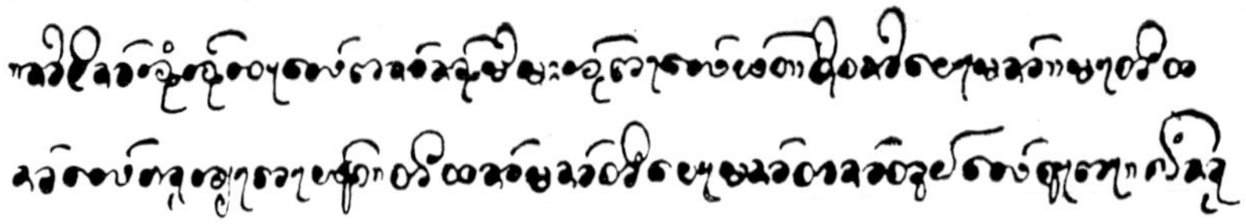

18.10*a*. Khamti current hand.

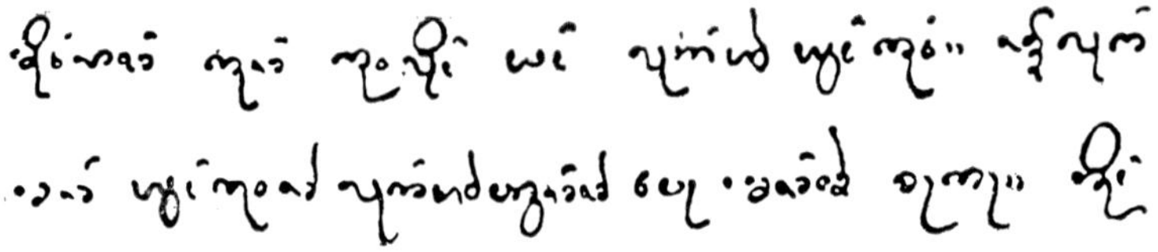

18.10*b*. Khamti printed script.

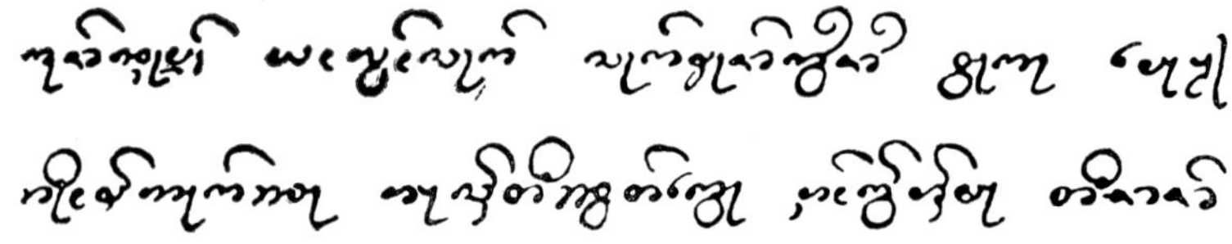

18.10*c*. Tairong Khamti.

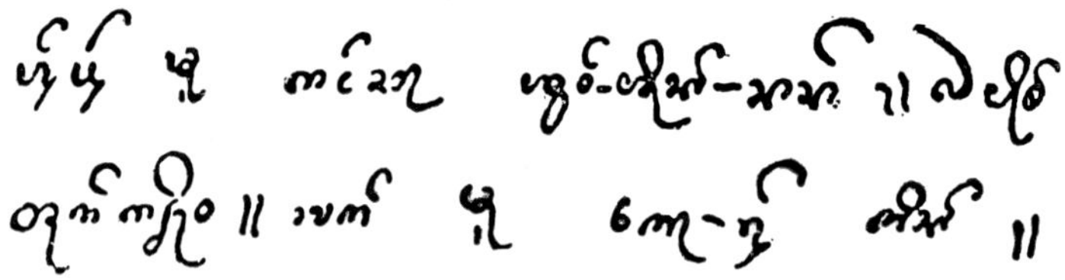

18.10*d*. Aitonia character.

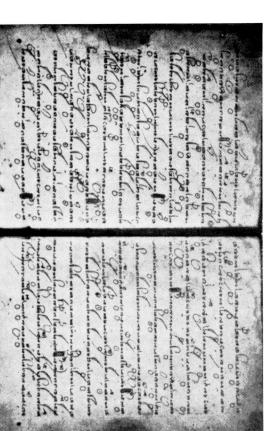

18.11. Javanese scripts. *a* 1. *Aksara Bud'da*, or 'Ancient Character'. 2. Another form of 'Ancient Character'. 3. *Aksara Jawa* or 'Javanese Character'. 4. *Aksara Pasang'an* or 'corresponding character'. 5. *Aksara Gedé* (some letters have peculiar forms). *b* A manuscript of 1790, *Damar Wulan* (India Office Library, *Jav. C.1*). *c* Modern writing.

293

18.12. Kalasan inscription from Java, in Sanskrit AD 778.

18.13. Calcutta incription of Erlangga (Old Javanese part) AD 1041.

18.14*a*. Written page of a Batak manuscript.

18.14*b*. Cover of the manuscript above, both written on the inner bark of *terap* tree (Cambridge University Library *Or. 930*).

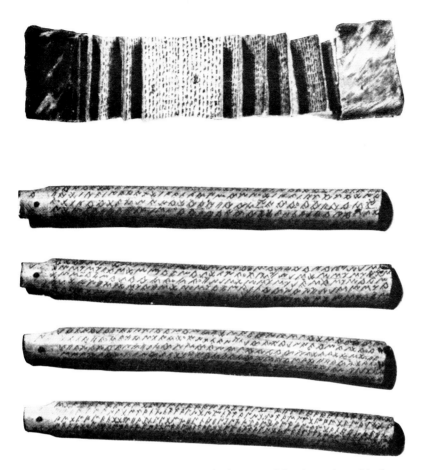

18.15. (Above) Batak book written on bark: part of the divination table for the 30 days of the month (below) portion of a *Story of Creation*, written on bamboo in Malay language using the Rèndjang characters of the Palembang and Benkulen districts of South Sumatra. The four sticks are 'numbered' (left) *ta*, *pa*, *la*, *sa*. (Explanation by P. Voorhoeve, University Library, Leyden).

a	e-i	o-u	ka	ga	nga	ta	da	na	pa	ba	ma	ya	la	wa	sa	ha	
																	1
																	2
																	3
																	4
																	5
																	6
																	7
																	8
																	9
																	10
																	11
																	12
																	13
																	14
																	15
																	16
																	17
																	18
																	19
																	20
																	21
																	22
																	23
																	24
																	25
																	26
																	27
																	28
																	29
																	30

18.16. The main alphabets of Further India, particularly of the Philippine Islands (based on F. Gardner, *Philippine Indic Studies*, 1943). 1–6, Old Javanese or Kavi. 7–8, Early Sumatra. 9, Batak character. 10, Buginese. 11–14, Tagalog. 15–16, Iloco. 17–18, Bisaya. 19, Pangasinan. 20, Pampangan. 21, Tagbanua. 22–26, Mangyan varieties. 27–30, Buhil.

A
E-I
OU
BA
CA
DA
GA
YA
LA
MA
NA
PA
SA
TA
I
UA
?

(b)

(a)

b

a

c

d

e

a	ya	o, ú	yo	o	yo	u	yu	ü	i	a

k	n	t	r(l)	m	p	s(d)	(ng)	tj	ch	kh	th	ph	h

f

18.17. *a* Specimen of Bisaya writing. *b* Tagbanua characters (*a* if read upwards according to Dr. Gardner; *b*, in Professor Kroeber's opinion it should be read downwards). *c Belarmino*, re-edited in 1895 by P. Lopez. *d* Buhil writing, 1941, copied from bamboo (F. Gardner, *Philippine Indic Studies*, 1943). *e* Specimen of Mangyan writing: it reads *Pagpunsion ti namatay no nakutkut ye ti but-ol*, meaning 'A feast is given to the dead, when his bones are dug up.' (F. Gardner and I. Maliwang, *Indic Writings*, etc., 2, pp. 17–18). *f* The Korean alphabet.

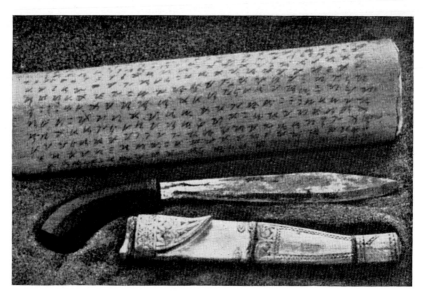

a

18.18. *a* Philippine bamboo manuscript, with
writing knife and its
container. *b* Left-handed
boy 'writing' with a knife
on a bamboo tube.

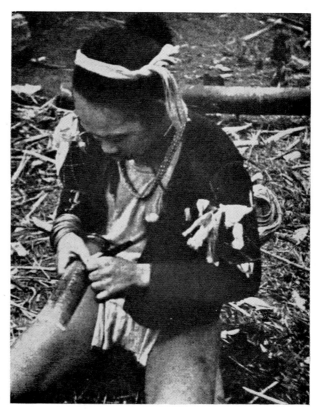

b

Letters	Phon. Value	Letters	Phon. Value	Letters	Phon. Value
ㅈ	ć (*fr.* tch)	ㄱ	k	ㅏ	a
ㅊ	ć'	ㄴ	n	ㅑ	ya
ㅌ	t'	ㄷ	t	ㅓ	ɔ (ŏ)
ㅋ	k'	ㄹ	ṙ– l	ㅕ	yɔ
ㅍ	p'	ㅁ	m	ㅗ	o
ㅎ	h	ㅂ	p	ㅛ	yo
ㅇ		ㅅ	s,– t	ㅜ	u (*fr.* ou)
				ㅠ	yu
				ㅡ	ə
				ㅣ	i
				ㆍ	å (ă)

18.19. The Korean alphabet.

EARLY GREEK ALPHABETS · 8th.-7th. CENT. B.C.					
ATHENS	THERA	CRETE	NAXOS	CORCYRA	BOEOTIA

19.1. Early Greek alphabets.

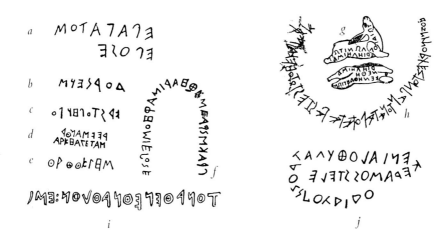

19.2. Early Greek inscriptions written from right to left; *a–f* from Thera; *g* Ionic votive inscription to Apollo; *h–j* inscriptions from Athens; *k* graffito on jug c. 725 B.C.; *l* graffito on pottery c. 7th cent. B.C.; *m* Bronze Aryballos, late 7th cent. B.C.; *n* Bronze lebes rim 600–525 B.C.

a

b

c

d

e

f

g

19.3. Early Greek inscriptions in *boustrophedon* style. *a* Stele from Lemnos, 6th cent. B.C.; *b* Archaic inscription from Corinth. *c,d* Graffiti: names inscribed on rock at Thera, late 8th century B.C.; *e* Inscribed will-block from Temple of Apollo Pythios, Gortyn, 600-615 B.C.; *f* Stone stele with text of sacred law from Magnesia, Thessaly, *c.* 550 B.C.; *g* Part of inscribed marble altar? *c.* 500-480 B.C.; from Attica.

304

ΣΕΜΑΦΡΑΣΙΚΛΕΙΑΣ
ΚΟΡΕΚΕΚΛΕΣΟΜΑΙ
ΑΙΕΙΑΜΤΙΛΑΜΟ
ΓΑΡΑΘΕΟΝΤΟΥΤΟ
ΛΑΧΟΣΟΝΟΜΑ

1

ΑΘΑΝΑΙΑΣ:ΙΑΡΑ:ΤΑΣΕΜΗΒΣΑΡΟΙ

2

ΝΑΙΡΕΝΑΡΟΝ
ΟΝΔΙΣΤΥΚΑΚΟΣ
ΛΕΓΕΙΟΥΔΕΘΠ
ΝΟΝΤΑΠΟΛΟΣ
ΑΝΘΡΟΠΟΝΛΥ
ΣΑΜΕΝΟΣ
ΚΑΜΑΤΟ

4

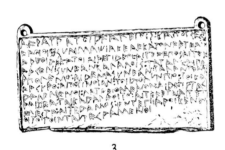

3

ϜϜΣΕΤΟΣΙΤΕΡΑΣΟΝΛΟΓΟΣ
ΝΕΝΑΣΤΑΣΔΑΜΑΤΡΣΤΑΣΘΕ:ΜΟΦΟΡΟΣ
ΜΕΥΝΣΕΡΟΣΕΣΔΥΜΕΝϜΣΕΑΣΑΕΓΕϜΕΡϟΟ
ΣΙϜΧΟϟΟΣΤΥΚΑΟΙΣΣΤΟΤΕΡΔΑΝϟΟϜΟΡϟΕ
ΣΤΑΣΔΑΡΥΝΑΣΓΡΣΑΚΟΝΤΑΕΣΔΕΝΕΑΦΑΕΤΟΣ
ΑΝΑΣΕΒΕΣΑΝΕΝΕΟΔΕΚΥΡΟΣΔΕΚΟϜΕΤΕΡΕΝΑ
ΟΔΕ

5

19.4. Early Greek inscriptions from left to right.
1 Grave pillar of Phresikkia, Attica, *c.* 540 B.C.
2 Inscription on a silver cup dedicated to the Megarian Athena, from Kozani, *c.* 500 B.C.
3 Bronze plaque with treaty between Elis and Heraea, *c.* 500 B.C.
4 Gravestone of Charon from Teithronion, Phocis, *c.* 500 B.C.
5 Bronze plaque with ritual inscription, Arkadian, *c.* 525 B.C.

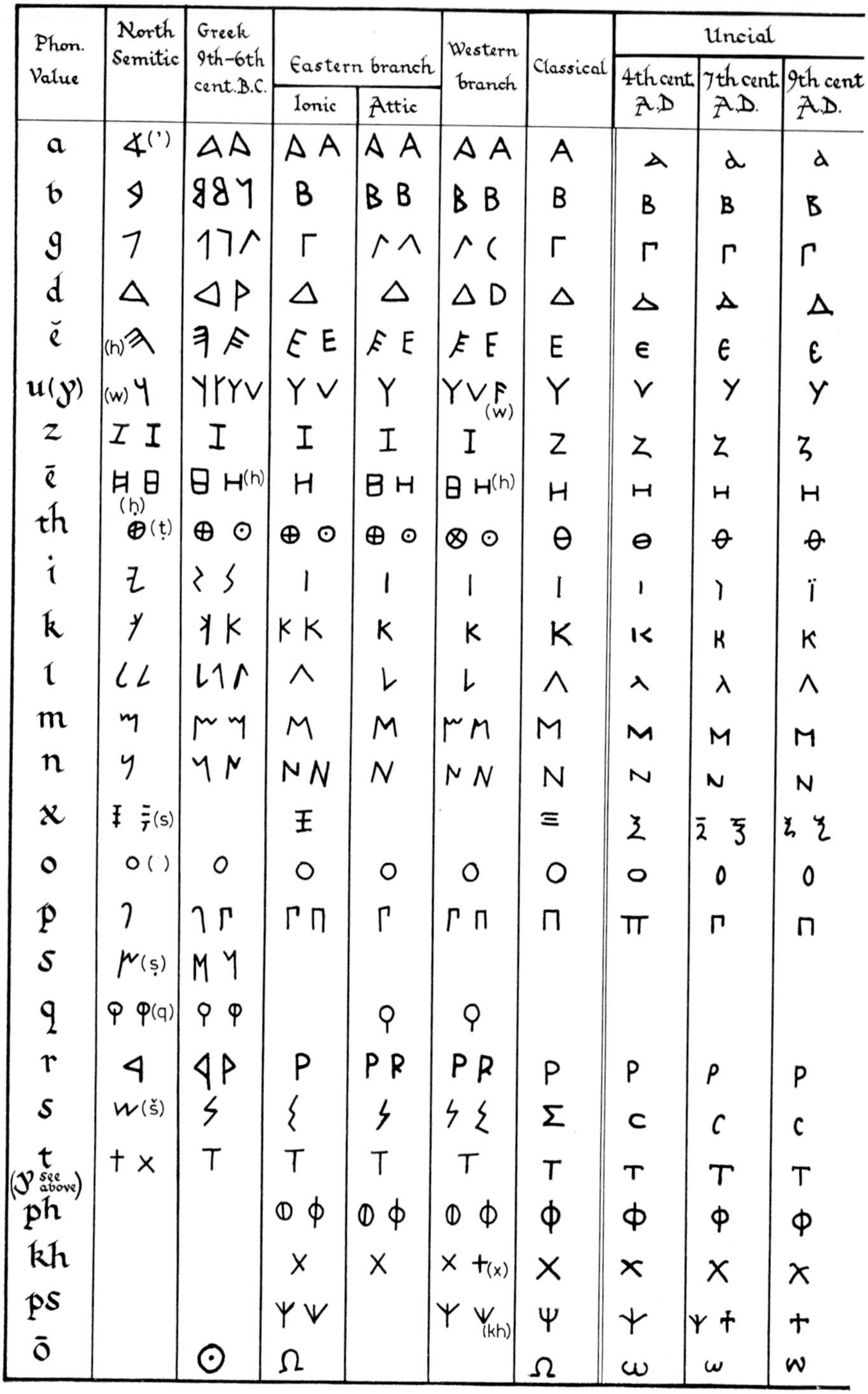

Phon. Value	North Semitic	Greek 9th–6th cent. B.C.	Eastern branch		Western branch	Classical	Uncial 4th cent. A.D.	Uncial 7th cent. A.D.	Uncial 9th cent. A.D.
			Ionic	Attic					
a	𐤊(')	ΔΛ	Δ A	Λ A	Δ A	A	⋏	ɑ	ɑ
b	𐤁	𐊇𐊇𐊈	B	B B	ß B	B	B	B	B
g	𐤂	𐊊𐊋Λ	Γ	Λ Λ	Λ ⟨	Γ	Γ	Γ	Γ
d	𐤃	◁Þ	Δ	Δ	Δ D	Δ	Δ	Δ	Δ
ĕ	(h)𐤄	⊒Æ	Ɛ E	⅀ E	⅀ E	E	ε	ϵ	ϵ
u(y)	(w)𐤅	Υ𐊚Υν	Y ν	Y	Y ν �𝔉(w)	Y	ν	Y	Y
z	I I	I	I	I	I	Z	Z	Z	Ʒ
ē	⊟ ⊟(h)	⊟ H(h)	H	⊟ H	⊟ H(h)	H	н	н	н
th	⊕(ṭ)	⊕ ⊙	⊕ ⊙	⊕ ⊙	⊗ ⊙	θ	θ	θ	θ
i	𐤆	⟨ 𝔰	I	I	I	I	ı	ı	ï
k	𐤊	𐊇K	K K	K	K	K	к	к	к
l	𐤋𐤋	Ⴑ𐊘Λ	Λ	∨	∟	Λ	ʌ	ʌ	ʌ
m	ᵐ	ᵐ ᵞ	M	M	ᵐM	M	M	M	M
n	𐤍	Ꙭ Ν	N N	N	N N	N	N	N	N
x	𐤎 𐤎(s)		𐊴			≡	⩎	⩎ ⅔	⅔ ⅔
o	○(ˁ)	○	○	○	○	O	o	o	o
p	𐤐	𐊡 Γ	Γ Π	Γ	Γ Π	Π	ᴨ	Γ	Π
s	𐤑(ṣ)	M Ᏹ							
q	𐤒 𐤒(q)	𐊴 𐊴		𐊴	𐊴				
r	𐤓	𐊴Þ	P	P R	P R	P	P	P	P
s	w(š)	𐊮	⟨	𐊮	𐊮 ⟨	⅀	c	c	c
t (y see above)	✝ ✗	T	T	T	T	T	T	T	T
ph			⊕ φ	⊕ φ	⊕ φ	φ	φ	φ	φ
kh			✗	✗	✗ ✝(x)	✗	✗	✗	✗
ps			Υ ν		Υ ν(kh)	ψ	ⴕ	Υ ✝	✝
ō		⊙	Ω			Ω	ω	ω	ω

19.5. Development of the Greek alphabet.

Greek cursive script			Greek minuscule			Modern		Modern
2nd cent. B.C	2nd cent A.D.	7th cent.	9th cent A.D.	10th–11th cent.	12th–14th cent	Capitals	small letters	letters in print
ᴀ ᴅ	ᴀ ᴠ	ᴜ ᴄᴇ	a	α	a δ	A A	a ᴀ	α
B U	ß	β u	u	B u	ußϨϲ	ℬ	ϐ β	β
ᴦ ᴦ	ᴦ ᴦ	Y ᴦ	γ	ᴠ ᴠ	ᴦ [ᴠ	ℊ	ᴦ	γ
Δ δ	δ ᴢ	δ δ	δ	Δ δ	δ Δ	𝒟	ᴦ	δ
ᴇ ᴇ	ᴇ ε	ξ ᴠϲ	ϭ	Ϲ ϧ	ϭϵϵ	ℰ ℰ	ε	ε
Y V	Y Y	V U	υ	ᴠ	υ ᴠ	𝒱	υ	υ
Z	ᴢᴢ	ϨϨ	ᴢ ᴢ	ᴢ ᴢ	ϨϨᴢᴢ	ℤ	ᴢᴢᴢ	ᴢ ᴢ
ʜ	ʜ	h ᴢ	h	h ᴜ ʜ	ʜ ʜ x ᴨ	ℋ	ᴨ ᴦ	η
θ	θ δ	θδℓ	θ	θ δ	θℓℓ	ℓ	δ	θ θ
I	I	ᴠ ᴠᴢ	ᴠ ᴢ	ᴜ ᴠ	ᴠ ᴢ	𝒥 𝒥	ᴠ	ι
ᴦ	ᴋ ᴜ	ᴜ ᴜ	ᴜ	ᴋ ᴋ	ᴋᴜx	𝒦	ᴜᴋ	ᴋ
λ	ᴦ	ℓ ℓ	ᴦ	ᴦ λ	λ λ	𝒜	λλᴢ	λ
ᴦ ᴜ	ᴜ ᴜ	ᴨᴜ	μ	μ ᴜ	ᴜ ᴜ	𝑀	μ	μ
N	ᴨ ᴨ	ᴠ N	ᴦ ᴦ	ᴠ N	N ᴦᴦ ᴠ	𝒩	ᴠ	ᴠ
ᴢ ᴢ	ᴢ ᴢ	ϩ ϩ	ᴢ	ᴢ ϩ	ϩϩϬ	ℨ	ϩϩ	ᴢ
o	o	o	o	o	o	𝒪	σ	o
Π	π	π ᴜ	ϖ	π ϖ	π ϖ	𝒥	ω	ϖ
ρ	ϼϩϩ	ℓ ℓ	ϼ	ϼϭϩ	ϼϭϼϩ	𝒫	ρ	ϼ
ᴄ	ϲ ϲ	ϲᴢϬ	σ ᴄ	σ(ϲ	σ ᴜ ϲ	ℒℒ	σ σ	ϛ ϲ
Y ᴦ	ᴦ	T T	T	T ᴦ	ᴦ T ᴦ	𝒥	ᴦ ᴦ	ϲ ᴦ
ϕ	ϕ	ϕ	ϕ	Ϸ ϕ	ϕ ϕ ϕ	℘	ᴦ ᴦ	φ
X	X	X	x	X	X	𝒳	x ᴦ	z
ᴦ	ᴦ	ᴦ	ᴦ	ᴦ ᴦ	Ψ	Ψ ᴦ	ᴦ	ψ
ω	ω	ω	∞	∞	ω	𝒲	ω	ω

19.6. Development of the Greek alphabet.

19.7. Greek monumental inscriptions of the Roman Imperial period.

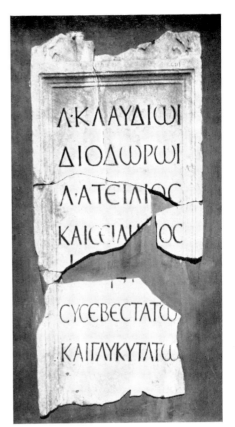

a

b

c

19.8. Greek monumental funerary inscriptions of the Roman Imperial period.

309

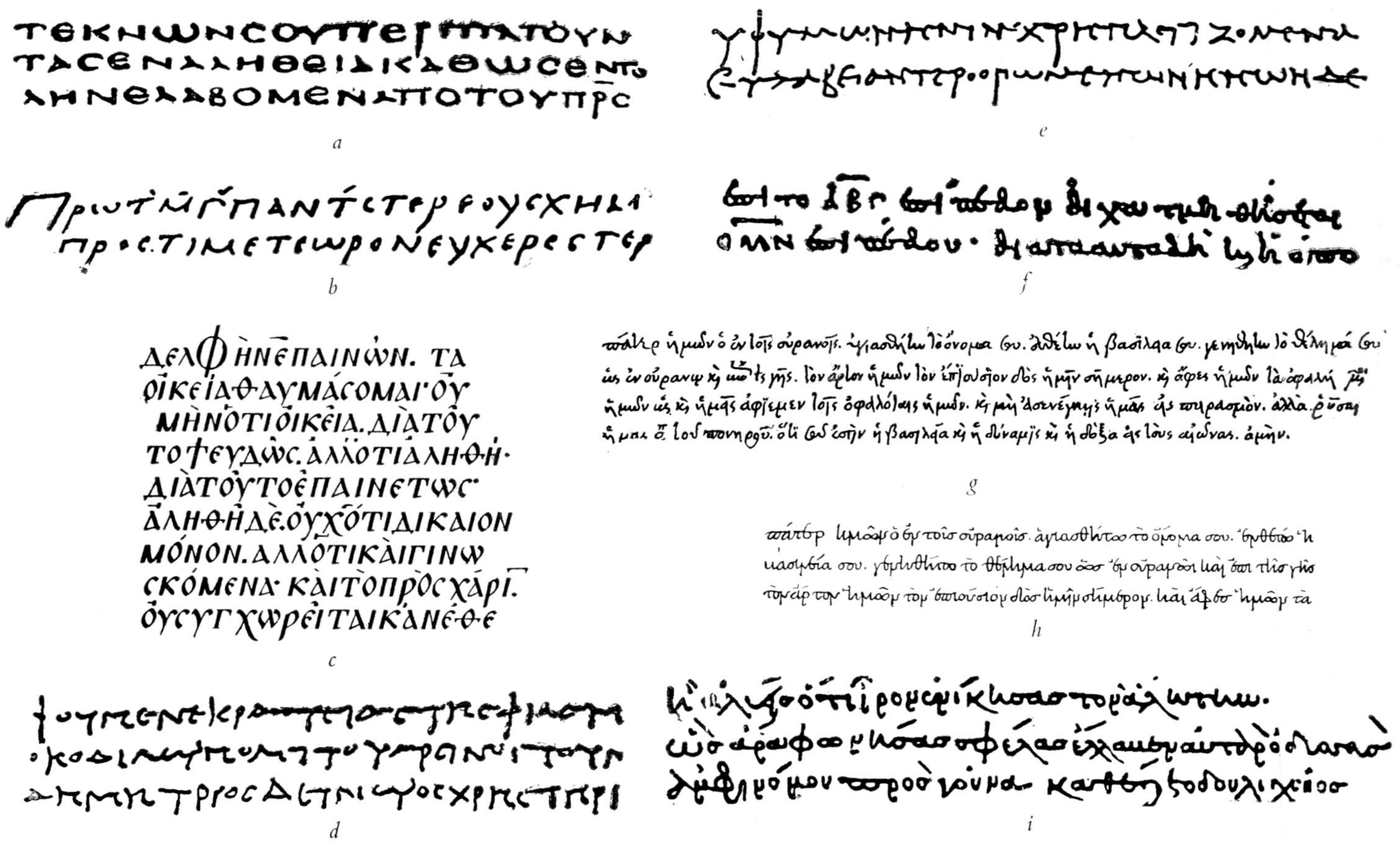

ΔΕΛΦΗΝΕΠΑΙΝΩΝ. ΤΑ
ΟΙΚΕΙΑΦΛΥΜΑΟΜΑΓΟΥ
ΜΗΝΟΤΙΟΙΚΕΙΑ.ΔΙΑΤΟΥ
ΤΟΓΕΥΔΩϹ.ΑΛΛΟΤΙΔΛΗΘΗ·
ΔΙΑΤΟΥΤΟΕΠΑΙΝΕΤΩϹ
ΔΛΗΘΗΔΕ.ΟΥϽϽΟΤΙΔΙΚΑΙΟΝ
ΜΟΝΟΝ.ΔΛΛΟΤΙΚΑΙΓΙΝΩ
ϹΚΟΜΕΝΑ·ΚΑΙΤΟΠΡΟϹΧΑΡΙ.
ΟΥΓΥΓΧΥΡΕΙΤΑΙΚΑΝΕΘΕ

19.9. Specimens showing the development of Greek script, from uncial style to modern current hand. *a* Fifth century A.D.; *b* seventh century A.D.; *c* ninth century A.D.; *d* 237 B.C.; *e* 163–162 B.C.; *f* A.D. 888; *g* fifteenth century A.D.; *h* tenth century A.D.; *i* thirteenth century A.D.; *j* nineteenth century. A.D.

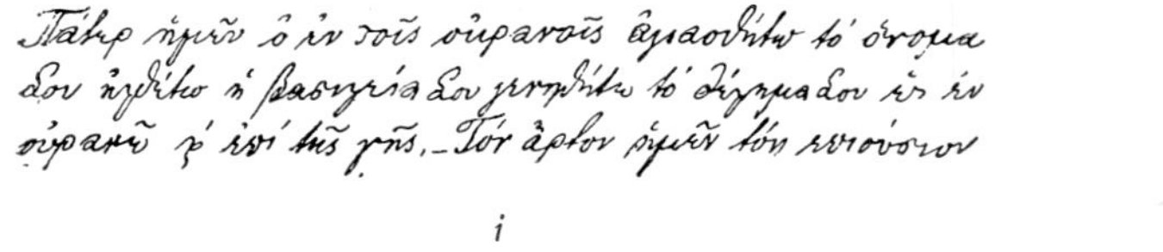

19.10 Greek uncial script: a page from the famous *Codex Sinaiticus* (fourth century A.D.).

This is perhaps the earliest Greek vellum codex extant. In 1933 it was purchased by the British Museum from the Soviet Government for £100,000.

19.11. Earliest preserved Greek manuscripts of the Bible: *a* Fragment of papyrus roll from Dervein. Height 7 cm. *b* Fragment of *Deuteronomy*, 2nd cent. B.C. (*Rylands Papyrus No. 458*).

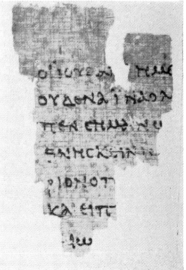

19.11. *c, d* St. John's Gospel, Ch. 18, first half 2nd cent. A.D. (*Rylands Papyrus No. 457*).

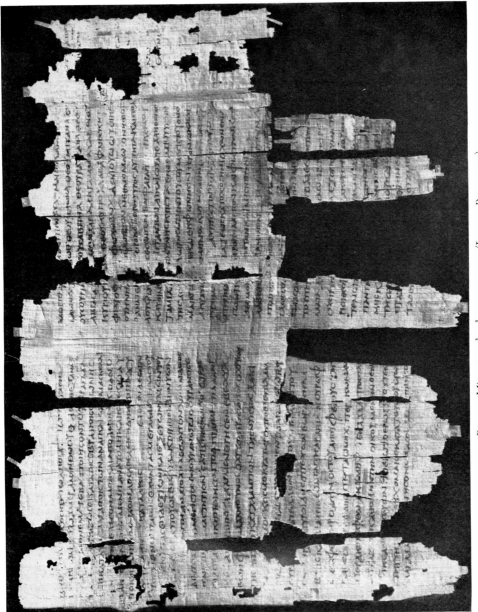

19.12. *Papyrus Mimaut*, 3rd–5th century A.D. (Louvre *Pap 1.2391*).

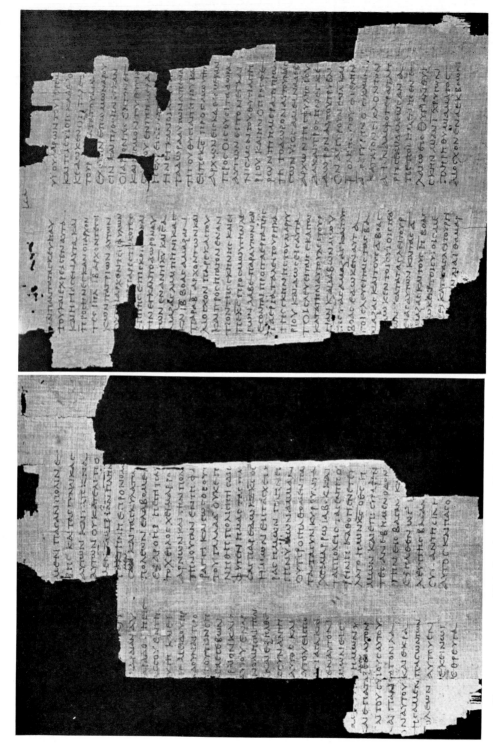

19.13*a. Deuteronomy* 2, 30–34 (Col. 1) and 2, 34–3, 1 (Col. 2). Fine literaay 19.13*b. Numbers* 7, 1–15. Fine Greek literary hand of late 1st or early 2nd hand of late 1st or early 2nd century. (Chester Beatty Pap. VI, fol. 10 recto). century. (Chester Beatty Pap. VI, fol. 10 verso).

19.14b. *Revelation* 13, 16-14, 4. Rough Greek hand of the late 3rd century (Chester Beatty Pap. III, fol. 7 recto).

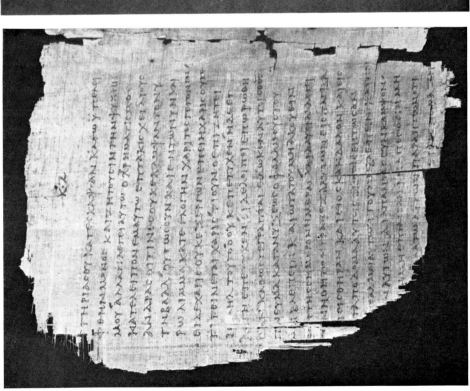

19.14a. *Romans* 11, 3–12, *c* A.D. 200 (Chester Beatty Pap. II, fol. 14 recto).

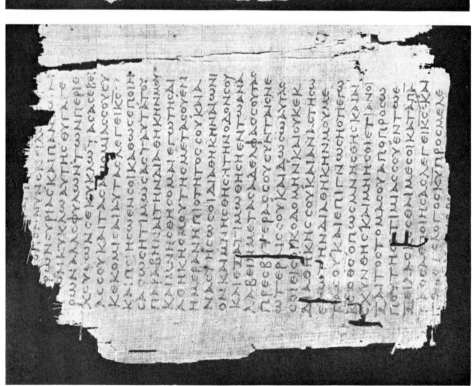

19.15a. Ezekiel 16, 57–17, 1. First half of 3rd century (Chester Beatty Pap. IV, fol. 16 recto).

19.15b Genesis 42, 27–35. Documentary Greek hand of the 3rd century (Chester Beatty Pap. V, fol. 20 recto).

19.16a. Portion of a poem by Bacchylides, variously attributed to the first century B.C. or A.D. (British Museum, *Pap. 733*).

19.16b. Portion of the three speeches by Hyperides against Demosthenes and for Lycophron and Euxenippus, 1st century A.D. (British Museum, *Pap. 108, 115*).

a

b

19.17. *a* One of the few extant documents in the Doric dialect. *b* fragment of a lost Greek tragedy, 3rd century A.D. (British Museum, *Pap. 695*). *c* fragment dating from the seventh year of Nero.

c

19.18. The *Sayings of Jesus*, fragment of a papyrus codex found at Oxyrhynchus, attributed to the third century A.D. (Bodleian Library, Oxford).

19.19a. Earliest extant Greek literary document on parchment: *Oration* by Demosthenes; late 1st century A.D. (British Museum, *Add. MS. 34473*).

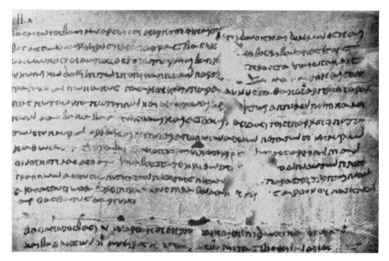

19.19b. Second earliest Greek document written on parchment. It is dated to 22–21 B.C., and was found with two other documents near Avrōmān (British Museum, *Add. MS. 38895B*).

19.20. Greek palimpsest; lower script, *Codex Z* (*Gospel of St. Matthew*), written in Greek uncials of the sixth century A.D. (Trinity College, Dublin, *MS. K.3.4.A., No. 28*).

a   *b*

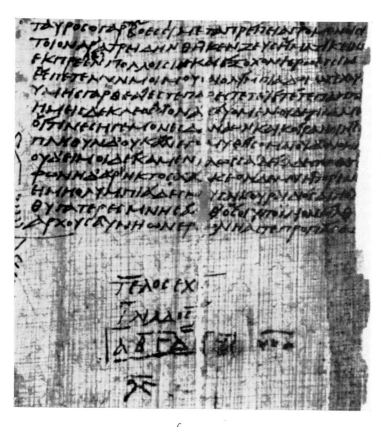

c

19.21. Homer manuscripts written on papyrus. *a* Berlin *Pap. 6869* (first century B.C.); *b* Fayyûm, No. 6 (period of Augustus); *c* British Museum *Pap. 126* (fourth century A.D.).

a

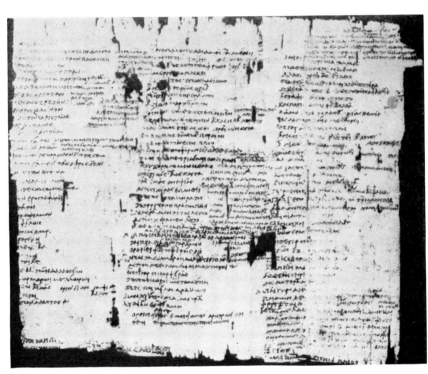

b

19.22. *a* The *Ambrosian Iliad* variously attributed to the third to fifth centuries A.D. (Ambrosian Library, Milan, *Codex F.205, inf.*), *b* Alcman (Louvre Museum, Paris, *Pap. E. 3320*).

a

b

19.23. a Parts of four poems by Alcaeus (flourished late 7th and early 6th centuries B.C.) written on papyrus in the 2nd century A.D. (Bodleian Library, MS. *Class. b.18* (P.)). b Timotheus, *Persae* (col. 5, v. 187–247), the earliest preserved literary papyrus, 4th century B.C.

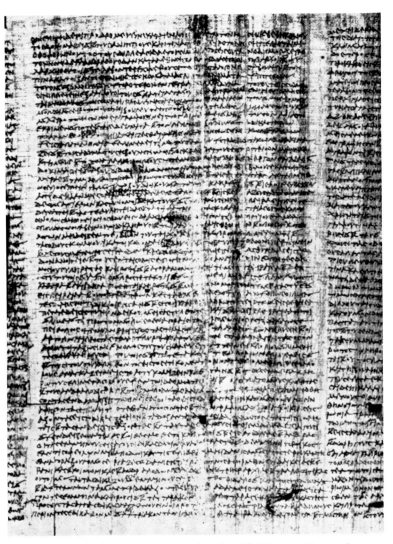

19.24. Aristotle, *Constitution of Athens* (British Museum, *Pap. 131*).

19.25. Herodas, *Mimes* (British Museum, *Pap. 135–3*).

19.26. *a Dialogues* by Plato written for Arethas of Patras in A.D. 896 (Bodleian Library, Oxford, *Clarke MS. 39*); *b* Thucydides, tenth-century copy (Laurentian Library, Florence, *Plut. 59.2*).

19.27a. Aristophanes (Vatican Library *Pal. Gr. 67*).

19.27b. Aeschylus (Laurentian Library, Florence, *Cod. 31.8*).

19.27c. Demosthenes, early 11th century A.D. (Laurentian Library, *Plut. 59.9*).

West Greek	Phrygian	Pamphylian	Lycian	Lydian	Carian Letters	Carian Syllables
Δ A (A)	Δ A (A)	A (A)	↑(E) P (A)	A (A)	A Δ P δ λ (A)	Ω (KO) ↑ (T I)
B (B)	B ß (B)	B (B)	B b (B)	8 (B)	d b (B-PF)	Ŧ Ŧ (TO) ʃ ʃ (PE)
Λ Γ (G)	Γ (G)	レ (G)	Γ ৭ (G)	⅃ (G)?	C < [ ) (G)	▽ (RA) ⋀ (RE)
Δ (D)	Δ (D)	△ (D)	Δ (D)	λ (D)	Δ (D)	⫪ ⋔ ✝ ✝ 人 (RI)
Ɛ E (E)	Ϝ Ɛ (E)	E (E)	)(TH) K(Y) K(C)	ʃ (E)	ʄ E ⪦ ⪥ ⋙ (E)	▽ ⋔ ⋔ Υ (RO)
Ϝ (W)	Ϝ Ϝ (V W)	Ϝ ⋔ (W)	Ϝ Ⅹ (Q) (V W)	⅃ (V)	Ϝ F ⋏ ⪦ ⪦ ⪦ ⪥ (V)	M M ⋔ (M (I))
I (Z)	ʃ ʃ ʃ ʃ ʃ (Z)	I (Z)	I (Z) K(C)		I I (Z)	)(Υ(NO) □ Ⅰ (YA)
I (I)	I (I)	I (I)	E (I)	I (I)	⊕ ⊗ (TH)	⋉ (YO?) ⊔ Ψ Ⴞ Ⴆ (VA)
k (K)	k K (K)	K (K)	Ψ ↓ Ψ Υ Υ (K)	⍋ (K)	K ⋊ ⅄ (K)	Φ ⊕ ⊖ ⊖ ⊖ (VO)
↳ (L)	Λ (L)	Λ (L)	Λ (L)	⅂ (L)	Γ Γ Λ ⅂ (L)	⋀ Ⅹ (VU)
⋔ (M)	⋔ M (M)	M (M)	M(M) Ⅹ (M̃)	M(Ã) ⋔ (M)	M ⋔ (M)	⋉ ⋉ (SE) ⋁ (?)
N (N)	N N (N)	レ (N)	N (N) Ŧ (Ñ)	Υ (N)	Υ Υ N ⋏ (N)	⪦ ⪦ Ⅰ Ⴆ Ⴆ Ⴆ D (HE)
O (O)	O O O (O)	0 (O)	0 (O)	O (O)	O °(O)	
Γ (P)	Ρ Ρ Λ Γ Γ (P)	Γ (P)	Γ (P)	+ (P)	Γ (P)	
Ρ (R)	Ρ Ρ (R)	P (R)	Ρ (R)	ঀ (R)	Ρ Ρ R ঀ ঀ C (R)	
⑀ (S)	⑀ ⑀ ⑀ (S)	⑀ (S)	ʃ (S)	Ŧ (S) (S)	M ⋔ W ⋉ (S)	
T (T)	T (T)	T (T)	T (T) Ψ (τ)	T(T) Ŧ (τ)	T (T)	
Υ Ⅴ (U)	⋔ Υ (U)	Υ Υ (U)	0 (U)	⅄ (U)	Ⅴ Υ Υ Υ (U)	**Ligatures**
Φ (PH)	Φ (PH)	Φ (PH)	◇ (KH)		Ⅹ ⋌ (H)	⋊ (MI + VU)
Υ ⋎ (KH)	Υ ⋎ (KH)	Ψ (KH)	◇ (KH)	↑ (Q?)	↓ Υ Υ Υ Ψ ⋎ (KH)	ঀ ঀ ঀ (KHE + VO)
			⋎ ⋎ ⋎ ↓ (Ã)	8 (F) ⋔	⋈ (TS-CH)	
			⋎ Υ Υ Υ (Ẽ) + (H)	ঀ (V)	ঀ ঀ (A E-KHE)	

19.28. The Asianic alphabets.

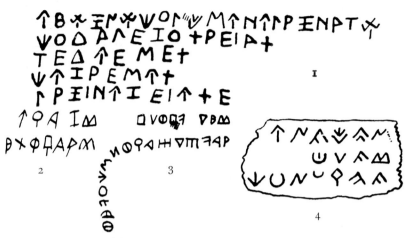

19.29a. (1) Lycian inscription, (2)–(4) Carian inscriptions.

19.29b. Carian inscriptions.

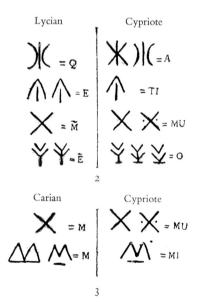

19.29c. (1) Lycian and Carian signs compared with Cretan signs, (2) and (3) and with Cypriote syllables.

LETTERS		NAME	PHON. VALUE	LETTERS		NAME	PHON. VALUE
MAJUSCULES	MINUSCULES			MAJUSCULES	MINUSCULES		
ⲁ	ⲁ	alpha	a	Ⲣ	ⲣ	ro	r
Ⲃ	ⲃ	vita	v (b)	Ⲥ	ⲥ	sima	s
Ⲅ	ⲅ	gamma	g̱	Ⲧ	ⲧ	tau	t
Ⲇ	ⲇ	delta	d	Ⲩ	ⲩ	ypsilon	y, u
Ⲉ	ⲉ	epsilon	ĕ	Ⲫ	ⲫ	phi	ph
Ⲍ	ⲍ	zita	z	Ⲭ	ⲭ	khi	ch=kḥ
Ⲏ	ⲏ	ita	i, ē̄	Ⲯ	ⲯ	psi	ps
Ⲑ	ⲑ	t̲ita	t̲	Ⲱ	ⲱ	omega	omega
Ⲓ	ⲓ	iōta	i	Ⲩ	ⲩ	šeı	š ⅏
Ⲕ	ⲕ	kappa	k	ϥ	ϥ	fai	f
Ⲗ	ⲗ	laula	l	ⳃ	ⳃ	khai	ḫ
Ⲙ	ⲙ	mi	m	Ⳉ	ⳉ	hori	h
Ⲛ	ⲛ	ni	n	Ⳅ	ⳅ	djandja	g̱
Ⲝ	ⲝ	xi	x	Ⳍ	ⳍ	chima	č (ancient)
Ⲟ	ⲟ	omicron	ŏ				
Ⲡ	ⲡ	pi	p	ϯ	ϯ	ti	ti

19.30. The Coptic alphabet.

19.31*a.* Coptic imprecation written on a rib.

19.31*b. Papyrus Q:* Oldest Coptic Gospel (St. John), 4th century A.D. (Bible House Library, London).

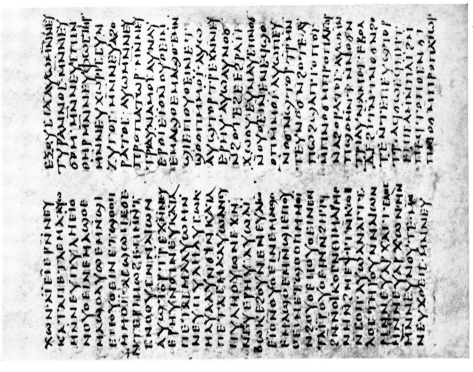

19.32b. *Pistis Sophia*, a treatise of Valentinus. Vellum MS. Late 4th or early 5th century (B.M.).

19.32a. Deuteronomy, Jonah and Acts, Coptic. Sa'idic Dialect. Papyrus, early 14th century (B.M.).

333

19.33. Specimens of Coptic books. *a* New Testament in Sahidic, on vellum, 5th or 6th century; *b Psalm 118*, v. 124–51; *c* Bohairic liturgical hymns, on paper, 14th or 15th century; *d* Arabic text written in Coptic Bohairic hand, 14th century.

19.34. Specimens from Herbert Thompson collection of Coptic manuscripts (University Library, Cambridge, *MS. Or. 1699*). *Above* (*left*), Apocryphal book on *Resurrection;* (*right*), *Homilies* by Shenūte. *Below*, *Martyrology* and *Homilies*.

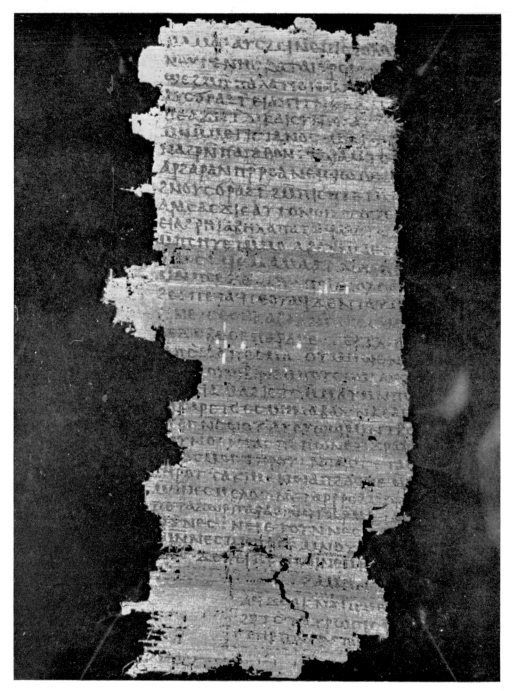

19.35. Leaf of a papyrus codex of the 4th–5th century A.D. containing the conclusion of a Manichean homily written in the Subachmimic dialect of Coptic (Chester Beatty Library).

19.36. Encomium of St. Menas dated A.D. 892/3 (from the Coptic MS. 590 in the Pierpont Morgan Collection). (*By permission of the Société d'Archéologie Copte*, Cairo).

19.37. Various Messapian inscriptions.

Phonetic value	Symbols	Numerical value
a, â	Αᴬᴬ	1
b (b?)	BᴃᴃБ	2
g, γ	ГГ	3
d, (d?)	ᴅᴅ	4
e	ЄЄ	5
q	ᵁᵁᵁ	6
z	ᴢᴢ	7
h	ʜʜ	8
p (θ)	ΦΦ	9
i	IᵢĪ	10
k	KK	20
l	λλ	30
m	MM	40
n	NN	50
j	GꟄ	60
u	ππ	70
p	ππ	80
—	Ч	90
r	ᴋᴋᴋ	100
s	SS	200
t	TT	300
w ü	YY	400
f	ꟻꟻ	500
χ (kh)	XX	600
hv (hw)	ΘΘ	700
o	ᴼᴼ	800
(sampi)	↑↑	900

a

b

c

19.38. *a* The Gothic alphabet. *b* Page from the *Codex Argenteus*. *c* The *Paternoster* according to the same *codex*.

Uncial Greek	Cyrillic	Bulgarian Glagolitsa	Croat. Glagolitsa	Names of the letters	Phonetic value	Num.
Λ	Ꙗ Λ			az	a	1
Ҍ Β	Б Β			buky	b	2
Γ	Γ			vedi	v	3
Γ	Γ			glagol	g	4
Δ	Δ			dobro	d	5
Є	Є			est', yest'	e – ye]	6
Τ (τσ)	Ж Ж			zhivete	zh	7
ʃ (ξ: ᵭς)	Ѕ Ѕ			zelo	z – dz	8
Ζ	Ζ			zemlya	z	9
Η	Η			izhe (ije)	ī	10
Ι Ï	Ï Ι			i	i	20
Τ (τι)	Ћ			dew' yerv' djerv' }	d'–dʲ t'–tʲ y	30
Κ	Κ			kako	k	40
λ	Λ Λ			lyudy	l	50
Μ	Μ Μ			myslite	m	60
Ν	Ν Ν			nash	n	70
Ο	Ο			on	o	80
Π	Π			pokoy	p	90
Ρ	Ρ			r'tsi	r	100
Ϲ	Ϲ			slovo	s	200

19.39. The Early Slavonic alphabets.

Uncial Greek	Cyrillic	Bulgarian / Croat. Glagolitsa		Names of the letters	Phonet. Value	Num.
T	T			tv'rdo	t	300
8 or ογ	ογ ƴ			uk	u	400
φ θ	ф		φ	fert thita	f th	500 9
X	X			kher	kh	600
ω	ω			ot	ō	700
ογ (ϭϭ) Sem. sh?	Ш		Ш	sha	sh	—
Ψ (ϭϭς) Sem.	ШТΨ			shta	sht	800
(Ϭ, ϹΖ, ϭϭς) Sem ts?	Ч			tsi	ts	900
(Ϲ, τϭ ς) Τ sem. ts?	Ƴ			ch'ro	ch	1000
Ϭ (οε)	Ь			yer	ŭ-y	—
Ϭι (οεϲι)	ЫІ ЬН		—	yery	y	—
Ϭ (ε)	ь		ТІ	yerek	ĭ	—
Gϯ	Ѣ, Ꙗ			yat'-yer'	ya-ye	800
IO	Ю			yu	yu	—
IΣ	ІЄ	—		ye	ye	—
Ι̂ Ι̃ (ιν)	Aϯ Î		—	e"s	eng	900
ο̇ ο+ιν	Ѫ		—	o"s	ong	—
I+A	ІѦ		—	ye"s	yeng	—
I+Ѫ	ІѪ		—	yo"s	yong	—
ξ Ξ ξ	Ξ ξ	—	—	ksi	ks	60
Ѱ Ѱ ϯ	Ѱ ⵕ	—	—	psi	ps	700
V	V Y		—	izhitsa	y-v-i ü	—

19.40. The Early Slavonic alphabets (continued).

PHON. VALUE	CYRILL.	RUSSIAN PRINT	RUSSIAN CURSIVE	BULGAR.	SERBIAN	UKRAIN	OLD RUM.
a	Ꙗ А	А	А	А	А	А	а
b	Б	Б	Б	Б	Б	Б	Б
v	В	В	В	В	В	В	В
g	Г	Г	Г	Г	Г	Г (Т)	Г
d	Д	Д	Д	Д	Д	Д	Д
ye	Є	Е	Е	Е	Е	Е (Є)	Е
zh (j)	Ж	Ж	Ж	Ж	Ж	Ж	Ж
z	З	З	З	З	З	З	Ѕ З
i	Н	И	И	И	И	И	Н
i	І	І	І			І (Ї)	І (Ї)
y	(Й й)	(Й й)	(Й)	Ј		(Й)	
k	К	К	К	К	К	Ќ	К
l	Λ л	Л	Л	Л	Л	Л	Λ
m	Ϻ м	М	М	М	М	М	М
n	N N	Н	Н	Н	Н	Н	N
o	О	О	О	О	О	О	О (ѡ)
p	П	П	П	П	ІІ	П	П
r	Р	Р	Р	Р	Р	Р	Р
s	С	С	С	С	С	С	С
t	Т	Т	Т	Т	Т	Т	Т

19.41. The main Slavonic alphabets of today.

342

PHON. VALUE	CYRILL.	RUSSIAN PRINT	CURSIVE	BULGAR.	SERBIAN	UKRAIN.	OLD RUM.
ty	Ћ				Ћ		
u (oo)	ȣ or	У у		У	У	У	ȣ or
f	Ф	Ф ℱ		Ф	Ф	Ф	Ф
kh	Х	Х 𝒳		Х	Х	Х	Х
ts	Ч	Ц Ц		Ц	Ц	Ц	Ч
ch	Ү	Ч ч		Ч	Ч	(Ц) Ч	Ү Ч
sh	ш	Ш Ш		Ш	Ш	Ш	ш
shch	ҷ ш ᴛ	Щ Щ		Щ		Щ	Ψ
mute	Ъ	Ъ ъ		Ъ	Ъ		Ъ
y	ꙑ	Ы ы		.			Ы
mute	ь	Ь ь		Ь	ь	ь	ь
ye	Ѣ	Ѣ ℒ		Ѣ			Ѣ
e	Э	Э Э					(Ι Е)
yu	Ю	Ю ю		Ю	Ю		Ю
ya	Я ꙗ	Я Я		Я	Я		Ꙗ
ph	Ѳ	Ѳ Ѳ					Ѳ (ft)
y	Ѵ	Ѵ ѵ					Ѵ ѵ
ü	Ѫ			Ж			Ѫ
iu	Ѧ ꙇ̑			Ι Ж			Ѧ ꙇ̑ ꙇ̑ ia in ꙃ ꙏ ks ps

19.42. The main Slavonic alphabets of today (continued).

a

ZHTKШHHTZHPГ
ШYßШYΛЄXШYM
CXHKYΠЄ·YNЄ:TШ
YΛCXH:ФM:ЄCTPШ
ГHNKYΠЄ:YKΣ:TШ
YΛCXH:∞NΔ:TШYPT
ШYNAΠHΛЄξШΠAN
ЄCTPYГHNKYΠЄ:K:
TШYΛCXH:M·AΛXACH
KYΠЄ:A·XΛШ YßPH N:A·

b

19.43. Cyrillic. *a* Traces of graffiti on the right column near the main entrance of the round church in Preslav. *b* Old Bulgarian inscription from the church in Bjal-Brjag, in the district of Preslav (Courtesy Acad. I. Goshev).

344

a

b

ДѢЛАТЪ·ЖДАЖГЪ·ВЫЖЕ
ВРАЗН·ВРАЗНГНЄСЪЛ
ГАШАЄЛОУ·ПОПНСАНОУ
ОУ̇ЛОУ·ІАКОСОУШТАА
ГОКСТЪСТВОЛЬСНАБЖН
ІА·ПОЛОЖЕННЄМЬНБЛА
ГОДАТНЖНАРНУОУТ·
ОБ́ЖЄНА·НЗНЖАНТЄЛА
ЗЬДАННЄ·НПРНЄПРΣС
ШТААГОВЪ̇ОЦН·ПРЄ̇Ж
ДЄНЄ́БЫБЪ̇ША·НБЫ̇БЪ̇
ШААГООТЪБЫТНА·НА
РНУОУШЄО̇ТЪНЄБЫТН·
ІА·БЫ̇БЪ̇·НЄ̇ТЪУЬ̇Ж
КЄНАБА·Н·ГАЛЪЖОУ
ТЬ·БОУСАВЪРАШАХЩЄ·

c

19.44. Old Bulgarian inscriptions. *a* Inscription of Aliates Stratelat, commander of the Byzantine garrison, in the round church of Preslav (A.D. 972). *b* Inscription of 'Črgubilja Mostič' after its reconstruction, 11th–13th century (Archaeological Museum, Sofia). *c* Sviatoslav-Izbornic, fol. 4 (A.D. 1073) (Courtesy Acad. I. Goshev).

19.45. Development of the Cyrillic monumental scripts. *a* Funerary inscription in Cyrillic script of A.D. 993 (dedicated by Tzar Samuel to his parents and brother); *b* manuscript of A.D. 1073; *c* manuscript of A.D. 1284; *d* prayer book of A.D. 1400; *e* manuscript of 15th century; *f* manuscript of 1561.

19.46. *a–e* Varieties of early Cyrillic alphabets. *f* Roumanian in Cyrillic character.

19.47*a*. Cryptic annotation in a manuscript of the 16th century.

19.47*b*. Cursive writing, 1555.

19.47*c*. Cursive variety of 1562.

19.47*d*. Manuscript of 1668.

19.47. Specimens of Cyrillic cursive writing.

348

19.48. *Gospels* written in 1429 by a monk named Gabriel; the text is in Cyrillic character, but it is accompanied by a Greek translation in cursive script (Bodleian Library, *MS. Can. Gr. 122*).

Language	Additional letters		Language	Additional letters
Moldavian	ё, щ, ъ,		Komi-Permian	i, ö,
Tajiki	й, ӯ, ғ, қ, х, ч, аз, дар,		Udmurt (Votyak)	ӝ, ӟ, ӥ, ӵ, ӧ,
Kurdish	ә, ö, h, г', ә', к', п', р', т', h', ч', ё, ц, ъ, ы, ю, я,		Mari (Cheremiss)	ä, ö, ӱ,
Ossetic	æ,		Mordvine-Erzya	-съ, -нъ,
Abkhasian	ҷ, қ, х, ч, э, ъ, ҕ, дә, цъ, жъ, жь, зә, б къ, ҟь, ҭә, тә, хъ, хе, цә, ҵе, цә, ашә, ачә, ҷ, шә, ё, й, щ, ъ, з, ю, я, ҙ, ҭ,		Mordvine-Moksha	-съ, -нъ, лх, рх,
Abasinian	гӀ, гӀв, кӀ, кӀв, лӀ, тӀ, фӀ, хӀ, хӀ, хӀв, чӀ, чӀ, чӀв, шӀ, ы, Ӏ, гъв, гӀв, джв, къъ, къв, кӀьв, хъв, гвв,		Nenets (Yurak)	нг, и,
Adigen	кӀ, лӀ, пӀ, тӀ, фӀ, цӀ, чӀ, шӀ, щӀ, ы, лӀ, лу, гъв, жъ, кв, пъ, хъ, хъ, чъ, шъ,		Selkup (Ostyako-Samoyed)	е', к', н', у',
Kabardian-Circassian (Cherkessian)	кӀ, кӀу, лӀ, пӀ, тӀ, фӀ, цӀ, щӀ, лу, жь, кхъ, кхъу, хъу,		Chuvash	ӑ, ӗ, ҫ, ӳ,
Chechen	гӀ, кӀ, пӀ, тӀ, цӀ, чӀ, ыь, Ӏӏ, аь, йо, ов, уь, юь, яь,		Turkmenian (Turkoman)	ж, н, ө, ү, е,

19.49. Cyrillic (Russian) alphabet adapted to non-Slavonic languages.

Azerbaijani	к, ч, в, ғ, ә,ј,ө, ү, һ, ё, ӥ, ц, щ, ъ, ь, з, ю, я,
Tatar	ө, ү, җ, ң, һ, ә,
Bashkir	ө, ү, һ, ә, ҙ,(з),ж, ҫ, (ҫ), ғ, ң,
Kumyk	гъ,гь, къ, нг, оь,уь,
Kara-Kalpak	ғ, қ, х,
Nogai	нъ, оь, уь, з м,
Kazakh	ғ, қ, ң, ө, ү, һ, і, ә,
Kirghiz	ң, ө, ү,
Altaic	ј, ҥ, ö, ÿ,

Ingush	гӏ, кӏ, пӏ, тӏ, хӏ,цӏ, чӏ, ыӏ, лӏ,ллаб, яв,
Avarian	гӏ, кӏ, тӏ,хӏ, цӏ,чӏ. ыӏ, г, к, т, х, ц, ч.
Darghi	гӏ, кӏ,тӏ, хӏ, цӏ, чӏ. ыӏ,
Lesghian	кӏ,пӏ, тӏ, цӏ, чӏ, ӏ.
Lakh	кӏ, пӏ, тӏ, цӏ, чӏ, ыӏ, аб,жв,уь,шв,
Tabasaran	кӏ, пӏ, тӏ, хӏ, цӏ,чӏ, ӏ, аб, об,
Vogul(Mansi)	нг,
Ostyak (Khantian)	ӄ, ӧ, ä, ӑ, ӈ, ö, е, ÿ, ә.
Komi (Zyryan) (Syryan)	ј,ö,

19.50. Cyrillic (Russian) alphabet adapted to non-Slavonic languages (continued).

Karachai	ў,
Balkar	нъ, нг, ў
Uzbek	ў, к, ғ,
Uighur	к, н, ғ, ү, ө, ж, ә, һ,
Yakut	ҕ, н, ө, һ, ү.
Tuva (Soyot or Uryankhai)	н, ө, ү,
Khakas	и, ч, ҷ, ғ, і, ö, ÿ,
Buryat	ө, ү, h, оо, өө, үү, үү, зз,
Kalmyk (Kalmuck)	ә, h, җ, н, ө, ү, ä, гъ, дж, нъ, ö, ÿ,

Tungus Proper (Evenki)	нг,
Lamut (Even)	з, ь, п, ә, и,
Gold (Nanai)	нг,
Chukcha (Luoravetian)	ӄ, ӈ,
Koryak (Nymylan)	к', н',
Nivkh (Gilyak)	'frequently used
Siberian Eskimo (Yuit)	г', к', н', х',
Dungan	ә, ж, н, ү,
Mongolian Proper	ө, ү, аа, оо, өө, үү, үү, зз,

19.51. The Cyrillic alphabets.

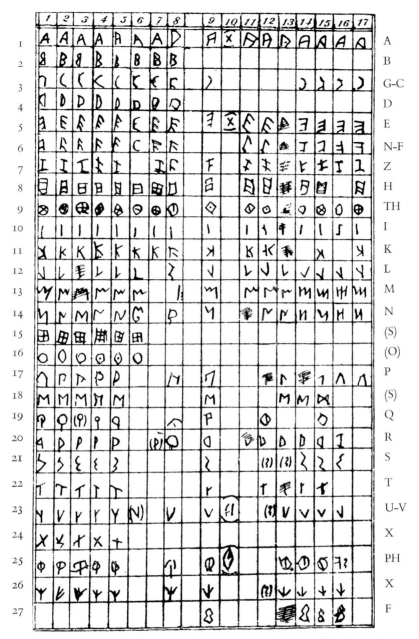

20.1. Etruscan sample alphabets (in columns). 1, Marsiliana. 2, Viterbo, 3, Cære. 4–5, Formello. 6, Colle. 7, Narce. 8, Leprignano. 9, Rusellæ. 10–13, Chiusi. 14, Bomarzo. 15–17 Nola.

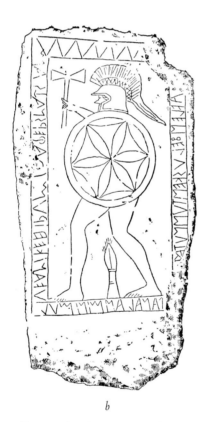

20.2 Etruscan inscription. *a* Marsiliana tablet. *b* The *stele* from Vetulonia. *c* The Perugia *Cippus*.

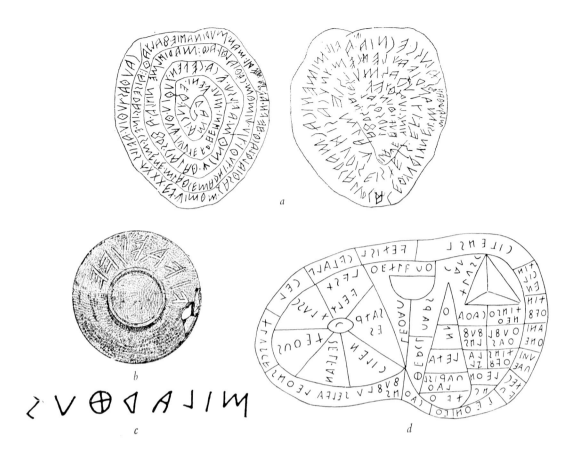

a

20.3. *a* The Magliano leaden tablet (left, obverse, right, reverse). *b* Etruscan partial syllabary from Orbetello. *c* Inscription on a vase. *d* The *Templum* of Piacenza. *e* The Etruscan 'classical' alphabet in all but final form. *f* Etruscan inscriptions from a 3rd century B.C. ossuary, from Chiusi (Vatican Museum).

	Lepontic	Sondrio	Bolzano	Magrè	Venetic
A	⋀ ⅂ ⋀ ⋀ ⋀	⋀⋀	⋀⋀⋀	⋀ ⋀ ⋀ Ⅴ Ⅴ	⋀⋀
B		B			
C		⟨ ⟩			
D					
E	ⴹ ⴼ ⴺ ⴺ ⴼ	ⴹ ⴺ	ⴼ ⴺ ⴹ	ⴼ ⴼⴹ ⴺ ⴺ	ⴺ ⴼ
V-W	(Ⅴ) (Y)		⋀ ⴹ ⴼ	ⴼ ⴼ ⴹ	ⴹ ⴼ
Z		⛄ ⛄ ⛄			✕ ✕
H			目	目	Ⱶ Ⅲ
Θ					✕
I	Ⅰ ⧢	Ⅰ	Ⅰ	Ⅰ ‖	Ⅰ
K	Κ Ⱪ Ⱪ ⴺΚ		ΚⱩ Ⱪ Ⱪ	Κ	Ⱪ Κ
L	Ⅴ Ⅴ Ⅴ Ⅴ L ⋀ ⋀	Ⅴ	⅂	⌐	⅂ ⋀
M	ⱴ ⱴ ⱶⱴ ⱴ	Ⱳ Ⱳⱴ	⋔ⱴ	⋔ⱴⱴⱴ	ⱴⱴⱴ
N	Ⲛ Ⱶ ⱴⱴ ⱴⱴⱴ	ⱴ	Ⲛ ⱴⱴⱴ	ⱴⱴ	ⱴⲚ
̈S	⋈				⋈
O	○ ○ ○ ○ ⌒ ⌒	○			◇ ○
P	⋀⋀	⋀	⋀⋀		⋀⋀⋀
Ś			⋔ⱱ	⋔	⋔
R	D ◁ ◁ ⊲◁		◁ ◁	◁ ◁ P P D	◁ ◁ P
S	Ƨ Ƨ ⴺ Ƨ S	Ƨ	Ƨ Ƨ	Ƨ Ƨ	Ƨ Ƨ
T	✕ ✕	✕	✕ ✕ Ⱶ ✕ ⱶ Ⱶ	✕ ⱶ Ⱶ	✕ Τ
U	Ⅴ ∪ ⱴ ⱴ Ⅴ	Ⅴ Y Ⅴ	Ⅴ	⋀ ⋀ Ⅴ	⋀
Φ			Φ	Φ	◇ ◇ Φ
X			Ⴤ ⋔	Ⴤ	Ⴤ
?				⛬ ⛬ ⛬	

20.4. North Etruscan and allied alphabets.

356

Phon. Value	Messapian	Picenian	Oscan	Umbrian	Siculan	Faliscan
a	Ꭺ Ꭺ Ꭺ	Ꭺ ↑	◁ ◁◁	Ꭺ Ꭺ Ꭺ	Ꭺ ↑↑	Я Я Я
b	B		ⱱ B	ⱱ	B B	
g	Γ	<) >	>	⅄		) > (ᴋ)
d	⊿	▷ Ᵽ ٩ ◁ ⊿	Я Я	✝	▷ ◁	◠
e	Ⅎ E	Ⅎ Ⅎ Ⅎ E	◄Ⅎ E	ϵ ⅄ Ⅎ	E Ⅎ	◄ ‖
v (f)	٦ F Ⅽ	Ⅽ ⅂ Ⅽ	⅂ ⅂ Ⅽ	⅂ ⅂ ⅃ ⅃ ⅂	Ⅽ	↑
z (ts)	I Z	≬ I ≬	I I	∓ ⅄ ∓		∓ ≱
h	ⱱ H ⅺ ⱶ	ⱱ‖‖◻⨅◻	ⱱ ⊟	⊘ ⊕	ⱱ ◧	ⱱ H ⱱ
θ (th)	⊗ ⊙	⊠ ◇ ⊗	Ⴀ ⱱ Ⴀ	⊙ (t)		
i	I	I ↑ (ᴋⅠⱶ)	I (ⱶ⅄ ? iᵉ)	I	I	I
k	ᴋ	ᴋ ⅄ ↗	↗ ᴋ	↗ ⅃ ᴋⅠᴋ ᴋ	ᴋ	↗
l	∧	∨ ⅃ Ⅼ	⅃ ⅃	⅃ ∨	⅂	⅃ Ⅼ ⅃
m	Ⳳ ⅄	Ⳳ ⱳ Ⳓ ⅄	ⱨ ⱳ	ⱨ ⱳ	Ⳳ ⅄	Ⳳ
n	⅄ ᴎ	⅄ ᴎ	ⱨ ᴎ	ⱨ ⱳ	ᴎ ᴦ ᴦ	ᴎ
s	+		(⟩ ↗)			
o	O	◻ ◇ ◇ ◇	(ⱽ ⱽ=ᵒ) (⅄ ⅄=ᵛ)		◻ ◇ ◇ ▽	◦
p	⅂ᴦ	⅂⅂Ⅼ⅃⅃	⅂ ⅂	⅂	⅂	٩ ⅂ ⅂
s	⅄	Ⳳ ⊠ ⋈ᴎ ? ? ? ?		Ⳳ		
q	٩ ⱷ					
r	٩⅄ ⅂ ᴘ ᴘ	٩ ◁ ▷ ◁ ◁	◁ ◁ ◁	◁ ◁ (٩:ř)	ⱱ▷◁٩⅂	Я
s	⅀ ⅀ ⅀ (sh ⅹ)	ⅉⱾ ⅀⅀⅀ ⅀	⅀ ⅀	⅀⅀ (sh ◍)	⅀ ⅀ ⅀	S Z
t	T	T ⱶ⅂ ⱶ⅃	ⱱ T	✝ ✝ ⅄ ✝	T	ⱶⱽ⅄
u		∧∨	Ⲩ ∨	∨	∧∨	∨
k	(ᴋs) X (ps) Ⲩ		X (⅀ ↗)	↗ ✝ ⅀ X		X X

20.5. Pre-Italic and Italic alphabets.

357

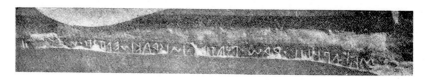

20.6a. The Picenian inscription of the 'Warrior' from Capestrano.

20.6b. Oscan inscriptions.

20.6c. The famous Faliscan inscription in two copies.

20.7. Noviliara funeral stele, written in Picenian, *c.* 550 B.C.

20.8. Eugubine tablet, table 5. Upper part is written in Umbrian script, lower part in Roman character.

PHON. VALUE	GERMANIC LETTERS	ANGLO-SAXON LETTERS	SCANDINAVIAN			DOTTED LETTERS
			EARLY SIGNS LETTERS	DANISH LATE SIGNS LETTERS	SWED. NORW. LATE SIGNS LETTERS	
f						
u						
þ						
å						
r						
k						
g						
w						
h						
n						
i						
j						
ė						
p						
r						
s						
t						
b						
e						
m						
l						
ng						
o						
d						
a						
ae						
y						
ea						
io						
c						
g						

21.1. Main branches of the Runic script.

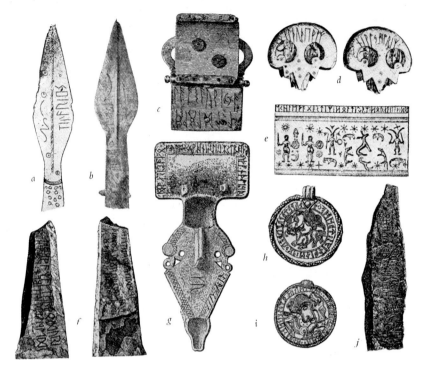

21.2. Early Runic inscriptions. *a* Spearhead from Kovel (Volhynia), attributed to the fourth century A.D.; *b* Spearhead from Dahmsdorf near Muencheberg (Brandenburg). *c* Clasp from Vi-mose in Fyn (S.-W. Denmark), attributed to the middle of the third century A.D.; *d* The end-clasp of a sword-sheath from Torsbjerg, attributed to *ca.* 300; *e* The 'Golden Horn' from Gallehus (northern Schleswig), of *ca.* A.D. 400. *f* The stone from Tune (S.-E. Norway), of the fifth century A.D.; *g* The brooch from Charnay (French Department of Saône and Loire; old Burgundian kingdom) of the fifth century A.D.; *h–i Bracteates* from Vadstena (Sweden) and Tjorkœ (Sweden) of the sixth–seventh centuries A.D. *j* Funerary inscription written from right to left, from Kyœlevig, or Strand (Ryfylke, Norway) of the sixth century A.D.

a

b

21.3. Metal and whale's bone used as writing material in England; (*below*) the *scramasax* or sword-knife, found in the Thames in 1857, and now in the British Museum; it probably belongs to about A.D. 800; (*above*) one side of the 'Franks Casket', attributed to about A.D. 650 or A.D. 700; the runes have been translated: 'The fish-flood (sea) lifted the whale's bones on to the mainland; the ocean became turbid where he swam aground on the shingle.'

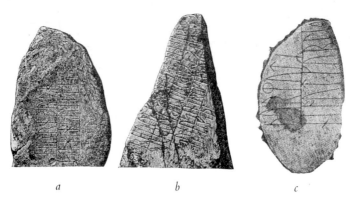

a   b   c

21.4. *a* Sepulchral stone from Kallerup, Denmark, 9th century A.D.
b Stone from the Odense region, Denmark, 9th century A.D. *c* Inscription from Nœrrenaerå, late 9th century A.D.

d   e

21.4. *d* The longest early Danish inscription from Glavendrup. *e* Alphabetic inscription, partly dotted, from Oestermarie Sogn (Bornholm).

21.4*f.* Funerary inscription from A°s, Sweden, of the 11th century.

21.4 Scandinavian Runic inscriptions

1. ∩ u   2. Þ þ (th)   3. ⊩ a   4. R r ,   5. ⟨ k   6. ✕ g   7. Ᵽ w   8. ᴎ h

9. ✛ n   10. | i   11. ⟩ j   12. ⟆ p   13. ⥿ (z)   14. ⅄ R (ř)   15. ⟨ s   16. ↑ t

17. ⬠ b   18. Ϻ e   19. ᴍ m   20. Γ l   21. ◇ ŋ (ng)   22. ⨂ o   23. ⋈ d   24. Ⱶ f

a

b ᛏᛙᛆᛍᛁᛂᛏᛁᛏᛎᛆᛝᛁᚢᛆᛙ

c ᛘᛋᛙᛘᛏᚱᛙ

d ᚠᚢᚢᚦᚦᛖᚱᚱᛦᚼᛁᛁ᛬ᛏᛁᛁᛙᛏᛏ᛬

e ᚠ∩ᚦᛂᚱᛘᚼᚼᚼ᛬ᛁᛅᛦᛙᚱ f u þ a r k h n i a s t b m l R

f ᛦ∩∩ᚦᚦᛂᚱᚱᛦᚼᚼᚼᚼ᛬ᛦᛂᛏᛏ

g ᛏ⟩᛬᛭᛭⟨ᛏ᛬᛭᛭᛬᛭᛭᛭ f u þ a r k h n i a s t b m l R

h
| \ | / | V \ | / | / | / |
| f | u | th | r | k | h | n | i | a | s | t | b | l | m | n. |

i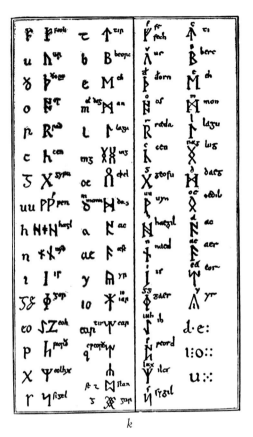

j ᛈᛁᛖᛆᚱᚱᚢᚾᛆᚱ

k

l a ⲓ᛬ᛙᛙᛙᛙ᛬ᛙᛙ᛬ᛙᛙᛙᛙᛙᛙ᛬᛬ᛙᛙᛙ᛬ᛙ᛬ᛙᛙ᛬ᛙᛙ᛬ᛙᛙᛙ   ·.·   ···   ·.·   ··.   d

21.5. *a* The Runic 'alphabet' according to Agrell; *b* Negau inscription, 2nd century B.C.? *c* Maria Saalerberg inscription, 1st century B.C.? Scandinavian varieities, *d* Roek; *e* Forsa; *f* Jæderen, Norway and Isle of Man; *g*, *h* Hælsinge, *i* Tjaldrunir (Roek inscription); *j* Kvistrunir (Maeshowe, Orkney) *k*; Anglo-Saxon Runic alphabet (*Codex Salisburgensis* 140); *l Corui* (Lat. Corvi) in (a) üsruna, (b) lagoruna, (c) stofruna, (d) hahalruna (St. Gallen MS. 270).

365

21.6a. Runic 'alphabet' of a manuscript of about A.D. 1300.

21.6b. Runic–oghamic inscription (Manx Museum).

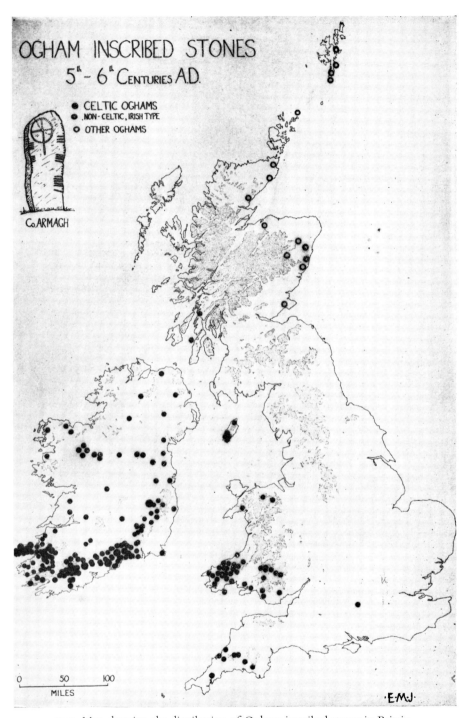

21.7. Map showing the distribution of Ogham inscribed stones in Britain.

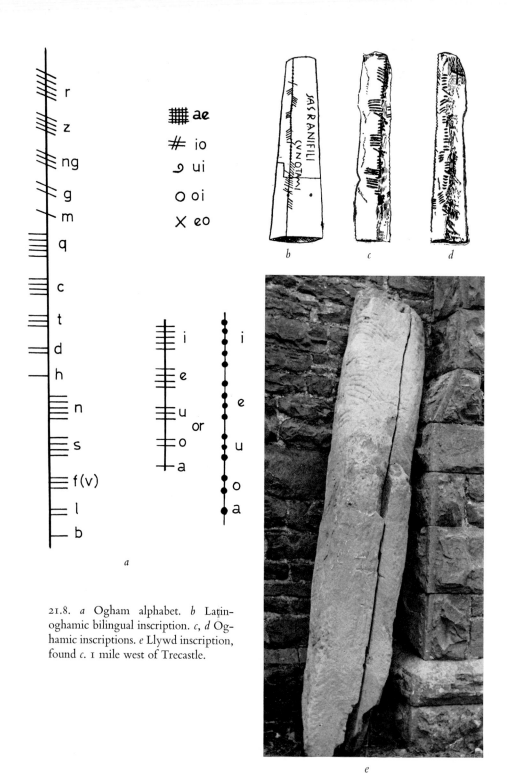

21.8. *a* Ogham alphabet. *b* Latin-oghamic bilingual inscription. *c, d* Og-hamic inscriptions. *e* Llywd inscription, found *c.* 1 mile west of Trecastle.

21.9. Silchester stone.

21.10. Left, Oghamic inscription. Right, Oghamic–Latin digraphic inscription (British Museum).

21.11a. Pictish Ogham.

21.11b. Pictish Ogham.

21.11c. Germanic Oghams.

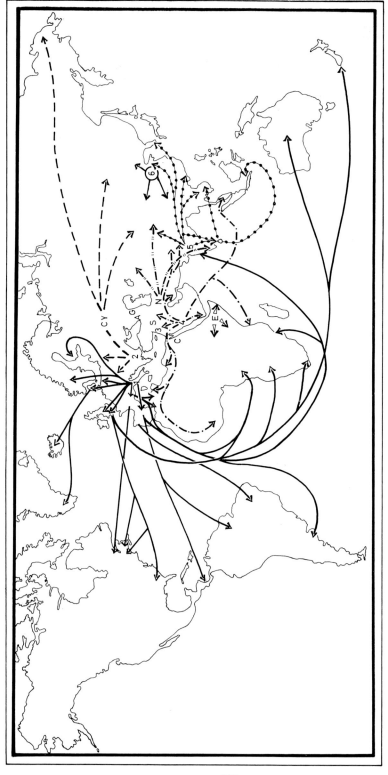

1 ——— Western Christianity: Latin. 2 Eastern Christianity: ——— CY-Cyrillic (including Russian); S-Syriac; ——— N-Nestorian;
A-Armenian; G-Georgian; C-Coptic; E-Ethiopic.   3 Judaism: Hebrew.   4 ——— Islām: Arabic. 5 ——— Buddhism: Pāli and
other scripts. 6 Confucianism: Chinese.

Map 3. Alphabet follows religion.

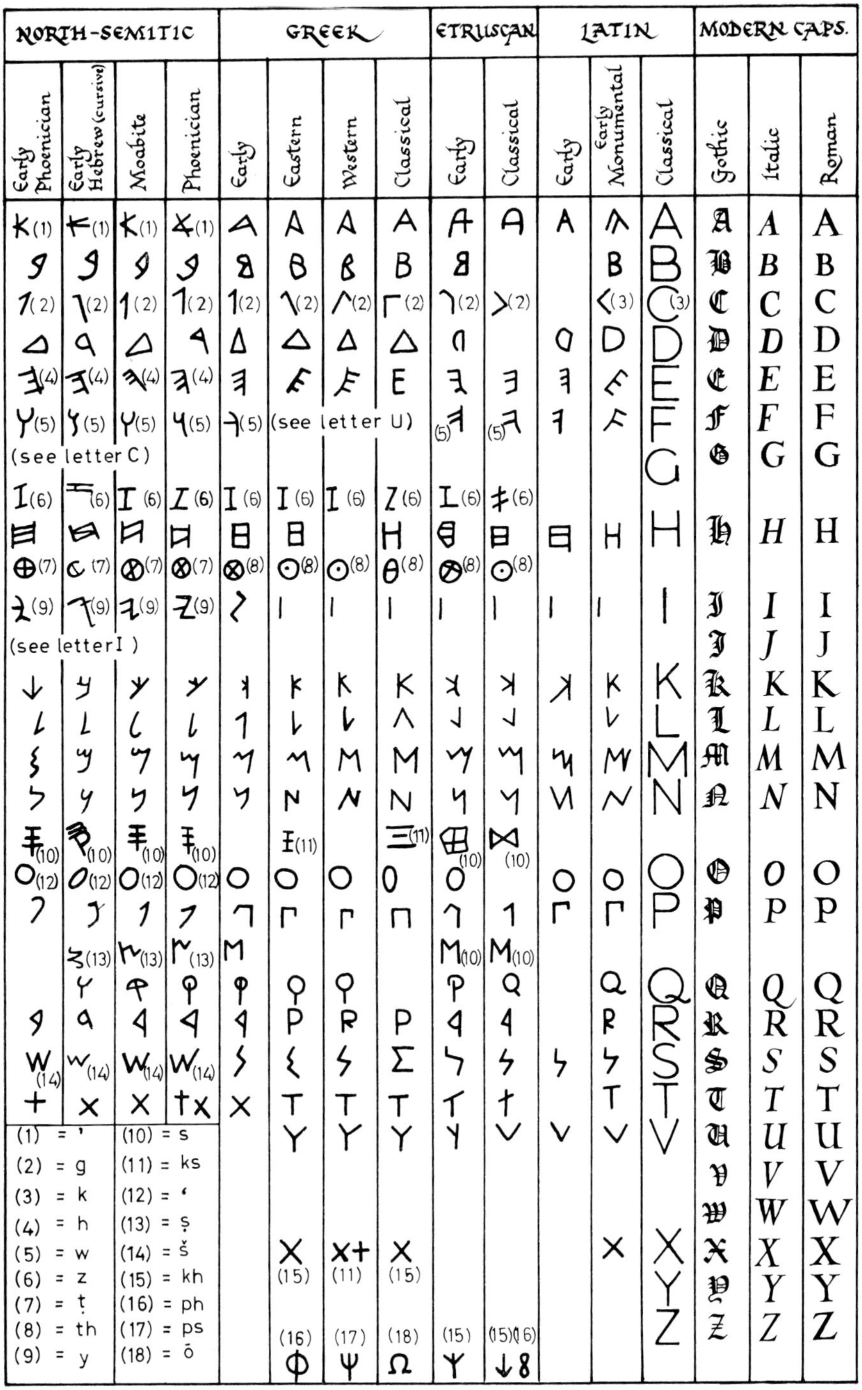
NORTH-SEMITIC
GREEK
ETRUSCAN
LATIN
MODERN CAPS.
Early Phoenician
Early Hebrew (cursive)
Moabite
Phoenician
Early
Eastern
Western
Classical
Early
Classical
Early
Early Monumental
Classical
Gothic
Italic
Roman
(see letter C)
(see letter U)
(see letter I)
(1) = '
(2) = g
(3) = k
(4) = h
(5) = w
(6) = z
(7) = ṭ
(8) = th
(9) = y
(10) = s
(11) = ks
(12) = ʻ
(13) = ṣ
(14) = š
(15) = kh
(16) = ph
(17) = ps
(18) = ō

22.1. From North Semitic to Modern caps.

22.2. Development of the Latin alphabet.

I—1, 4th cent. B.C. 2, 3rd cent. B.C. 3, 4th cent. A.D. 4, Later variants of the Latin monumental script. 5, Rustic capitals, 3rd cent. A.D. 6, Modern capitals.

II—1, Inscriptional uncial, 3rd cent. A.D. 2, Roman monumental uncials, 3rd cent. A.D. 3, Gallic uncials, 5th cent. A.D. 4, Roman uncials, 7th cent. A.D. 5, Irish semi-uncials, 7th cent.

III—1, Cursive writing, 2nd cent. A.D. 2, Current hand, 3rd cent. 3, Gallic cursive, 6th cent. 4, Caroline hand (8th-9th cent.). 5, Early 'black letter' or Gothic, 13th cent. 6, Irish minuscule. 7, Anglo-Saxon minuscule. 8, Italic type. 9, Roman type.

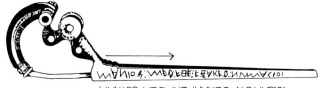

MANIOS:MED:FHEFHAKED:NUMASIOI

Manius me made (for) Numasius

22.3a. The Præneste fibula, 7th century B.C.

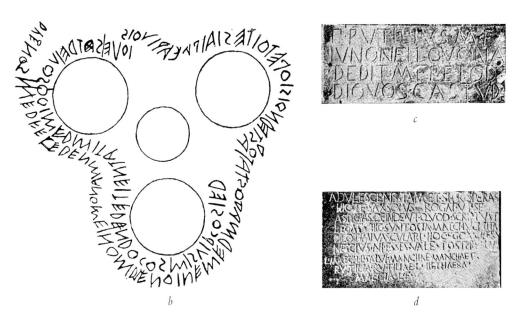

22.3. b The inscription of Duenos, 6th century B.C. *c* Dedication to Juno Lucina; from Norba, 4th century B.C. *d* Roman funerary *carmen*, of the period of Silla.

22.3. e Dedication to Juno; from Pisaurum, 4th century B.C. *f* Funerary inscription of Consul L. Cornelius Scipio, 259 B.C. *g* Dedication to Feronia, 4th century B.C.

22.3. Early Latin inscriptions.

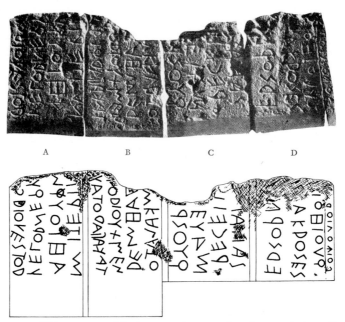

22.4*a*. Oldest preserved Latin text: photograph and transcription of the *cippus* from the Roman forum. Late 7th or early 6th century B.C.

22.4*b*. Funerary inscription of Consul Lucius Mummius, the conquerer of Corinth. 146 B.C.

22.5. One of the four faces of the *cippus* from the Roman forum (see also 22.4*a* c).

22.6. Specimens of Roman lapidary capitals.

22.7a. Bilingual Latin-Umbrian text from Todi, Vatican Museum (C.I.L. I, 1408).

22.7b. Marble slab from Arch of Claudius, Capitoline Museum, Rome (C.I.L. VI, 921).

PMVMMIOPFGALSI
SENNAERVTIANO
COSAVGVRIPROCOS
PROVINCASIAELEGATOAVG
PR·PR·MOESIAESVPERIORIS
PRAEFALIMENTPERAEMILIAM
PRAEFAERSATVRNIILEGECVI
VICTRICPRAETORITRPLQVAESI
TRIBLEGVMACEDXVIROSTI
TIBIVDICPATRONOMVNICI
PICVRIANIHVSALFOHER
CVLANIIAVGVSTALES
L   D   S   C

22.8b. Roman monumental script, Tombstone of Agrippina the Elder (C.I.L. VI, 886) who died in A.D. 33, and was buried by her son Caligula in A.D. 37 (Museo Nuovo Capitolino) Courtesy E. Wasmuth Verlag and E. Nash).

DIVIVLIAMINI
C ANTONIO
M·F·VOLTRVFO
FLAMINIDIVIAVG
COLCLARENSISET
COLIVLPHILIPPENS
SCHVNDEMIIVNCIR
TEMOSIDVLIATANE
TRIBMLCOHVXIVOLVN
IMORTRMIILEGVII
GEMINAEEQVITAVM
SSVBVORVM
VIC   II

22.8a. Roman monumental script of the 1st century A.D.: dedication to C. Antonius Rufus, from Alexandria Troas (British Museum).

380

22.9a. Roman inscribed wooden tablet.

	Pompeii	Alburnus Major
A		
B		
C		
D		
E		
F		
G		
H		
I		
K		
L		
M		
N		
O		
P		
Q		
R		
S		
T		
U-V		
X		
Y		
Z		

22.9b. Varieties of the early Roman cursive script (wax tablets from Pompeii and Alburnus Major).

22.10. Two pages from a 'book' (codex) of wax tablets, from Pompeii, A.D. 58.

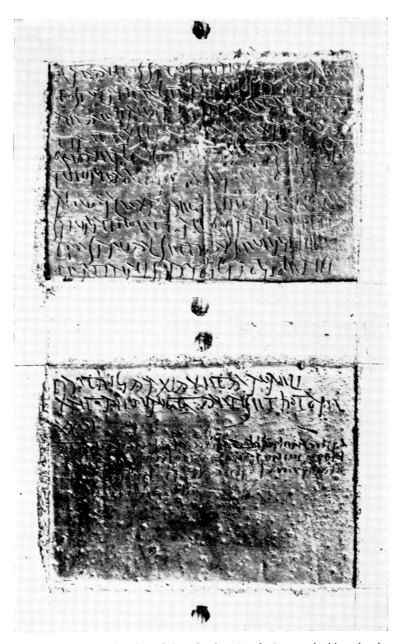

22.11. Roman wooden diptych (6 inches by 4¾ inches): waxed tablets, dated to the seventh year of Septimius Severus (A.D. 198). The text, in Latin cursive, and a woman's signature, written for her, in incorrect Greek, occupy the two sides of the interior of the diptych, which are here represented (*above*, page 2 of the diptych; *below*, page 3). Bodleian Library, at Oxford, MS. *Lat. Class.*, f. 9–10.

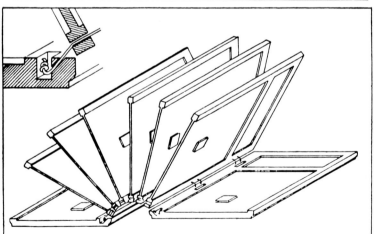

22.12. (*Above*) 'Page' from a *heptaptych* (British Museum, *Add. MS.* 33270); (*below*) *Octoptych* from Herculaneum, as reconstructed by M. Paolini.

22.13a. Triptych from Pompeii, dated A.D., 10.5.54.

22.13b. Latin papyrus, belonging to the 1st century A.D.

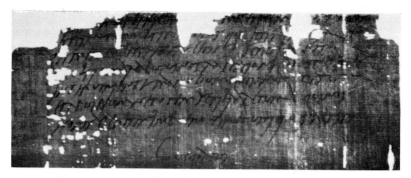

22.14*a*. Latin letter dated 7th October, A.D. 167 (British Museum, Pap. 730).

22.14*b*. Latin papyrus written on both sides: (left) obverse, military document of
A.D. 163–72; (right) reverse, fragment of an unknown grammatical treatise, early
3rd century A.D. (Archaeology Museum, Michigan University).

22.15 Inscription of Pupus Torquatianns. Roman cursive script, 3rd century A.D. (Vatican Museum).

22.16a. *Vatican Virgil* (Vatican Library, *Cod. Lat. 3225*).

22.16b. *Codex Vaticanus Vergilius*, folio 17r.

UICUMTEGREMICACCIPIETLAETISSIMADIDO
REGALISINTERMENSASLATICEMQUELACUM
CUMDABITAMPLEXUSADQUEOSCULADUICIAFIGET
OCCULTUMINSPIRESIGNEMFALLASQUEVENENO
PARETAMORDICTISCARAEGENETRICISETALAS

22.17a. *St. Gall Virgil*, in an elegant capital book hand of the 4th century A.D. (St. Gall, *Cod. no. 1394*).

ETIAMSUMMATAROCUTILLARUMCULMINATUMANE
MAIORISQUECADUNTALTISDEMONTIBUSUMBRAE

POETA   CORYDON
POEFORMOSUMCORYDONPASTORARDEBATALEXIN
DELICIASDOMININECQUIDSPERARETHABEBAT
TANTUMINTERDENSASUMBROSACACUMINAFAGOS
ADSIDUAEVENIEBATIBIHAECINCONDITASOLUS

22.17b. *Roman Virgil* (Vatican Library, *Cod. Lat. 3867*, fol. 3 *verso*).

389

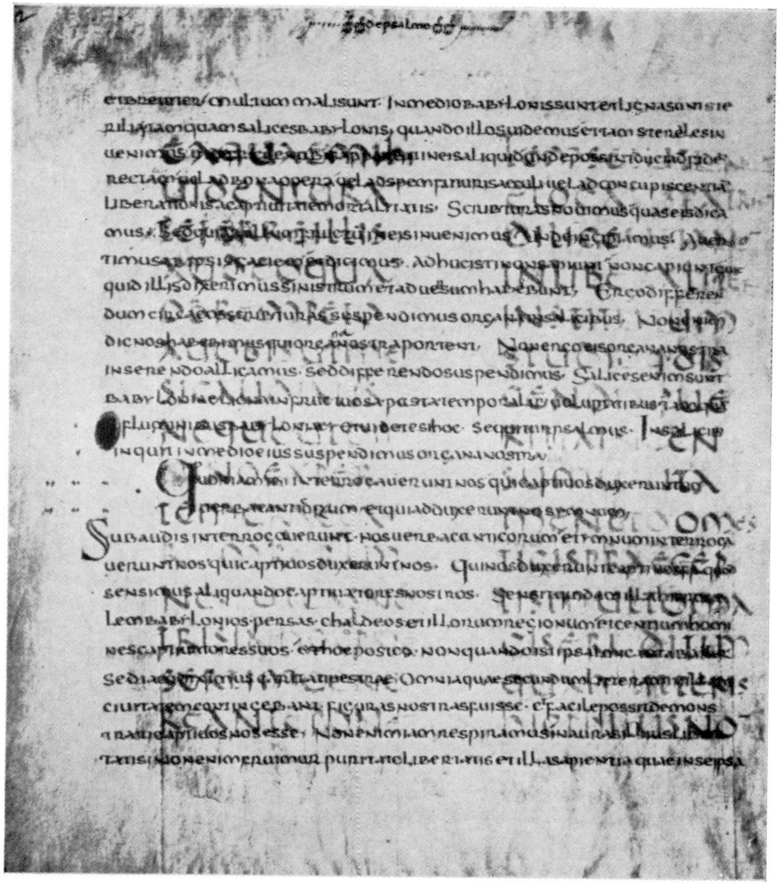

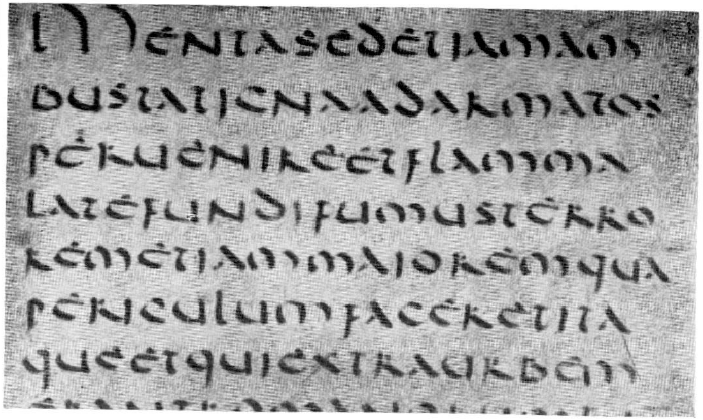

22.18. *a* (left) Palimpsest of Cicero's *De Republica.* Primary script, uncials of 4th or 5th century A.D., written in Italy. Re-written in 7th century, in Bobbio, to copy Augustine, *In Psalmos.* (Vatican Library, *Cod. Lat. 5757*). *b* (above) *Livius Lateranensis* (Livy, XXXIV), portion of a fragment consisting of seven pieces of parchment, forming a leaf and a half. 4th or 5th century A.D. In 1906 it was found in a cypress box made for Pope Leo III. 795–816. (Vatican Library, *Cod. Lat. 10696*).

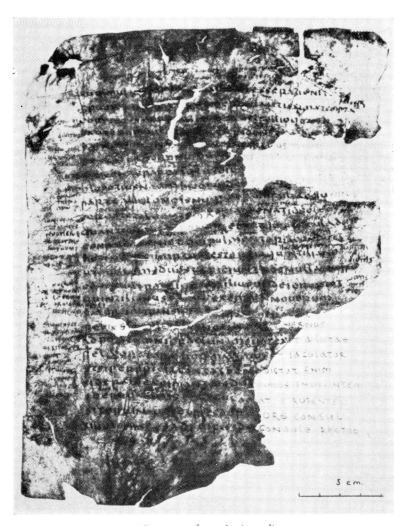

22.19 Fragment from Antinopolis.

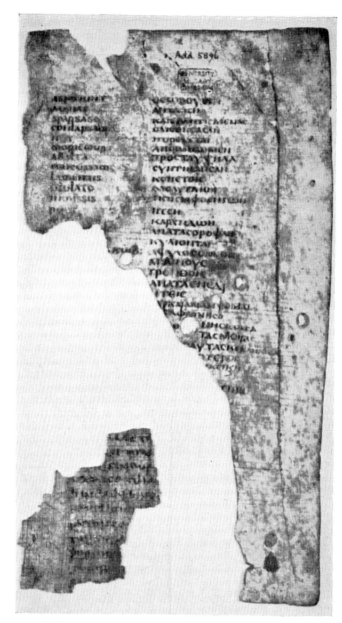

22.20. (*Above*) Virgil, Aeneid; fragment from a papyrus codex, written in half-uncial of the 5th century A.D. (University Library, Cambridge, *Add. MS. 4031*); (*insert*) *Latin-Greek lexicon for Aeneid* (University Library, Cambridge, *Add. MS. 5869*). Incomplete folio from a parchment codex written in uncials of the 6th century A.D. Both from Oxyrhynchus.

22.21. *Codex Bezae* (University Library, Cambridge, Nn. II, 41; fol. 304 *verso* and 305 *recto*).

22.22. *a* (above) The earliest Christian *Chronicle*. Jerome's Latin version of the *Chronicle* of Eusebius. The oldest known manuscript written in uncials, chiefly in three hands of the 5th and 6th centuries. (Bodleian Library, Oxford. MS. *Auct. T. II, 26*, fol. 121). *b* (left) *Codex Laudianus*, uncials, 6th century, probably written in Sardinia.

22.23. Primasius, *in Apocalypsium*, half-uncial of the 7th or 8th century (Bodleian Library, Oxford, *MS. Douce 140*).

22.24. *Codex Vercellensis* or *Eusebianus*, assigned to St. Eusebius, bishop of Vercelli, who died in 371 A.D. It is apparently the earliest preserved *Vetus Latina* codex (Capitulary Archives, Vercelli, North Italy).

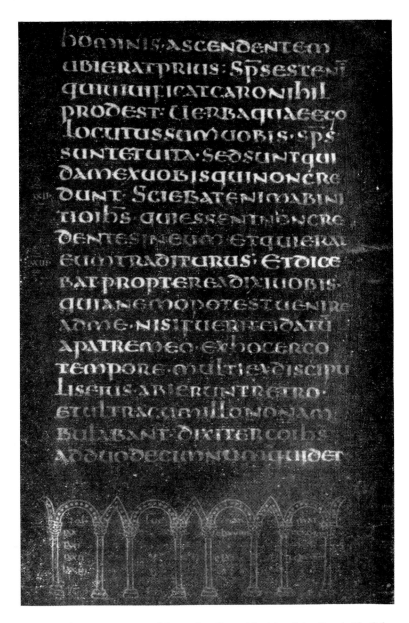

hominis ascendentem
ubierat prius: Sps est eni
qui uiuificat caro nihil
prodest: uerba quae eco
locutus sum uobis. sps
sunt et uita. sed sunt qui
dam ex uobis qui non cre
dunt. Sciebat enim ab ini
tio ihs qui essent non cre
dentes. et quis erat
eum traditurus: et dice
bat propterea dixi uobis.
quia nemo potest uenire
ad me. nisi fuerit ei datu
a patre meo. ex hoc ergo
tempore multi ex discipu
lis eius abierunt retro.
et ultra cum illo non am
bulabant. dixit ergo ihs
ad duodecim num quid et

22.25. *Codex Brixianus*, 418 folios of 20 lines. Uncials of the first half of the 6th century. Written in silver on purple stained vellum, the opening lines of the chapters being in gold. Contains Eusebius Caesariensis, *Canones evangeliorum* and the *Four Gospels* in the order of the *Vetus Latina* (Queriniana Library, Brescia, North Italy).

22.26. *Codex Palatinus*: (230 folios are preserved). The manuscript shown here is written in two columns of 20 lines, in silver on well prepared and deeply dyed parchment, the opening lines of *St. John* and *St. Luke* being in gold. Attributed to the 5th century A.D., and apparently the earliest preserved purple *Gospel* of the *Vetus Latina* (Trinity College, Dublin, *N. iv. 18*).

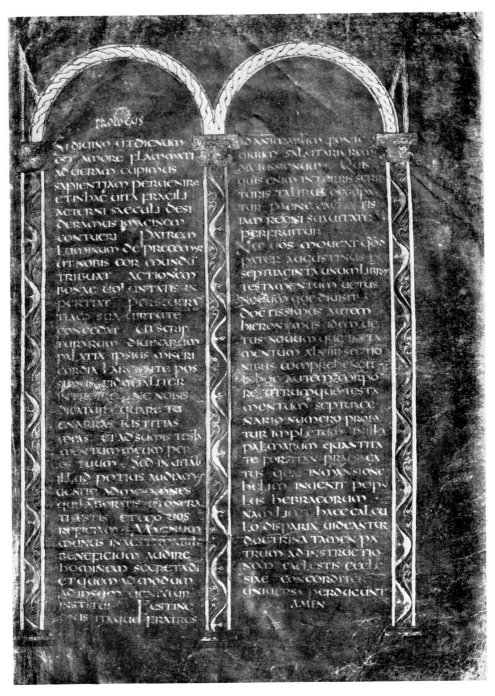

22.27. Codex Amiatinus, *c.* A.D. 700.

ecaelo filius sedhabeat
hominisqui uitamaeter
estincaelo nam nonerit
etsicutmoses misitds filiu
exaltauitser suuminmun
pentemindе dumutiudicet
serto itaexal mundum sed
tarioportet utsaluetur
filiumhomi mundusper
nis utomnis ipsum quicre
quicreditin ditineum non
ipsononpe iudicatur
reat sedha quiautem non
beatuitamae creditiamiu
ternam sic dicatusest
enimdilexit quinoncre
dsmundum ditinnomine
utfiliumsu unigeniti
umuniceni filiidi hoc
tumdaret estautem
utomnisqui iudicium quia
creditineum luxuenit
nonpereat inmundum

22.28. *Codex Claromontanus,* written in uncials of the 7th century, contains the Vulgate version (Vatican Library, *Cod. Lat. 7223,* fol. 230 *recto*).

22.29. *a* *Codex Ottobonianus*, contains the *Pentateuch* in Vulgate version with parts in *Vetus Latina*. N. Italy, 7th or 8th century A.D. (Vatican Library, *Off. Lat. 66*, fol. 52 *recto*). *b* Oldest complete copy of *Hexameron* by Ambrose. Written in 8th century minuscule at Corbie (Corpus Christi College, Cambridge, MS. 193).

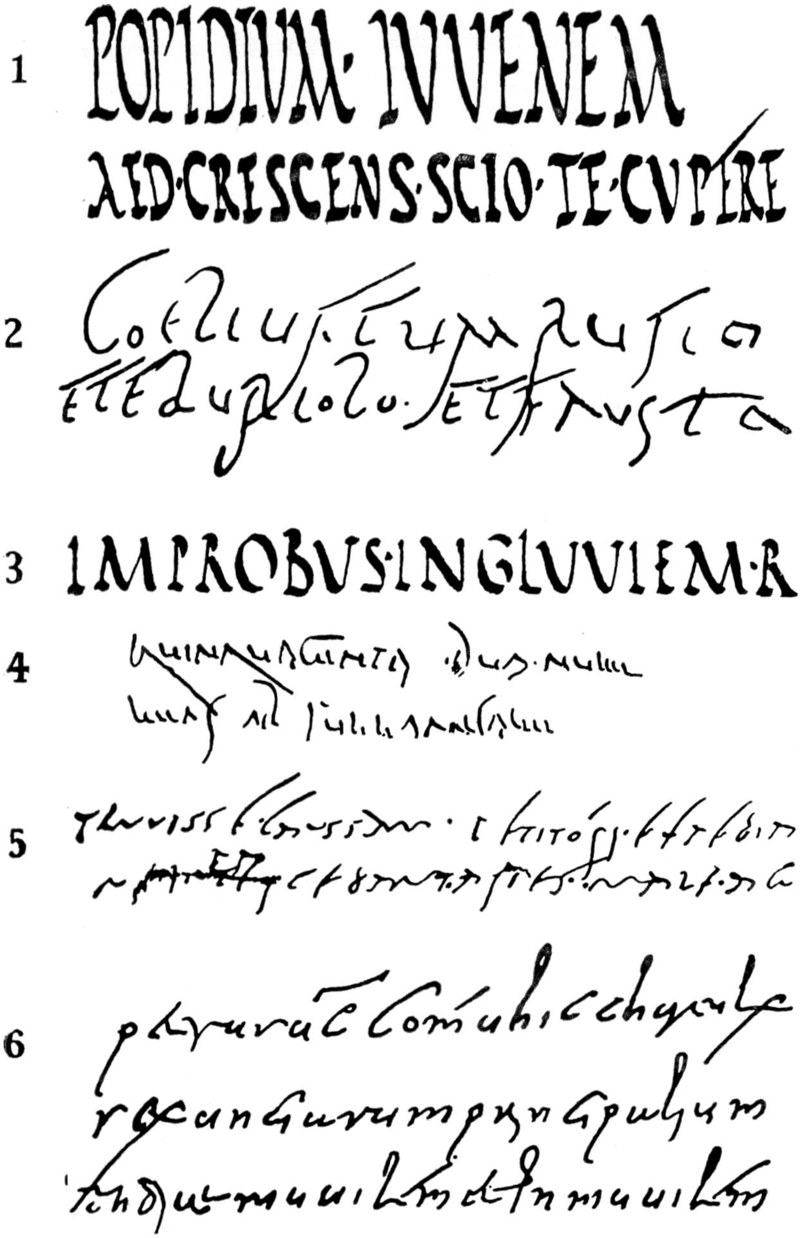

1 POPIDIVM· IVVENEM

AED·CRESCENS·SCIO·TE·CVPIRE

2 *(handwritten script)*

3 IMPROBVSINGLVVIEMR

4 *(handwritten script)*

5 *(handwritten script)*

6 *(handwritten script)*

22.30. Specimens of Latin scripts, I (G. Battelli, *Lezioni di Paleografia*, Città del Vaticano, 1936).

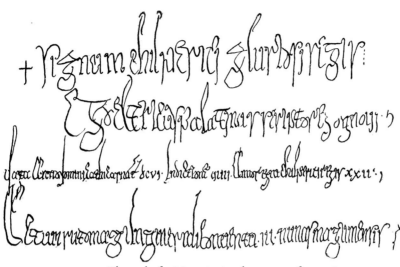

22.31*a*. The end of a Merovingian document of A.D. 583.

2l athain ḟil hi nimib, Noemthan thainm. Toṟt oc ḟlaithiuṟ. Oio oo toil i tálmain amail ata in nim. Tab ṇ oun moiu an ṟaṟao lathi. Ocuṟ loṣ oun an ḟiachu amail

22.31*b*. Specimen of Irish script, 9th century A.D.

1, Rustic capitals, A.D. 79
    (Pompeii, painted wall-inscription)

2, Majuscule cursive, A.D. 79
    (Pompeii, graffito)

3, Rustic capitals
    (MS., fifth century A.D., Vergil; *Cod.*
    Vat. Lat. 3867)

4, Majuscule cursive, A.D. 57
    (Wax tablet, Naples)

5, Majuscule cursive, A.D. 51–54
    (*Papyrus Claudius*, Berlin)

6, Minuscule cursive, seventh century A.D.
    (*Papyrus Marini XC*; document from
    Ravenna)

Popidium . iuvenem
aed [*ilem*] *. Crescens . scio . te . cupere*
Coelius . cum Rufio
et Eburiolo . et Fausto
improbus . ingluviem . r[*anisque*]

quinquaginta . dua . num [=]
mos ob fullonicam
tenuisse . caussam . petitori . expedia [*t*]
ne procedant [corrected from *intercedant*]
    artes . male . ag [*entibus*]
Petrus vir clarissimus com. uhic chartule
sex unciarum principalium
[*subs*] *tantiae muvilem et inmuvilem*

a   aromuociuarolldmniteæro
odromanæ lorumurrupdus

b   proferrem nonqueror quia
ro redtamen quaerella seum

c   solis profunuacionib æpro
funuacionib cuncas:

d   Et cu unus sit iudex sensus cerebri
quiinrinsæcur psidæ pme te tu

e   Siquir hr eorum quippue errenoruntur aeccl
aut prnuerbitegr autdiaconus porthanc depi

f   cauit interualla ramorum amplitudinis ratio
umbre cuiusque arboris quoniam has quoque

g   q̃ suo principi se obligasset: sed in decretali nra nusue por
tius obligationes cernuntur, et Imperialis sublimitas in

h   UAEAUTEMPRAES
NANTIBUSETIACTA

22.32. Specimens of Latin scripts, II (G. Batelli, *Lezioni di Paleografia*, etc.).

ne·uolumtate·di pat

22.33a. Anglo-Irish semi-uncials of the 7th century A.D. Gospel of St. Chad, now at Lichfield.

& predicatione uof faciat implere digna con

22.33b. Winchester School hand, 11th century (Bibliothéque National, Paris).

abrdrfghiklmnopqrzfstuwrhz

22.33c. The 'black letter' or Gothic hand.

---

a, Minuscule semi-cursive, eighth century A.D.
(St. Maximus, Milan, Bibl. Ambros.)

b, Semi-uncials, prior to A.D. 509–510
(St. Hilarius; Rome, Arch. Cap. di S. Pietro)

c, Visigothic, A.D. 954
(Escorial, Madrid)

d, Germanic pre-Caroline, eighth–ninth century A.D.
(St. Gregory, Bibl. Ap. Vatic.)

e, Anglo-Saxon minuscule as employed on the continent; Mainz, Germany, eighth–ninth century A.D.
(Bibl. Ap. Vatic.)

f, Round humanistic or renaissance hand, fifteenth century A.D.
(Plinius, Bibl. Ap. Vatic.)

g, Cursive humanistic, fifteenth century A.D.
(M. Salamonio, Bibl. Ap. Vatic.)

h, Uncials, fourth century A.D.
(St. Gallen)

. . . arum votiva solemnitate so [let]
[*qu*]*od remanet et suavius sapere*
proferrem non queror quia
[*igno*]*ro sed tamen quærella fam*[osa]

solis profanatoribus et pro[—]
fanationibus cunctis
Et cum unus sit iudex sensus cerebri
qui intrinsecus presidet permeatu[s]

si quis autem eorum qui præesse noscuntur.
æccl[esiae]
aut . praesbiter . aut . diaconus post hanc defi-
[*nitionem*]
[*diiudi*]*cavit intervalla ramorum*
amplitudinis ratio
umbræ cuiusque arboris . quoniam has quoque
quam suo principi se. obligasset: sed in decretali
nostra mutue po[—]
tius obligationes . cernuntur. et imperialis
sublimitas in-
Vae autem praeg[—]
nantibus et lactan[—]

1

2

3

4

5

6

7

8

9

10

11

22.35. *Sacramentary* by Gelasius written at Corbie in the 8th century (Vatican Library, *Reg. Lat. 316*, fol. *46 recto*).

22.34. Specimens of manuscripts written in 'national' hands. (*1*) Merovingian (in France), 7th century A.D.; (*2*) Merovingian, 8th century; (*3*) Visigothic minuscule (in Spain), 945; (*4*) Visigothic cursive script, before 779; (*5*) Visigothic, 11th century; (*6*) Roman minuscule, 9th century (*Vitae Sanctorum: Farfa codex*); (*7*) North Italian pre-Caroline minuscule (*Codex 490*, Capitulary Library, Lucca); (*8*) Idem, late 8th century; (*9*) Idem, 8th–9th century (upper part, uncial script); (*10*) Beneventan script, from Cassino, 8th century; (*11*) Idem, 11th century.

22.36. Priscian manuscript written in England, presumably at Canterbury, 'in a very fine hand' of the 8th century (Corpus Christi College, Cambridge, MS. 144).

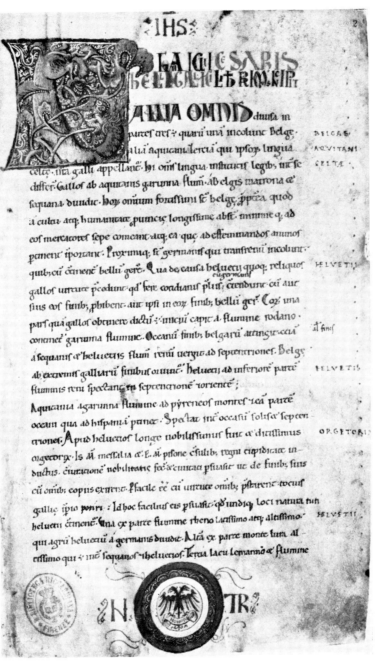

22.37. Caesar C.V. *Commentaria* 11th century (Bibl. Ricc. Florence).

22.38. (*Above*) A 12th-century codex of Terence, from south-west France (Vatican Library, *Vat. Lat. 3305*); (*below*) Plautus (British Museum, *Royal MS. 15, C. xi*, fol. 56).

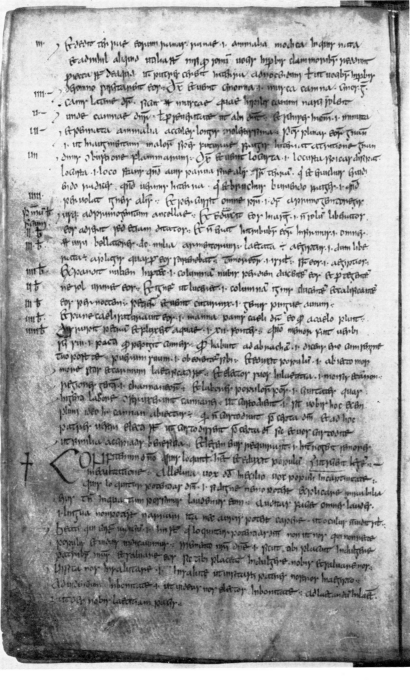

22.39. Codex Palatinus, 8th century A.D. (Trinity College Library, Dublin).

22.40. *a Book of Kells.* St.
Matthew's Gospel Folio 12r
(Trinity College Library,
Dublin). *b Book of Dimma,*
p. 31 (Trinity College Lib-
rary, Dublin).

22.41. (*Above*) Origines, *Homiliae in Lucam*, 8th- or 9th-century minuscule (Corpus Christi College, Cambridge, MS. 334). (*below*) *Varia Medica*, including Hippocrates and Galenus (University Library, Glasgow, *Hunterian MS. T.4.13*, fol. 99 *recto*; it is written in 'a curious and awkward mixed minuscule (Visigothic, Beneventan, Caroline . . . . .') (Lowe)).

413

22.42. St. Cyril of Alexandria (d. 444), *Thesaurus adversus haereticos*, transl. by Alphonsus Jorge of Trebizonda. The illuminated border shows in the upper part the Catalan royal arms, and in the lower part those of Naples. The codex, written in Italy, belonged to Alfonso V the Magnanimous (1416–58), king of Aragon, Sicily and Naples (Central Library, Barcelona, MS. 561, fol. 1).

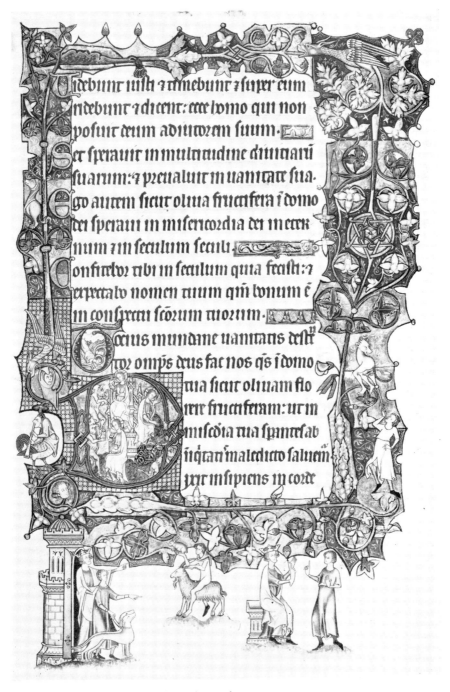

idebunt iusti z timebunt z super eum
ridebunt z dicent: ecce homo qui non
posuit deum adiutorem suum.
er sperauit in multitudine diuitiarū
suarum: z preualuit in uanitate sua.
go autem sicut oliua fructifera i domo
dei sperabi in misericordia dei in eter
num z in seculum seculi.
onfitebor tibi in seculum quia fecisti: z
expectabo nomen tuum qm bonum e
in conspectu sanctorum tuorum.
ocius mundane uanitatis deser
tor omps deus fac nos qs i domo
tua sicut oliuam flo
rere fructiferam: ut in
misedia tua sperantes ab
sitq̄ta māledicto salutem
perit insipiens in corde

22.43. *Ormesby Psalter*, psalm 52, v. 8–11, *c.* 1300–25.

22.44a. *Luttrell Psalter:* Gothic 'liturgical hand', *c.* 1340.

22.44b. *A Book containing divers Sortes of Hands,* by John de Beauchesne and John Basildon, 1571.

22.45. English Court hands: note the Saxon letters surviving.

ABCDEFGHIJKLMNOPQRSTUVW
abcdefghijklmnopqrstuvwxyz

ABCDEFGHIJKLM
abcdefghijklmnopqrstuv

ABCDEFGHIJKLMNOPQRSTUVWXYZ
abcdefghijklmnopqrstuvwxyz

ABCDEFGHIJKLMN
abcdefghijklmnopqrstuvwx

ABCDEFGHIJKLMNOPQRSTUVWXYZ
abcdefghijklmnopqrstuvwxyz

ABCDEFGHI JKLMNOPQRSTUVWXYZ
abcdefghijklmnopqrstuvwxyz

ABCDEFGHIJKLM
abcdefghijklmnopqrstuvw

ABCDEFGHI JKLMNOPQRSTUVWX
abcdefghijklmnopqrstuvwxyz

ABCDEFGHIJKLM
abcdefghijklmnopqrstuvw

ABCDEFGHIJKLMNOPQRSTUVWXYZ
abcdefghijklmnopqrstuvwxyz

ABCDEFGHIJKLMNOP
abcdefghijklmnopqrstu

ABCDEFGHIJKLMNOPQRSTUVW
abcdefghijklmnopqrstuvwxyz

ABCDEFGHIJKL
abcdefghijklmnopqrst

ABCDEFGHIJKLMNOPQRSTUVWXYZ
abcdefghijklmnopqrstuvwxyz

ABCDEFGHIJKLMNO
abcdefghijklmnopqrstuvwxy

ABCDEFGHIJKLMNOPQRSTUV
abcdefghijklmnopqrstuvwxyz

ABCDEFGHIJKLM
abcdefghijklmnopqrst

22.46. Mid 20th century type. Text faces.

ABCDEFGHIJKLMN OPQRSTUVWXYZ abcdefghijklmnopqrs tuvwxyz

ABCDEFGHIJKLM NOPQRSTUVWXY abcdefghijklmnopq rstuvwxyz

ABCDEFGHIJKL MNOPQRSTUV WXYZ

22.47. Mid 20th century type. Display and title faces.

MISTRAL

ABCDEFGHIJKLMNOPQ
RSTUVWXYZ
abcdefghijklmnopqrstuvwx

ASHLEY

ABCDEFGHIJKLMNOPQRSTUVWX
YZ

abcdefghijklmnopqrstuvwxyz

PEPITA

ABCDEFGHIJKLMNOP
QRSTUVWXYZ
abcdefghijklmnopqrstuvwxyz

FRANCESCA RONDE

ABCDEFGHIJK
LMNOPQRSTUV
abcdeefghijklmnopqrstuvwxyz

22.48. Mid 20th century type. Script faces.

ABCDEFGHIJKLM NOPQRSTUVWX abcdefghijklmnop qrstuvwxyz

ABCDEFGHIJKLM NOPQRSTUVWXY abcdefghijklmnop qrstuvwxyz

22.49. Mid 20th century type. Script faces.

Development of lower case — comparative table of letterforms.

Roman Cursive Majuscule	Roman Cursive Minuscule	Roman Uncials	Roman Semi-Uncials	Anglo-Saxon Majuscule	Caroline Minuscule	"Gothic"	Venetian Min.(Italic)	N.Italian Min.Roman	Mod. Lower Case Gothic	Mod. Lower Case Italic	Mod. Lower Case Roman
λ	u	A	a	a	a	a	a	a	a	a	a
	ẞ	B	b	b	b	b	b	b	b	b	b
	c	C	c	c	c	c	c	c	c	c	c
	d	D		d	d	d	d	d	d	d	d
	E	E	e	e	e	e	e	e	e	e	e
F	v	F	f	f	f	f	f	f	f	f	f
5	h	G	s	s	s	g	g	s	g	g	g
H	i	H	h	h	h	h	h	h	h	h	h
I		I	l	l	l	i	i	l	i	i	i
		J				j	j		j	j	j
		K				k	k		k	k	k
		L				l	l		l	l	l
l	m	M	l	l	l	m	m	l	m	m	m
	n	N	m	m	m	n	n	m	n	n	n
	d	O	n	n	n	o	o	n	o	o	o
O	f	P	o	o	o	p	p	o	p	p	p
P	u	Q	p	p	p	q	q	p	q	q	q
	v	R	q	q	q	r	r	q	r	r	r
	T	S	r	r	r	s	s	r	s	s	s
	4	T	s	s	s	t	t	s	t	t	t
T		U	t	t	t	u	u	t	u	u	u
		V	u	u	u	v		u	v	v	v
u		W				w			w	w	w
x	x	X	x	x	x	x	x	x	x	x	x
y	y	Y				y	y		y	y	y
z	z	Z				z	z		z	z	z

22.50. Development of lower case.

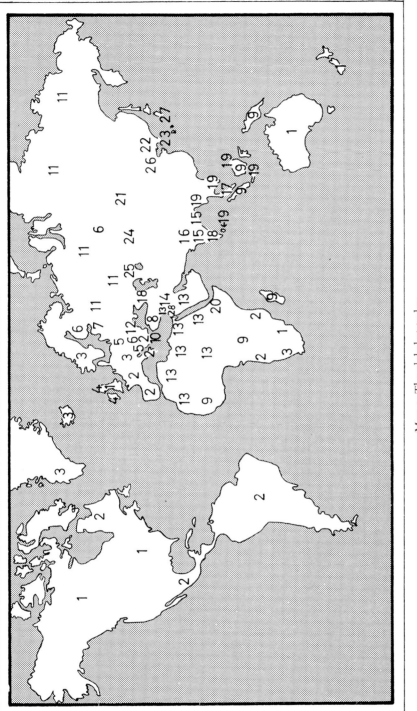

Map 4. The alphabet today.

1. English
2. Romance Branch
3. Germanic Branch (excl. English)
4. Celtic Branch
5. W.-Slavonic Branch
6. Finno-Ugrian Branch
7. Baltic Branch
8. Modern Turkish

9. Recent Adaptations of Latin Alphabet
10. Greek Alphabet
11. Cyrillic: Russian Alphabets
12. Cyrillic: Serbian and Bulgarian Alphabets
13. Arabic Alphabet
14. Persian–Arabic Alphabet

15. Urdu Alphabet
16. Pashtu Alphabet
17. Malay–Arabic Alphabet
18. Armenian and Georgian Alphabets
19. Indian and Further Indian Branch
20. Ethiopic Script
21. Mongolian Alphabet
22. Manchurian Alphabet

23. Korean Alphabet
24. Turco–Tatar Languages in Arabic Characters
25. Turco–Tatar Languages in Russian characters
26. Chinese Scripts
27. Japanese Scripts
28. Hebrew Alphabet.

III. The Alphabet by rote
42 characters§

1.	æ	ae	25.	ʧh	ith
2.	b	bee	26.	ʃh	thee
3.	ʧh	chee	27.	ʃh	ish
		(see)	28.	ȝ	zhee
4.	d	dee	29.	ŋ	ing
5.	ee	ee	30.	aa	ahv
6.	f	ef	31.	a	at
7.	g	gae	32.	e	et
8.	h	hae	33.	i	it
9.	ie	ie	34.	o	ot
10.	j	jae	35.	u	ut
11.	k	kae	36.	au	aul
12.	l	el	37.	ω	foot
13.	m	em	38.	ꞷ	brood
14.	n	en	39.	ou	owl
15.	œ	oe	40.	oi	oil
16.	p	pee			
		(kue)		———	
17.	r	rae			
18.	s	ess	41.	ʑ	zess
19.	t	tee	42.	wh	whae
20.	ue	ue			
21.	v	vee			
22.	w	wae			
		(eks)			
23.	y	yae			
24.	z	zed or zee			

22.51. Augmented Roman alphabet.

helpiŋ ϸe bliend man

loŋ agœ ϸær livd a
bliend man. hee livd whær
trees and flouers grœ; but
ϸe bliend man cœd not see
ϸe trees or flouers.

ϸe pœr man had tœ feel
ϸe wæ to gœ wiϸ his stick.
tap-tap-tap went his stick on
ϸe rœd. hee waukt slœly.

22.52. Specimen of writing in the INITIAL TEACHING
ALPHABET.

hamlet

bie William ſhækspeer

from act ſhree, ſeen wun

hamlet: tω bee, or not tω bee: ſhat is ſhe kwestion:
　Wheſher 'tis nœbler in ſhe miend tω suffer
　ſhe slings and arræs ov outræjus fortuen,
　. Or tω tæk arms agænst a see ov trubls,
　and bie oppœsing end ſhem. tω die: tω sleep;
　nœ mor; and bie a sleep tω sæ wee end
　ſhe hart-æc, and ſhe ſhousand natueral ſhocks
　ſhat fleſh is ær tω, 'tis a consummæſhon
　devoutly tω bee wiſht. tω die, tω sleep;
　tω sleep: perchans tω dreem; ie, ſhær's ſhe rub;
　for in ſhat sleep ov deſh whot dreems mæ cum,
　When wee hav ſhuffld off ſhis mortal coil,
　Must giv us paus: ſhær's ſhe respect
　ſhat mæks calamity ov sœ long lief;
　for hω wωd bær ſhe whips and scorns ov ſhem,
　ſhe oppressor's rong, ſhe proud man's contuemly,
　ſhe pangs ov dispieſed luv, ſhe lau's delæ,
　ſhe insolens ov offis, and ſhe spurns
　ſhat pæſhient merit ov ſhe unwurſhy tæks,

22.53. Hamlet in INITIAL TEACHING ALPHABET.

426

	Bi-labial	Labio-dental	Dental and Alveolar	Retroflex	Palato-alveolar	Alveolo-palatal	Palatal	Velar	Uvular	Pharyngal	Glottal
Plosive	p b		t d	ʈ ɖ			c ɟ	k g	q ɢ		ʔ
Nasal	m	ɱ	n	ɳ			ɲ	ŋ	N		
Lateral Fricative			ɬ ɮ								
Lateral Non-fricative			l	ɭ			ʎ				
Rolled			r						R		
Flapped			ɾ	ɽ					R		
Fricative	ɸ β	f v	θ ð s z ɹ	ʂ ʐ	ʃ ʒ	ɕ ʑ	ç j	x ɣ	χ ʁ	ħ ʕ	h ɦ
Frictionless Continuants and Semi-vowels	w ɥ	ʋ	ɹ				j (ɥ)	(w)	ʁ		

		Front	Central	Back	
Close	(y ʉ u)	i y	ɨ ʉ	ɯ u	
Half-close	(ø o)	e ø	ɘ	ɤ o	
Half-open	(œ ɔ)	ɛ œ	ɜ ɞ	ʌ ɔ	
Open	(ɒ)	a	æ ɐ	ɑ ɒ	

(Secondary articulations are shown by symbols in brackets.)

OTHER SOUNDS.—Palatalized consonants: ṭ, ḍ, etc.; palatalized ʃ, ʒ: ƒ, ʒ. Velarized or pharyngalized consonants: ɫ, ḍ, z, etc. Ejective consonants (with simultaneous glottal stop): p', t', etc. Implosive voiced consonants: ɓ, ɗ, etc. r fricative trill. σ, ϱ (labialized θ, ð, or s, z). ʮ ʯ (labialized ʃ, ʒ). ƪ, ƫ, ƈ, ƕ (clicks, Zulu c, q, x). l (a sound between r and l). ŋ Japanese syllabic nasal. ƕ (combination of x and ʃ). ʍ (voiceless w). ɩ, ʏ, ɷ (lowered varieties of i, y, u). ɜ (a variety of ə). ɵ (a vowel between ø and o).

Affricates are normally represented by groups of two consonants (ts, tʃ, dʒ, etc.), but, when necessary, ligatures are used (ʦ, ʧ, ʤ, etc.), or the marks ⌒ or ‿ (t͡s or t‿s, etc.). ⌒ also denote synchronic articulation (m͡ŋ = simultaneous m and ŋ). c, ɟ may occasionally be used in place of tʃ, dʒ, and ʒ, 2 for ts, dz. Aspirated plosives: ph, th, etc. r-coloured vowels: eɹ, aɹ, ɔɹ, etc., or eˏ, aˏ, ɔˏ, etc., or ɚ, aˏ, etc.; r-coloured ə: aɹ or aˏ or ɹ or ɹˏ.

LENGTH, STRESS, PITCH.— ː (full length). ˑ (half length). ˈ (stress, placed at beginning of the stressed syllable). ˌ (secondary stress). ˉ (high level pitch); ˍ (low level); ʹ (high rising); ˏ (low rising); ˋ (high falling); ˎ (low falling); ˆ (rise-fall); ˇ (fall-rise).

MODIFIERS.— ˜ nasality. ˳ breath (l̥ = breathed l). ˬ voice (s̬ = z). ˙ slight aspiration following p, t, etc. ˌ labialization (n̩ = labialized n). ̪ dental articulation (t̪ = dental t). ˴ palatalization (z̴ = ʒ). ˒ specially close vowel (e̗ = a very close e). ˓ specially open vowel (e̖ = a rather open e). ˔ tongue raised (e˔ or ẹ = e). ˕ tongue lowered (e˕ or ẹ = ɛ). ˖ tongue advanced (u˖ or u̟ = an advanced u, t̟ = t̟). ˗ or ˍ tongue retracted (i˗ or i̱ = ɨ, ṯ = alveolar t). ˙ lips more rounded. ˒ lips more spread. Central vowels: ï (= ɨ), ü (= ʉ), ë (= ə), ë (= ɵ), ö (= ɵ), ɛ̈, ö̈. ˌ (e.g. n̩) syllabic consonant. ˑ consonantal vowel. ʃ variety of ʃ resembling s, etc.

22.54. The INTERNATIONAL ALPHABET. Revised to 1951.

Nyanja

'Nyanja' is a Bantu term; the word is variously spelt ('Nyanza,' 'Nyasa,' 'Nyassa,' etc.). The Nyanja are a Bantu negroid people of eastern central Africa, living mainly in the Nyasaland Protectorate, lying between northern Rhodesia, Portuguese East Africa, Tanganyika Territory and the Lake Nyasa. The Nyanja dialects, spoken by over 1,500,000 people, are the most interesting group of the whole Bantu family of languages. According to Sir Harry H. Johnston, there are 'two hundred and twenty-six distinct Bantu languages of present times.' These are spoken in nearly the whole of the southern third of Africa, and constitute a very distinct type of speech 'which, as contrasted with others amongst the groups of negro tongues, is remarkable as a rule for the Italian melodiousness, simplicity and frequency of its vowel sounds, and the comparative ease with which its exemplars can be acquired and spoken by Europeans' (Johnston).

Tamvelani Bwana Diringer,

Ndikondwera ndí kulola kuti kalatai ífalítsídwe m'bukhu wanu wa A B C, monga císanzo ca malembedwe a Cinyanja, ndíganiza cifuno canu cidzakwanila.

Ndine wanu,

Bennett E. Malekebu.

Twi

This language is known by many terms: Twi (originally Kwi or Ekwi, Okwi), Oji or Odshi, Tyi, Chwee or Tshi, Amina, Ashanti, etc. It is a Sudanese form of speech, belonging to the great prefix-pronominal group, and is spoken by about 1,000,000 people living in the Gold Coast Colony and in part of the French colony of the Ivory Coast. Twi, like most African languages, is divided into a number of dialects. Indeed, 'Akuapem, Asante, Akyem and Fante as well as other closely related dialects form the Akan group of languages,' but 'the name Twi has been used for the whole of this group excluding Fante.' 'It would be wise now to adopt Twi as the general name, and in making reference to special forms of the language, to call them Akuapem Twi, Asante Twi, Akyem Twi, etc.' (I.C. Ward). Twi has been written for over 100 years.

Ɔdɔfo Dr. Diringer,

Eyɛ me Thomas Boatin a meboa wɔ Asante Kasa kyerɛ mu wɔ "School of Oriental and African Studies" wɔ London na merekyerɛ wo.

Meda wo ase wɛ wo krataa a woakyerɛ me no ho.

Woabisa me nsa ano krataa sin yi a wopɛ sɛ wode yɔ Twii-ŋkyerɛ ŋhwesɔɔ wɔ wo ŋwoma a ɛfa ŋkyerɛ-Nsɛnkyerɛnce ho no mu. Mede anigye reyɔ wo adesrɛdeɛ. na mewɔ andisasɔɔ sɛ eyi bɛkerɛ deɛ wohwehwe.

Mekyia wo.

Conclusion I. Latin Script adapted to African Languages

Yoruba

The Yoruba are a higher grade and commercially-minded negro people speaking a Sudanese language. They number about 3,000,000 and inhabit the south-west corner of Nigeria from the sea to Jebba and from Dahomey to the borders of the Bini State. The Nago of the Dahomey coast region and, partly, the Bini, are related to them. The Yoruba language ranks as one of the three chief languages of Nigeria. The first Yoruba dictionary, compiled by (an ex-slave and afterwards bishop) Samuel Crowther, was published in 1843.

Dr. Diringer,

Alagba,

Mo gbe pe e fe ki nko iwe kekere kan ti e ó tè sinu iwe yin leri 'Alphabet,' lati fi se apere bi àá ti ikowe l'ede Yoruba.

Tayotayo ni mo fí kowe yi ni sókí, mo si rò pe yio bá, l'ona ti e fe lò o si.

Ke epe o!

Emi ni

E. L. Lasebikan.

Efik

This interesting Sudanese language, spoken by some 50,000 people in Calabar, Nigeria, was reduced to writing about the middle of the last century. *See* also p. 29 f., 148 ff., and 564 f.

Edima Ete,

Mmenem esit ndinwam ye ekpri ŋwed emi ndisin ke ŋwed fo emi abaŋade A B C, ndiwut nte ewetde usem Efik, mmodori enyin nte emi eyekem ye udwak fo.

Okuo ke akpanikɔ,

Nyoŋ Ekanem.

Conclusion 2. Latin script adapted to African languages.

⊤ 1 airi	𝖠 15 fingo	L△ 29 ɛdipikn
4 2 grɛid	ᚼ 16 tiɛtɔ	L7 30 ɛdipaːriːd
⚏ 3 sɛːtaː	ꓕ 17 ʌigɛt	LH 31 ɛditrita
▽ 4 aidü	ꓕ 18 kisani	LH 32 ɛdikanapt
⯎ 5 dʒitɔ	Є 19 siːtriːk	LHH 33 ɛdifaigi
⅄ 6 tarisi	LΘ 20 ɛdiːtiɔ	LX 34 ɛdifudipt
↓ 7 fuda	LL 21 ɛdiari	L△ 35 ɛdifiŋgo
↑ 8 ɛitia	L1 22 ɛdigrɛid	LH 36 ɛditiɛtɔ
△ 9 pikn	L⅂ 23 ɛdisɛːtaː	Lꓕ 37 ɛdiʌigɛt
⊤ 10 paːriːd	L▽ 24 ɛdiaidu	L⯎ 38 ɛdikisaːni
H 11 tritaː	L⯎ 25 ɛdidʒitɔ	LЄ 39 ɛdisiːtriːk
H 12 kanapt	L⅄ 26 ɛditarisi	4Θ 40 krɛido
HH 13 faigi	L↓ 27 ɛdifuda	△Θ 60 sɛtado
X 14 fudipt	L↑ 28 ɛditia	▽Θ 80 aidudo
	⯎Θ 100 dʒitɔdo	

a   *b*

Here is the Obɛri Ɔkaimɛ script reduced to roman type with the addition of ɔ and ŋ. The question-mark represents an unrecognizable symbol.

1. D. ɔksiritues drins fra nimazidiŋ ? umilen ?
2. ? peprit dɛi wɔkri fra dzjias o, gizin, dei kalikist
3. bolin elimontas pdzjoprim amitriŋ seniɔ vɔida
4. ruzɔrd mium slanint fra dzjas o, gizin,
5. ventaismint gizin atiɛfpts kn riks dzjibreant
6. ? nɔminent badzjba fra kenod duma arien seslin enedium
7. nipdzjin pinstrik anivad (symbol for ' or ') zu rotri kivziɔ
8. bisanetksi b ? eam beda riks futrim (symbol for ' or ') bulɔ dapori
9. ? alimoti eis kɔlen abel saprivos andea dei
10. kalamiusiŋ eis kɔlen abel dei ? ramuksi fɔŋ
11. nip ? zin snani zu vus kɔruvik diup etuals seraus
12. kɔlenkist pos dzba talimaiŋ liu ? ad dei rituel
13. ksirin dei ? ɔmi ? en kn dei marr due apinkɔri

c

Conclusion 3. Oberi Okaime script. *a* Numerals, *b* a portion of the script, *c* transliterations.

VOWELS		OLD PHONETIC SYMBOLS	WADE SYSTEM	INTERNATIONAL PHONETIC SYMBOLS	APPROXIMATE ENGLISH SOUND
PRINT	SCRIPT				
A a	*a a*	ㄚ	a	a·	a (as in ar)
O o	*o o*	ㄜ	o	ɔ·	aw (as in law)
E e	*ɛ e*	ㄜ	ê,o	ɘ·	er (as in her)
I i	*ɡ i*	ㄧ	i	i·	ee (as in bee)
U u	*U u*	ㄨ	u	u·	oo (as in too)
Y y	*Y y*	ㄩ	ü	y·	German ü

CONSONANTS		OLD PHONETIC SYMBOLS	WADE SYSTEM	INTERNATIONAL PHONETIC SYMBOLS	APPROXIMATE ENGLISH SOUND
PRINT	SCRIPT				
B b	*B b*	ㄅ	p	p	b (but not voiced)
P p	*P p*	ㄆ	p'	p'	p (strongly aspirated)
M m	*m m*	ㄇ	m	m	m
F f	*F f*	ㄈ	f	f	f
D d	*D d*	ㄉ	t	t	d (but not voiced)
T t	*J t*	ㄊ	t'	t'	t (strongly aspirated)
N n	*n n*	ㄋ	n	n	n
L l	*L l*	ㄌ	l	l	l
G g	*g g*	ㄍ	k	k	g (hard, but not voiced)
K k	*K k*	ㄎ	k'	k'	k (strongly aspirated)
Ŋ ŋ	*ŋ ŋ*	ㄫ	ng	ŋ	ng (final)
H h	*H h*	ㄏ	h	x	h (aspirated, partly like ch in Scottish loch)
Ч ч	*U u*	ㄐ	ch(i)	tɕ	j
Q q	*2 q*	ㄑ	ch'(i)	tɕ'	ch
X x	*X x*	ㄒ	hs(i)	ɕ	sh (palatal)
Z z	*Z z*	ㄓ	ch	tʂ	j or dg'
Ç ç	*C ç*	ㄔ	ch'	tʂ'	ch (strongly aspirated)
Ş ş	*S ş*	ㄕ	sh	ʂ	sh (as in shore)
R r	*R r*	ㄖ	j	ʐ	r (tending towards the z in azure)
Z z	*Z z*	ㄗ	ts(tz)	ts	ds (but not voiced)
C c	*C c*	ㄘ	ts'	ts'	ts (strongly aspirated)
S s	*S s*	ㄙ	s,ss,sz	s	s
J j	*J j*	ㄧ	y	j	y
W w	*W w*	ㄨ	w	w	w

Conclusion 4. Adaptation of alphabetic scripts to Chinese.

Final		Old Phonetic Symbols	Wade System	Inter— national Phonetic Symbols	Approxmate English Sound
a:	ai	ㄞ	ai	aɪ	long i (as in eye)
	au	ㄠ	ao	ao	ow (as in how)
	an	ㄢ	an	an	an (as in can)
	aŋ	ㄤ	ang	aŋ	ang (as in sang)
o:	ou	ㄡ	ou	ou	o (as in note)
e:	ei	ㄟ	ei	eɪ	ay (as in way)
	en	ㄣ	en	ɔn	un (as in French)
	eŋ	ㄥ	êng	ɔŋ or ʌŋ	(no exact equivalent)
i:	ia	ㄧㄚ	ia	ia	yah
	ie	ㄧㄝ	ieh	ie	ye (as in yes)
	iau	ㄧㄠ	iao	iao	yow (as in yowl)
	iu	ㄧㄡ	iu	iɔu	u (as in unite)
	ian	ㄧㄢ	ien	iɛn	e en (as in the end
	in	ㄧㄣ	in	in	een (as in keen)
	iaŋ	ㄧㄤ	iang	iaŋ	yan (as in yankee)
	iŋ	ㄧㄥ	ing	iŋ	ing (as in sing)
u:	ua	ㄨㄚ	ua	ua	wah
	uo	ㄨㄛ	uo	uɔ	wa (as in water)
	uai	ㄨㄞ	uai	uaɪ	wi (as in wife)
	ui	ㄨㄟ	ui (uei)	uɔɪ	wee
	uan	ㄨㄢ	uan	uan	oo an
	un	ㄨㄣ	un	uɔn	oo n
	uaŋ	ㄨㄤ	uang	uaŋ	oo ahng
	uŋ	ㄨㄥ	ung	uŋ	oo ng
y:	ye	ㄩㄝ	yüeh	ye	(no equivalent)
	yan	ㄩㄢ	yüan	yan	(no equivalent)
	yn	ㄩㄣ	yün	yɔn	(no equivalent)
	yŋ	ㄩㄥ	yung	iuŋ	yoong

Conclusion 5. Adaptation of alphabetic scripts to Chinese.

written	printed	sounded as	written	printed	sounded as	written	printed	sounded as
A a	A a	a in at	*Q,o*	Q o	oa in oat	*ð,ə*	ð	ð	th in these
A q	A q	a .. alms	*L s*	S s	ur .. fur.	*S s*	S s	s in so
O o	θ o	a .. all		Consonants		*Z z*	Z z	s .. is
O o	O o	o .. olive	*C c*	C c	c in cot	*ʃ ʃ*	Σ ʃ	sh .. show
W u	W u	oo .. foot	*G g*	G g	q .. go	*Z z*	Z z	s .. pleasure
Y y	Y y	oo .. food	*T t*	T t	t .. to	*L l*	L l	l .. low
I i	I i	i .. ill	*D d*	D d	d .. do	*L l*	L l	ll .. welsh
E ɛ	E ɛ	ee .. eel	*P p*	P p	p .. put	*M m*	M m	M .. me
E e	E e	e .. ell	*B b*	B b	b .. but	*N n*	N n	n .. no
A a	A a	ai .. aim	*F f*	F f	f .. foe	*N n*	N n	hn .. almost
i	i	i .. isle	*V v*	V v	v .. vase	*Y ŋ*	Y ŋ	ng .. wing
O o	O o	oi .. oil	*C ç*	C ç	ch .. chin	*R r*	R r	r .. row
U u	U u	u .. us	*J j*	J j	j .. jade	*R r*	R r	hr .. welsh
8 r	8 r	ow .. owl	*T t*	T t	th .. thin	*K k*	K k	ch .. german

Besides the above letters there are three vowel marks, ′ = h, ` = y, and ‾ = w only found over vowels, hence their name. These marks are quite often found united over vowels, thus uă = uhwa, meaning ashes; ūâ = wuhya, meaning a door; and ūă = wuhwa, meaning tinder of birds' down. The effect of these marks always precedes the vowels over which they are found.

Conclusion 6. The Yámana (Yahgan) Phonetic Alphabet.

Conclusion 7. Inscriptions written in unknown scripts. *a–c* The so-called proto-Arabic inscriptions from 'Ur of the Chaldees.' *d* Another enigmatic inscription from Mesopotamia. *e* Spurious (?) inscription from Peru. *f–g* Enigmatic inscriptions from Spain.

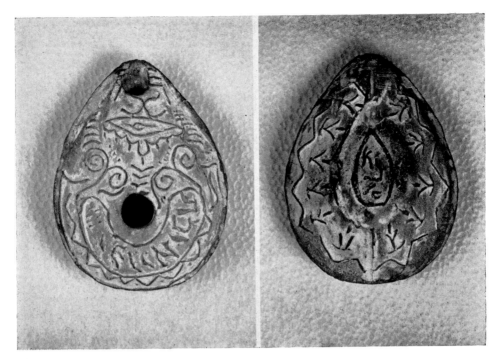

Conclusion 8. *a* (above) obverse and
reverse of an 'inscribed' lamp: a forgery.
b (left) Little bronze lamina inscribed
in a script unknown to the excavators,
which has actually turned out to be
Hebrew. Discovered about 1930 at
Minturnae, Italy in the joint excava-
tions of the University of Pennsylvania
Museum and the Associazione Inter-
nazionale per gli Studi Mediterranei,
Rome.

Conclusion 9. The Shapira forgery. Two pages of the line and wash drawing by C. D. Ginsburg, of Shapira's Deuteronomy manuscript (British Museum *Add.* 41294, fol. 35).

SYSTEM	UNITS										100	1000	MISCELL.
	1	2	3	4	5	6	7	8	9	10	100	1000	
CUNEIFORM	𒁹	𒐀	𒐁	𒐂	𒐅	𒐆	𒐇	𒐈	𒐉	𒌋	𒐕	𒌋𒁹	10,000 𒌍𒁹
EGYPTIAN HIEROGL. *	I	II	III	IIII	III/II	III/III	IIII/III	IIII/IIII	III/III/III	∩	◎	𓆼	⌐10,000
HIERAT. *	I	II	III	—	ʿ٦	⁝⁝	乙	=	⫽	∧	⁄	20 40 ⋏ ⁒
CHINESE ANCIENT	—	=	三	四	五	六	七	八	九	十	百	千	
CURRENT *	I	II	III	X	४	⊥	⸗	⸬	文	+	丹	千	𢀛 10,000
PHOENICIAN	I	II	III	IIII	II III	III III	I III III	II III III	III III III	—	Þ	N 20
SYRIAC	I	٢	٢I	٢٢	→	⊢	⊢	٢→	٢٢→	⅂	∪	
PALMYRENE	⁄	⁊⁊	⁊⁊⁊	⁊⁊⁊⁊	Ⅎ	⅂Ⅎ				⅂	⅂⁊	⅂Ⅎ⁊	
KHAROSHTHĪ	ˉ⁊ or I	ˉ‖ or II	ˉ‖‖ or III	⅂X	IX	IIX		XX		2⁊ or ⁊	⅄I	3 20
BRAHMĪ	—	=	≡	半	⅁	⅍	⊃	3	3	∝	3	8 20
MAYA *	०	००	०००	००००	❘	•❘	••❘	•••❘	••••❘	❘❘		⊖ ZERO
ETRUSCAN *	I	II	III	IIII	Λ	IΛ	IIΛ	IIIΛ	XI	X	⋇	(X)	XX 20
ANCIENT ROMAN *	I	II	III	IIII	V	VI	VII	VIII	IX	XX or X	C	(X)	50 ↓↓⊥L
CHIOGGIA *	I	II	III	IIII	Λνυ U or	VI	VII	VIII	IX	XOA or	⊕	⊗	500 ⋀ⵣ
CLASSICAL ROMAN *	I	II	III	IIII	V	VI	VII	VIII	IX	X	C	M	XX 20
MEDIEVAL ROMAN *	7	77	777	7777	V	V7	V77	V777	7X	X	Ⳑ	G	℧ 500

* SELECTED

Conclusion 10. Numerical notation, preceding the arabic numerals.

	1	2	3	4	5	6	7	8	9	0
Deva-nagari letters (2nd. cent A.D.)		ट	ᅀ	◡	⊔	⊔	ᴎ	४	௮	
Arabic numerals (10th.cent.)	I	२	३	૪	૭	৮	৴	৭	੭	০
Arabic numerals (M S. A.D. 976) (Latin M.S., Escorial Library)	I	८	६	४	੮	৬	৲	8	9	
Arabic numerals (Western Type)	I	८	3	૪	৭	6	৲	8	9	০
Arabic numerals (Eastern Type) To-day	∫	⼷	⼷	ৎ	৷	੭	⋁	∧	੭	·
	I	⼷	⼷	৷	◬	੭	⋁	∧	੭	·
	I	2	⼷	℀	੪	੭	⋁	∧	੭	০
	I	⼷	⼷	ৎ	০	੭	⋁	∧	੭	·
"Apices" of Boëthius (11th & 12th centuries)	I	2	५	∞	G	ᒷ	⼉	8	9	
	I	⼷	⼷	⼉⼉	੪	⼉	∧	8	9	
	I	⼷	ਮ	B	੪	ᘃ	⼉	୪	੭	
	I	⼷	⼷	∞	੪	ᒷ	∧	8	9	⊚
	I	⼷	⼷	∞	੪	ᴎ	∧	8	9	
Numerals of John Basingestockes (d.1252)	੭	੪	੭	੪	੪	੭	⊥	⌙	⍀	
Arabic-Byzantine numerals (12th. to 15th. cent.)	I	⼷	⼷	৷	੪	੭	⋁	∧	੭	
	I	⼷	⼷	ৎ	0	੪	⋁	∧	੭	·
	I	2	3	ৎ	੪	6	⋁	୪	੭	০
M.S. from France 2nd. half of 12.cent.	I	⼷	੫	ৎ	B	੬	⋁	੪	੭	০
Italian M S., Florence, first half of 14th.cent.	I	z	3	4	ſ	6	7	8	੭	০
Italian MSS. of 15th. cent.	1	2	3	4	੪	6	7	8	9	0

Conclusion 11. Development of arabic numerals.

Conclusion 12. Medieval musical notation: *Mozarabic Antifonarium*, 11th century (Leon Cathedral, Spain).

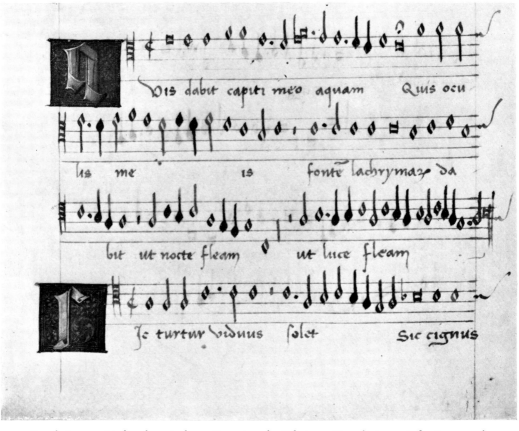

Conclusion 13. Medieval musical notation: Agnolo Poliziano, *Trenodio in morte* for Lorenzo the Magnificent, *c.* 1486 (Civic Library, Cortona, Italy).

Conclusion 14. Musical notation: Giuseppe Maria Angelieri, *Messa in Quattro*, Milan, 1691.

vector of magnitude A **A**

scalar product of **A** and **B**   **A.B**

vector product of **A** and **B**   **A × B, A ∧ B**

nabla or del, $\left(\mathrm{i}\dfrac{\partial}{\partial x} + \mathrm{j}\dfrac{\partial}{\partial y} + \mathrm{k}\dfrac{\partial}{\partial z} \right)$ ∇

Laplacian operator, $\left(\dfrac{\partial^2}{\partial x^2} + \dfrac{\partial^2}{\partial y^2} + \dfrac{\partial^2}{\partial z^2} \right)$ ∇^2

$$F_j \simeq F' + 2(f + \delta f_j)(\cos\theta - \delta\theta_j \sin\theta),$$

$$\Delta_j = 2f\{(\delta f_j/f)\cos\theta - \delta\theta_j \sin\theta\}.$$

$$\Delta_j = -2f\sin\theta\, \delta\theta_j.$$

$$\sigma_l^n = \sum_s m^s [\tfrac{1}{3}(\alpha_1^s + \alpha_2^s + \alpha_3^s) + \tfrac{2}{3}(\pm\beta_1^s \pm \beta_2^s \pm \beta_3^s)]$$

$$\sigma_t^n = \sum_s m^s [\tfrac{1}{3}(\alpha_1^s + \alpha_2^s + \alpha_3^s) - \tfrac{1}{3}(\pm\beta_1^s \pm \beta_2^s \pm \beta_3^s)]$$

Conclusion 15. Mathematical notation.

$$\xi = F(t) \cdot F(t+s)$$

$$\xi \neq 0 \text{ if } s < T; \ \xi = 0 \text{ if } s > T$$

$$Z = \frac{2\pi L^2}{h^3}(2mkT)^{3/2} \int_0^\infty z^{3/2} e^{-x} dx$$

$$Z = \left(\frac{2\pi mkT}{h^2}\right)^{3N/2} \frac{1}{N!} \int \exp\left(\frac{-\Phi}{kT}\right) \cdot dV_N$$

$$\Phi = \sum_{pairs} \phi_{ij}(r_{ij}) = \sum_{i>j} \phi_{ij}(r_{ij}) = \tfrac{1}{2} \sum_{i=1}^{N} \sum_{j=1}^{N} \phi_{ij}(r_{ij})$$

$$ZnSO_4 \cdot 7H_2O \rightarrow ZnSO_4 \cdot 6H_2O \xrightarrow{100°C} ZnSO_4 \cdot H_2O$$

$$\xrightarrow{250°C} ZnSO_4$$

$$\xrightarrow{750°C} ZnO + SO_4$$

Conclusion 16. Scientific notation.

A Angström, answer. **A1**, first class (of ships). **A.A.**, Anti-Aircraft, Automobile Association. **A.A.A.**, Amateur Athletic Association, American Automobile Association. **A. and M.**, Ancient and Modern (hymnal). **A.A.U.**, Amateur Athletic Union (U.S.). **A.B.**, Able-bodied seaman. **A.B.A.**, Amateur Boxing Association. **Ab. init.**, *ab initio* (L., from the beginning). **Abl.**, ablative. **Abp.**, archbishop. **A.C.**, Aircraftman, alternating current, *ante Christum* (L., before Christ). **A/c**, account. **Acc.**, accusative. **A. Cdre**, Air Commodore. **A.C.F.**, Army Cadet Force. **ACTH**, Adrenocorticotrophic hormone. **A.D.**, *anno domini* (L., in the year of the Lord). **Ad.**, Admiral(ty). advertisement. **A.D.C.**, aide-de-camp. **Add.**, addenda. **Adj.**, adjective. **Ad. lib.**, *ad libitum* (L., as much as desired). **Adm.**, Admiral(ty). **Admin.**, administer(ed), administration, administrative(ly). **Adv.**, Advent, adverb. **A.E.A.**, Atomic Energy Authority. **A.E.C.**, Atomic Energy Commission (U.S.). **Aeg.**, *aegrotat* (L., he is ill), Allied Electrical Industries. **Aet.**, *aetatis* (L., of the age). **A.E.U.**, Amalgamated Engineering Union. **A.F.**, audio-frequency. **A.F.L.–C.I.O.**, American Federation of Labor–Congress of Industrial Organizations (U.S.). **A.F.S.**, Auxiliary Fire Service. **A.G.**, air-gunner. **A.H.**, *anno hegirae* (L., in the year of the Hegira – Mohammedan calendar). **A.I.**, Appleton layer. **Ala.**, Alabama. **Alas.**, Alaska. **alt.**, altitude. **Alta.**, Alberta. **A.M.**, Air Ministry. **a.m.**, *ante meridiem* (L., before noon). **amp.**, ampere. **AMVETS**, American Veterans of World War II & Korea. **Anniv.**, anniversary. **anon.**, anonymous. **A.O.C. (in-C.)**, Air Officer Commanding (in-Chief). **A.P.**, Associated Press. **approx.**, approximate(ly). **Aq.**, *aqua* (L., water). **arch.**, archaic, architecture. **archbp.**, archbishop. **Ariz.**, Arizona. **Ark.**, Arkansas. **A.R.P.**, Air Raid Precautions. **Arr.**, arranged, arrive(s). **A.S.**, Anglo-Saxon, anti-submarine. **a.s.l.**, above sea-level. **A.S.P.C.A.**, American Society for the Prevention of Cruelty to Animals. **assist.**, assistant. **assoc.**, associate(d). **assn.**, **assocn.**, association. **A.S.S.R.**, Autonomous Soviet Socialist Republic. **asst.**, assistant. **A.T.C.**, Air Transport Command (U.S.), Air Training Corps. **A/t**, anti-tank. **at. no.**, atomic number. **A.T.S.**, Auxiliary Territorial Service. **at. wt.**, atomic weight. **A.U.C.**, *anno urbis conditae* (L., 'in the year of the founding of the city' [Rome], 753 B.C.). **Aug.**, August, **aux.**, auxiliary. **A.V.**, Authorized Version (of the Bible). **avdp.**, avoirdupois. **A.W.O.L.**, absent without leave.

B Born, brother. **B.A.**, Bachelor of Arts, British Academy, British Association (for the Advancement of Science), Buenos Aires. **Bac.**, *baccalaureus* (L., bachelor). **Ball.**, Balliol College, Oxford. **b. and b.**, bed and breakfast. **B.A.O.R.**, British Army of the Rhine. **Bart.**, baronet. **Bart's**, St. Bartholomew's Hospital, London. **B.B.C.**, British Broadcasting Corporation (originally Company). **B.C.**, Before Christ, borough council, British Columbia, British Council. **B.Ch.**, Bachelor of Surgery (L., *chirurgiae*). **B.C.L.**, Bachelor of Civil Law. **B.Com.**, Bachelor of Commerce. **B.D.**, Bachelor of Divinity. **Bde.**, brigade. **b.e.**, bill of exchange. **B.E.A.**, British European Airways. **Beds**, Bedfordshire. **B.E.F.**, British Expeditionary Force. **B.E.M.**, British Empire Medal.

B.Eng., Bachelor of Engineering. **Berks**, Berkshire. **b.f.**, brought forward. **bk.**, book, bank. **b.l.**, bill of lading. **B.Litt.**, Bachelor of Letters (L., *Litterarum*). **B.LL.**, Bachelor of Laws (L., *Legum*). **B.M.**, Bachelor of Medicine, British Museum. **B.M.A.**, British Medical Association. **B.M.C.**, British Motor Corporation. **Bn.**, battalion. **B.O.A.C.**, British Overseas Airways Corporation. **B. of E.**, Bank of England. **bor.**, borough. **bos'n**, boatswain. **B.O.T.**, Board of Trade. **bot.**, botany(ical). **B.P.**, British Pharmacopoeia. **b.p.**, boiling point. **Bp.**, bishop. **B.R.**, British Railways. **Brec**, Breconshire. **Brit.**, British. **Bros.**, brothers. **B.R.S.**, British Road Services. **B.S.A.**, Birmingham Small Arms (Company). **B.Sc.**, Bachelor of Science. **B.S.I.**, British Standards Institution. **B.S.T.**, British summer time. **Bt.**, baronet. **B.T.U.**, Board of Trade Unit. **Bucks**, Buckinghamshire. **B.U.P.**, British United Press. **bus**, omnibus (L., for all). **B.V.M.**, Blessed Virgin Mary. **Byz.**, Byzantine.

C *Centum* (L., hundred). **C.** capacitance, Centigrade, Central, coulomb. **c.**, centimetre, chapter, cubic, *circa* (L., about). **C.A.**, Consumers' Association. **cal.**, calorie. **Calif.**, California. **Cambs**, Cambridgeshire. **Can.**, canon. **Cantab.**, *Cantabrigiensis* (L., member of Cambridge University). **cap.**, capital, chapter. **Capt.**, captain. **car.**, carat. **C.A.T.**, College of Advanced Technology. **cat.**, catalogue. **C.B.**, confined to barracks, county borough. **C.C.**, Coastal Command, county council(lor), cricket club. **c.c.**, cubic centimetre, cubic contents. **C.C.C.**, Central Criminal Court, Commodity Credit Corporation (U.S.). **C.D.**, Civil Defence, Contagious Diseases (Acts), *Corps Diplomatique* (Fr., diplomatic body). **C.D.C.**, Commonwealth Development Corporation. **C.E.**, Chancellor of the Exchequer. **C.E.G.B.**, Central Electricity Generating Board. **C.E.M.A.**, Council for the Encouragement of Music and the Arts. **cent.**, century. **cet. par.**, *ceteris paribus* (L., other things being equal). **C.F.**, Chaplain to the Forces. **c.f.**, carried forward, cubic foot (feet). **cf.**, *confer* (L., compare). **C.G.**, centre of gravity. **cg.**, centigramme. **C.G.S.**, centimetre-gramme-second (system of units), Chief of the General Staff. **C.G.T.**, Confédération Générale du Travail (Fr., general confederation of work; equivalent of British T.U.C.). **C.H.**, Companion of Honour. **c.h.**, central heating. **Ch.**, chaplain, church. **Ches**, Cheshire. **C.I.**, Channel Islands. **C.I.A.**, Central Intelligence Agency (U.S.). **C.I.D.**, Criminal Investigation Department. **C.I.G.S.**, Chief of the Imperial General Staff. **C.-in-C.**, Commander-in-Chief. **C.I.O.**: see **A.F.L.–C.I.O.** **Cl.**, classical. **cm.**, centimetre. **C.M.G.**, Companion of the Order of St. Michael and St. George, Congressional Medal for Gallantry (U.S.). **C.M.S.**, Church Missionary Society. **C.N.D.**, Campaign for Nuclear Disarmament. **C.O.**, Colonial Office, commanding officer, conscientious objector, Crown Office. **Co.**, company, county. **c/o**, care of. **C.O.D.**, cash on delivery, Central Ordnance Depot. **C. of E.**, Church of England. **C.O.I.**, Central Office of Information. **Col.**, colonel, colonial, Colorado. **Col-Gen.**, colonel-general. **Coll.**, college. **Com.**, Communist, commissioner. **Comdt.**, commandant. **Comecon**, council for mutual economic aid (Communist).

Comm., commodore. **Comp.**, comparative, compositor, compound. **Compa.**, company (on £5 notes). **con.**, *contra* (L., against). **conf.**, conference. **conj.**, conjugation, conjunction. **Conn.**, Connacht, Connecticut. **Cons.**, Conservative. **contd.**, continued. **Co-op.**, Co-operative. **Cor.**, Corinthian(s), coroner. **C.O.R.E.**, Congress of Racial Equality (U.S.). **Corpn.**, corporation. **cos.**, cosine, **cox**, coxswain. **C.P.**, Common Prayer, Communist Party. **c.p.**, carriage paid, candle-power. **Cpl.**, Corporal. **cr.**, created, credit. **C.R.C.**, Civil Rights Commission (U.S.). **cresc**, *crescendo* (Ital., becoming louder), crescent. **c/s**, cycles per second. **C.S.C.**, Civil Service Commission, Conspicuous Service Cross (U.S.). **C.S.E.**, Certificate of Secondary Education. **cts.**, cents, centimes. **cttee.**, committee. **cu.**, **cub.**, cubic. **C.U.P.**, Cambridge University Press. **C.V.O.**, Commander of the Royal Victorian Order. **C.W.S.**, Co-operative Wholesale Society. **cwt.**, hundredweight.

D Five hundred (Roman). **d.**, daughter, *denarius* (L., penny), died. **D.A.**, District Attorney (U.S.). **dat.**, dative. **dau.**, daughter. **dB**, decibel. **D.B.E.**, Dame Commander of the Order of the British Empire. **D.C.**, *da capo* (Ital., from the beginning), direct current, District of Columbia (U.S.). **D.C.L.**, Doctor of Civil Law. **D.C.V.O.**, Dame Commander of the Royal Victorian Order. **D.D.**, Doctor of Divinity. **deb.**, debenture. **dec.**, deceased. **Del.**, Delaware. **del.**, *delineavit* (L., he drew); dele., delete. **Dept.**, department. **Deut.**, Deuteronomy. **D.F.**, Defender of the Faith. **D.F.C.**, Distinguished Flying Cross. **D.F.M.**, Distinguished Flying Medal. **D.G.**, *Dei Gratia* (L., by the grace of God), Director General, Dragoon Guards. **D.I.**, Defence Intelligence. **diam.**, diameter. **dim.**, *diminuendo* (Ital., becoming quieter). **dip.**, diploma. **dir.**, director. **dist.**, district. **div.**, division, divorced. **divi.**, dividend. **dl.**, decilitre. **D. Litt.**, Doctor of Letters (L., *Litterarum*). **D.M.**, Doctor of Medicine. **D. Mus.**, Doctor of Music. **D.N.A.**, deoxy-ribonucleic acid. **D.N.B.**, Dictionary of National Biography. **do.**, ditto. **D.O.M.**, *Deo Optimo Maximo* (L., to God the best and greatest). **Dom.**, Dominican, Dominion, *Dominus* (L., lord, master). **D.O.R.A.**, Defence of the Realm Act. **doz.**, dozen. **D.P.**, displaced person(s). **D.R.**, dead reckoning. **Dr.**, debtor, doctor. **dr.**, dram, drawer (of a cheque). **D.S.**, *dal segno* (Ital., [repeat] from the mark). **D.Sc.**, Doctor of Science. **D.S.O.**, Distinguished Service Order. **d.s.p.**, *decessit sine prole* (L., died without issue). **D.T.**, delirium tremens. **Dunelm**, *Dunelmensis* (L., of Durham). **Duo.**, duodecimo (12). **D.V.**, *deo volente* (L., God willing).

E Earl, east, eastern, English, second class (of ships). **e.**, eldest. **E. & O.E.**, errors and omissions excepted. **Ebor**, *Eboracensis* (L., of York). **E.C.A.**, Economic Co-operation Administration. **Eccl.**, (Book of) Ecclesiastes. **Econ.**, economics. **Ed.**, editor, edited, educated, Edward. **E.D.C.**, European Defence Community. **Edin.**, Edinburgh. **educ.**, educated, education. **E.E.C.**, European Economic Community. **E.F.T.A.**, European Free Trade Association. **e.g.**, *exempli gratia* (L., for the sake of example). **e.h.f.**, extra high frequency. **el.**, electric, element. **eld.**, eldest. **E.M.F.**, electro-motive force. **E.M.U.**, electro-magnetic unit. **E.N.E.A.**, European

Conclusion 18. Systems of shorthand from antiquity to the present day.

Conclusion 19. Modern shorthand: Pitman system.

what · when · whether · which · who · whose · why · wish · wished · with · within · without · wonderful-ly · word · would · writer · yard · year · you · young · your

think · third · this · those · though · thus · thyself · till · to · to be · told · too, two · toward · towards · trade · tried · truth · under · usual-ly · valuation · very · was · we

significance · significant · signification · signify-ied · southern · speak · special-ly · spirit · subject-ed · subjection · subjective · sure · surprise · surprised · tell · thank-ed · that · the · their, there · them · themselves · therefore · thing

a, an · ah! · the · aye, eh? · of · to · all · two, too · on · but · O! oh! owe · he · and · should · awe · ought, aught · who · how · with · when · what · would · beyond · you · why

information · hand · under · sent · language · owing · thing · young · Lord · your · year · yard · word · are · our, hour · ourselves · rather · writer · we · whether · wonderful-ly

me · him · myself · himself · most · more · remark-ed · Mr. · mere · importance-ant · improved-d-ment · impossible · in · any · own · influence · influenced · next · nor · near · opinion · northern

Conclusion 20. Stenography. Sample from a shorthand typewriter. The passage from *Hamlet*, act three, scene one, is read from top to bottom by columns, and from left to right (Courtesy Miss Vivien Rigden).

Conclusion 21. The semaphore alphabet.

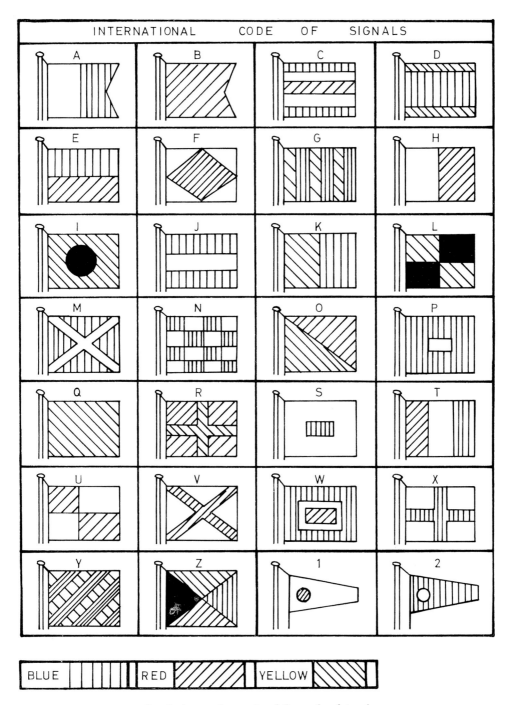

Conclusion 22. International flag code of signals.

MORSE CODE

A · —	H · · · ·	O — — · —	V · · · —	3 · · · — —
B — · · ·	I · ·	P · — — ·	W · — —	4 · · · · —
C — · — ·	J · — — —	Q — — · —	X — · · —	5 · · · · ·
D — ·	K — — —	R · — ·	Y — · — —	6 — · · · ·
E ·	L · — · ·	S · · ·	Z — — · ·	7 — — · · ·
F · · — ·	M — —	T —	1 · — — — —	8 — — — · ·
G — — ·	N — ·	U · · —	2 · · — — —	9 — — — — ·

Conclusion 23a. Morse Code.

BRAILLE

Conclusion 23b. Braille.

450

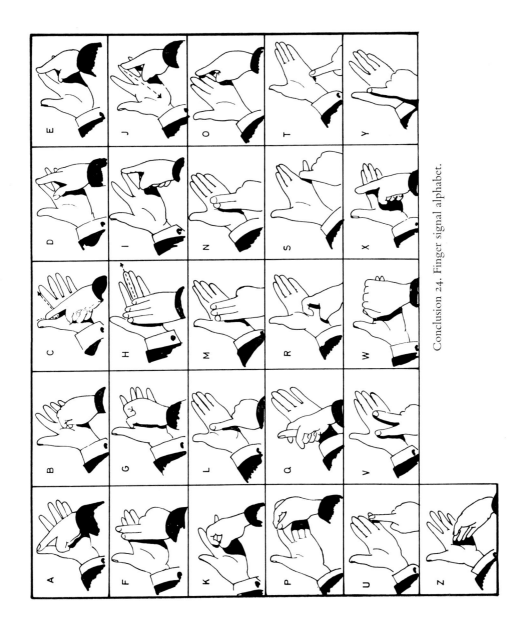

Conclusion 24. Finger signal alphabet.

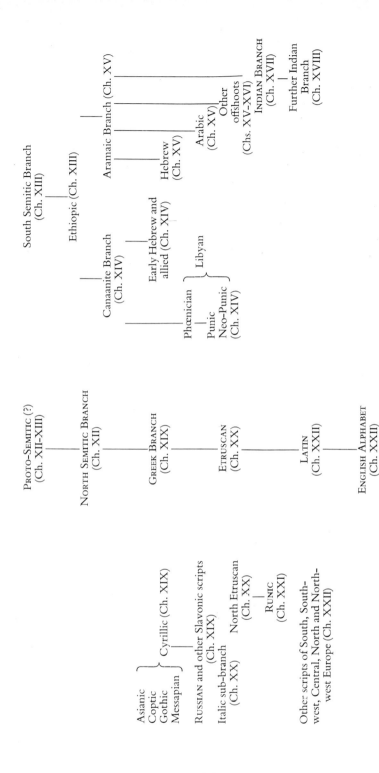

Conclusion 25. The origin of the English alphabet and its relationship to other main alphabetic scripts.